You Can Work It Out!

YOU CAN WORK IT OUT!

The Power of Personal Responsibility in
Restoring Relationships
2nd Edition

Dr. Chuck Lynch

Unless otherwise noted, Scripture quotations are from the NEW AMERICAN STANDARD BIBLE, copyright © 1960, 1962, 1963, 1968, 1971, 1972, 1973, 1975, 1977 by The Lockman Foundation, and are used by permission.

Scriptures noted AMPLIFIED BIBLE are from The Amplified New Testament. Copyright © 1958 by the Lockman Foundation (used by permission).

Library of Congress Cataloging–in–Publication Data

Lynch, Chuck, 1942–
    You can work it out! : the power of personal responsibility in restoring relationships / Chuck Lynch — 2nd ed.
        p. cm.
    Includes index.
    ISBN 1-4536-5402-x
    1. Interpersonal relations—Religious aspects—Christianity. 2. Responsibility—Religious aspects—Christianity. I. Title.
BV4597.52.L86 1999
248.4—dc21
                                                        99–37225
                                                            CIP

Printed in the United States of America.
1 2 3 4 5 6 7 8 9 QPV 04 03 02 01 00 99

To John and Alice Bourdon—
Two dear friends who applied these principles
and totally changed their marriage and ministry

CONTENTS

ACKNOWLEDGMENTS

It was while flying at 37,000 feet that Mark Sweeney, the new vice president for manuscript acquisition at Word Publishing, first read my primitive draft of *Circles of Responsibilities*. I am indebted to Mark for accepting this project and for his creativity in giving it a more descriptive title, *You Can Work It Out!: The Power of Personal Responsibility in Restoring Relationships.*

Words fail to express my deepest appreciation to the outstanding editorial staff of Word Publishing. Ami McConnell did another masterful job as senior editor. Holly Halverson smoothed every verbal pothole an author could create and straightened each hairpin turn of the manuscript.

I cannot say thank you enough to my dear wife, Linda, who harnessed her schoolteaching skills to spend hundreds of hours polishing and proofreading each revision. Her encouragement and support helped me make it through the many deadlines.

If gleaming golden trophies were handed out for Volunteer of the Year, Patricia Maxfield would win hands-down. She single-handedly transcribed more than six hundred handwritten pages and turned my hieroglyphics into intelligent computer text. She gladly made reams of corrections without complaint.

I deeply appreciate George Maxfield, who carefully checked and cross-checked the hundreds of Scripture references.

It would be impossible to list and adequately thank the friends who read and critiqued the various manuscript stages. I repeatedly heard, "I wish I'd had this book five (ten, twenty) years ago."

I continue to be grateful to my literary agents, Sealy Yates and Tom Thompson, for their professional counsel.

Finally, there is a special group of people to whom I will be eternally indebted: the dear friends who let me tell their stories. *You Can Work It Out!* is not a monument to an author but a memorial to his friends. I reminded each one years ago that someday God was going to greatly benefit others because of the personal pain they worked through. To them I say thank you, as they join me in giving all the glory to our awesome God.

Introduction

"Yeah, sure! Right! It would take a miracle to fix this relationship." I believe you. Your particular conflict may have the word *impossible* written all over it. Maybe you've tried everything. Nothing worked. You're at a dead end. The situation is overwhelming, incredibly complicated, and at a full stop.

Good. Then this book is for you.

Or instead, you may have a relative, friend, or coworker who has her back against a wall. You want to help or at least encourage her, but you don't know what to do or say. From the outside her conflict looks like a tangled mess. It probably looks the same from the inside. Good news—this book is for you too. Whether you are facing an embroiled conflict or wanting to help someone work through one, you have come to the right place.

For almost forty years, God has allowed me the privilege of serving people who have faced unimaginable conflicts. Two realities have impressed me over the decades: first, that God's Word is tremendously practical, and second, that God is absolutely faithful to His Word. Let me explain.

God is no stranger to conflict. In fact, the majority of the Bible is about conflict in one form or another. It starts early in Genesis and does not end until the last book of the New Testament, Revelation. God created man and woman. He knows how they tick. God knows what it takes to work out the painful and complicated situations they get into. And He has provided very practical tools to equip us to cooperate with what He does best—bring peace from turmoil and reconciliation from alienation.

When people tell me how they are dealing with a conflict, they may admit that they have yelled from time to time or just shut down. Parents sometimes describe nagging their kids to do something and then doing it themselves. I always ask, "Does this pattern work for you?" and the answer, inevitably, is "No." It has never worked, isn't working now, and won't work in the future. Yet they are determined to stick to the dysfunctional pattern. This could be one reason God allows conflicts to persist—to expose dysfunctional strategies and encourage people to consider a biblical alternative. His ways of handling conflict are clearly not our ways. And our ways do not work.

We are free to re-create the proverbial wheel. But most of our homemade approaches to conflict consist of riding square wheels—and they create one uncomfortable ride. God reveals to us that there are methods of conflict resolution that seem right to us but end in death (Prov. 16:25). There is spiritual death, which is the separation of sinful man from a holy God. There is physical death, which is the separation of our spirit from our body. Then there is relational death, which is the separation of two or more individuals from each other. Divorce is only one painful example of this.

But God has documented in His Word what does work in producing reconciliation and peace. What we need to do is identify the ways of God in working out a conflict and utilize them to the fullest. *You Can Work It Out!* does just that. The principles I have gleaned over these years I have shared with hundreds of people who found they worked—not because they were my ways but because they were God's ways.

This book will take you through the steps of conflict resolution. Where do you start with a solution-defying conflict? In these pages you will meet a couple whose conflict would have stretched the wisdom of Solomon. But you will learn a simple procedure that will allow you to identify what is really happening. It is like taking an x-ray of the family that shows where the damage is and how it should be treated.

The next step is to assign circles of responsibility: decide who is supplying words, habits, and attitudes that are not working in the relationship and replace them with ways that work. Then you will learn an empowering procedure that allows you to actively tap into God's infinite resources; as you learn to assume your responsibilities, you will find healing and closure.

You will be encouraged to learn also that God has His own circle of responsibilities. These are specific things that only He can do in effecting a reconciliation. If you try to do what only God can do, you will fail.

It is vital to understand that there is one thing that distinguishes those who succeed from those who fail at dealing with conflict: God has not promised to bless the "hearers" of His Word, just the "doers." You will observe a power surge in the lives of those who identify and fulfill what is in their circle of responsibilities.

Some of the other practical issues we will tackle:

- What can you do when others within a conflict do not cooperate? I will describe a specific discipline that will prevent anyone from stealing your power, joy, or peace.
- What if others won't assume or fulfill their responsibilities? God has provided clear tests to help us determine whether we should take up the slack.
- What will God think of me if I do everything I know to do

from His Word and the conflict remains? When one client, Susan, learned the answer to that question, she was elated. It freed her to be an effective single mother to her three daughters.

- What benefit will it be to me to know and apply the ways of God to my problems if the others in the conflict do not change? There are at least eleven life-changing benefits to you personally when you apply God's tools in a difficult situation.

Convinced? Not yet? That is why I have asked John and Alice Bourdon to relate their personal story. There was enough pain in their relationship to last ten lifetimes. But they identified the ways of God, assigned and assumed their own responsibilities, and plugged into the power of God. I have since referred scores of couples, stuck in their own impossible situations, to these people helpers. Not only did these principles change John and Alice's marriage, they drastically altered their ministry.

I have a twofold purpose for this book. First, I want to share from Scripture how you can work out difficult personal conflicts. Second, I want to encourage you to help someone else with the tools you will learn. I'm in your corner, my friend, cheering you on. You can work it out as God enables you through the power of personal responsibility.

Chuck Lynch

ONE

Yes, It Is Possible!

"Read this one, Grandpa!" exclaimed my grandson. We were leafing through a book of nursery rhymes. Half reading and half from memory I began:

> Humpty Dumpty sat on a wall,
> Humpty Dumpty had a great fall,
> All the king's horses and all the king's men,
> Couldn't put Humpty together again.

Then came the endless barrage of questions.
"Why did he fall, Grandpa?"
"Did he get hurt?"
"Is he going to be okay?"
Each answer from Grandpa only unleashed more questions from Taylor's inquisitive mind. He could not accept the fact that Humpty Dumpty could not be fixed and be "all better." In Taylor's child world, everything can be fixed. In the real world, it may not be that easy.

It is one thing to attempt to explain to a three-year-old why Humpty Dumpty cannot be fixed, and quite another to explain to Billy why his daddy is not going to be living at home anymore, why Mommy is spending time with a man that's not his daddy, or why half the church will not be worshiping together again after an ugly split.

Yes, it is one thing to try to piece together broken eggshells. It is quite another to try to mend fractured marriages or to resolve complicated, deeply involved relational problems with spouses, kids, or in-laws. So much more is at stake! Tim, a pastor-friend of mine, knew this firsthand.

Scrambled Eggs

Pastor Tim heaved a big sigh on the phone. His plea was simple and desperate: "Help! I have a couple in my church on the verge of divorce. The husband is an alcoholic. He works late hours. He is physically and verbally abusive to his wife. Their kids are in our Christian school. The oldest son is on probation for fighting and the next oldest is suspended for stealing money from the candy sale fund-raiser. The only daughter is twelve going on eighteen. She is heading for some big-time moral trouble. Mom is a screamer and controller. She is very critical and does not seem to care when or where she vents her anger on the kids, or on anyone else for that matter.

"Man, where do you even start with a mess like this?"

Good question. Tim was experiencing the same initial frustration you might feel if your child announced he wanted fried eggs instead of scrambled—just after you'd whipped the last two eggs together. Untangling a family mess seems as impossible as trying to unscramble eggs.

Those who are willing or able to attempt to unravel these complicated, heart-wrenching conflicts are rare—understandably so. Who has not been burned trying? True, "Blessed are the peacemakers, for they shall be called sons of God" (Matt. 5:9). Believers sometimes fail to realize, however, that Matthew 5:9 is followed by verse 10: "Blessed are those who have been persecuted for the sake of righteousness. . . ." Even the Old Testament prophets who attempted to reconcile the rebellious nation, Israel, with a righteous God were killed for their efforts (Matt. 23:37).

AVOIDANCE IS NORMAL

The hesitancy to get involved in messy conflicts is nothing new. Even the master reconciler, the apostle Paul, faced this same reluctance of others to get involved in arbitrating a bitter conflict among believers in the new churches he established. The church at Corinth was Exhibit A of the kind of snarled knots even saints can work themselves into.

The apostle had just poured eighteen months of his life into establishing and discipling this new fledgling church in Corinth, Greece. Upon his departure from Corinth, Paul felt he had left this young church well-grounded and with responsible, capable leadership. But bad news traveled fast. Months later he learned that major conflicts had broken out between members. That wasn't the worst of it; they were now resorting to the pagan law courts to resolve their issues instead of resolving them within the confines of the church. Out of his frustration, Paul firmly wrote, "Is it so, that there is not among you one wise man who will be able to decide between his brethren, but brother goes to law with brother, and that before unbelievers?" (1 Cor. 6:5–6). Were life's problems so complicated and beyond the Corinthians' powers of negotiation that they had to turn to godless courts to resolve their conflicts?

In interpersonal relationships, usually the absence of biblical truth is not the problem. Rather it is the lack of practical wisdom to *apply* that truth to specific difficult situations that continues to place churches in turmoil, homes in chaos, and in-laws at swords' points. Picking up the pieces or identifying the facts in a conflict is one thing; doing something significant with them is quite another.

Conflict Is Not a Stranger

Unfortunately, conflict is no stranger to Christians. In the Bible it is clear that God is not shy about documenting this reality. The Book of James, one of the first written in the New Testament, hit it head-on. The author briefly mentioned one of the first important keys in making the impossible—untangling squabbles—possible: "But let everyone be quick to hear, slow to speak and slow to anger; for the anger of man does not achieve [produce] the righteousness of God" (James 1:19–20).

This key is very basic. It is often overlooked because of its simplicity. But it confirms what we experience: conflicts erupt when a firestorm of heated words replaces listening attentively and acknowledging another's perspective. Rage replaces reason. Primary issues get lost amid the angry exchanges. Solutions evaporate.

I often ask a couple in counseling how their last fight got started. Glancing at each other, they struggle to recall the opening shots of their recent skirmish. The reason is simple. They spent a couple of minutes on the initial issue, then shifted defensively into name-calling, issue hopping, and blame shifting.

In his book, James readily confronted the strife resulting from favoritism and prejudice. Then in chapter 4 he came down hard on the misuse of words that can so easily fan the flames of conflict. James was not subtle. He asked, "What is the source of quarrels and conflicts among you?" He then cut to the core: lust, murder, envy, fighting, quarreling, prayerlessness, wrong motives, and selfish pleasures. He strongly asserted, "Do not speak against one another, brethren," and concluded, "Who are you who judge your neighbor?" (James 4:1–3, 11–12). Finally in chapter 5 James exposed the greed of the rich who exploit the poor.

All these complicated, emotionally charged issues serve as only a hint of the spectrum of problems that plagued the infant church and have, unfortunately, carried over to the contemporary church and family. My own father walked out of a deacon board meeting that had erupted into a fistfight. Not even as our Lord ministered among His own people did He escape strife. And the disciples within His inner circle were not strangers to conflict either. It was sinister and selfish—and pervasive.

As the dark shades of the last hours of Jesus' life on earth began to draw to a close, Satan made his move. He had put it in the heart of Judas to betray Jesus treacherously for the price of thirty pieces of silver. Meanwhile, Jesus had gathered the disciples for their last meal together. It was during this Passover meal that He established a memorial that we celebrate today: "the Lord's table" or the Communion service. The wine served at the meal became a reminder of His blood that was spilled out to establish a new covenant between God and man. The bread was a memorial of His body given sacrificially for man's sin (Luke 22:19).

What an incredible experience that had to be for those disciples—but not for all of them. An underlying greed for power erupted. Again, an argument arose among Jesus' followers as to which one was the greatest (Luke 22:24). This jealous competition had been a running battle among the disciples from almost day one (Luke 9:46). They expected that Jesus would establish a new kingdom, so there were many important positions to vie for (Matt. 20:20–24). And even after Jesus quelled this argument and went to His death, conflict did not end with the cross.

It raised its head again just after the infant church was birthed. Right in the middle of a spiritual high—the coming of the Holy Spirit—a very practical problem surfaced. A complaint arose between the non-Palestinian Jews and the native Jews. The non-Palestinian Jews felt "their widows were being overlooked in the daily serving of food" (Acts 6:1). The believers had communally pooled their resources. It was their intent to share all equally (Acts 4:32). This perceived neglect was a very sensitive issue. How would the disciples work it out graciously and fairly? A specific principle of Scripture served as the basis in resolving this tense issue—the fulfillment of personal responsibility.

The twelve apostles summoned the congregation of believers and explained, "It is not desirable for us to neglect the word of God in order to serve tables" (Acts 6:2). It was not that they were unwilling to do so. Jesus taught them to serve others (Matt. 20:26–27). But each disciple had a priority responsibility to establish the infant church in the Word of God. The solution was simple. "Select from among you, brethren, seven men of good reputation, full of the Spirit and of wisdom, whom we may put in charge of this task" (Acts 6:3). Because the disciples knew what was their primary responsibility, they could delegate others to clear up the inequities in the food distribution. And so they worked it out.

Even successful first-century churches were not strangers to problems. Although the apostle Paul had a great deal of praise for the church at Philippi, friction existed. He enlisted the efforts of the whole church family to assist two hardworking women, Euodia and Syntyche, to learn how to work out their conflicts and to live in harmony in the Lord (Phil. 4:2–3). Yes, it is possible.

Great men and women of faith in the Old Testament did not escape conflict either. It was serious. Consider the bitter marital discord between Moses and his wife, Zipporah. Moses had failed in his responsibility to circumcise his son (either Gershom or Eliezer), and God was about to take Moses' life for this failure. Seemingly out of anger, Zipporah, his wife, took a flint and cut off her son's foreskin. Then after she disgustedly threw it at Moses' feet she said, "You are indeed a bridegroom of blood to me" (Exod. 4:24–25). Sense the bitter disdain?

What about the man after God's own heart, King David? As David led the procession returning the ark of the Lord to Jerusalem, he was "leaping and dancing." When he excitedly returned to bless his own household, he was abruptly met by his irate, embarrassed wife, Michal. Unleashing upon him a string of stinging rebukes, she said, "How the King of Israel distinguished himself today! He uncovered himself today in the eyes of his servants' maids as one of the foolish ones shamelessly uncovers himself!" (2 Sam. 6:20).

David defensively replied that he did this before the Lord. Then he did something that many of us do in arguments. He issue hopped. He shifted the focus off his behavior and reminded her that God chose him to be king in her father's place. The charge of exhibitionism hurt David deeply. Apparently this fight resulted in some kind of marital separation; Michal remained childless until her death (2 Sam. 6:23). It's a shame. They could have worked this out.

Scripture also describes the results of conflict between employee and employers (Matt. 20:1–16; James 5:4) and citizens and government (Rom. 13). Did you know that less than 10 percent of the New Testament deals directly with evangelism, while a majority of the balance focuses on how to please God, how to get along with people, and how to unravel and work out impossible situations? Obviously, we need the help.

WHAT'S THE DIFFERENCE?

"So if Christian families, churches, and organizations have problems, what's the difference between them and the rest of society?" A disillusioned friend of mine asked this question. I had hired him to serve on the public relations staff of a small midwestern Christian college. He had had many years of experience dealing with the general public in a high-stress retail business, but none interacting with believers in a Christian vocational context.

What a rude awakening! He had visualized all the administration, staff, and faculty to be Spirit-filled, loving, cooperative, and kind, all through each "glorious" working day. That perception lasted less than a month. I will never forget the bewildered look on his face as he challenged me to explain the kinds of behavior he was experiencing from well-seasoned saints.

"I don't get it," he unloaded with exasperation. "I didn't expect to run into this kind of petty behavior in a Christian organization." His bubble was popped.

A veteran church leader himself, he was no stranger to religious politics or problems. But problems and conflicts in a Bible college? How could it be? The answer is simple. Christians have the same basic conflicts and complicated struggles as those who boast of no religious affiliation. What makes the difference is how Christians respond to conflict and what tools they use to resolve it. Christians start with the premise "You can work it out!" God has already given all the tools to do so (2 Pet. 1:3–4).

Tools to Live By

God has designed and granted us powerful tools that He expects us to use to work out the most solution-defying conflict. These biblical tools have several common features. First, they are universal. They can be utilized with both fellow believers and those who make no profession of faith in Christ. The tools transcend all cultural and religious boundaries.

Next, God's tools of conflict resolution reflect His character. God always acts consistently with His character. He expects believers to relate to each other, not according to their own selfish nature, but according to the new nature they received from Him.

The tools He gives us to unravel difficult problems also reflect His ways. Moses grew to understand God's ways through the difficult experience of leading Israel to the Promised Land. He learned the character and ways of God through the many conflicts he experienced with the people of God, Israel.

Moses also had a personal desire to learn the ways of God. He revealed the reason in his heartfelt prayer, "Let me know Thy ways, that I may know Thee, so that I may find favor in Thy sight" (Exod. 33:13). Friend, as you work through hurtful relationships, you are in for an exciting adventure. You are going to discover the power of personal responsibility. But you are going to learn something else. You are going to learn to know God. As you use His ways, like Moses you will learn to know Him.

One of the most consistent comments I have heard as I have observed hundreds struggle through to victory is, "This has drawn me closer to God." This will be one of the most encouraging personal benefits of your struggle as you seek to restore a shattered relationship.

Furthermore, these tools or principles are always based on truth. Why? Because God is truth and He gives grace only for the truth. Jesus came full of grace and truth (John 1:14). He always acted in the sphere of truth and reality, never in denial.

And finally, these tools are spiritual in nature, for two reasons. First, God is a spirit. His very essence is spirit (John 4:24). Second, in our conflicts we are actually dealing with spirit-beings who are acting upon physical beings. The apostle Paul confirms this when he says, "For our struggle is not against flesh and blood" (Eph. 6:12). You may object: "Paul doesn't know my brother-in-law and all the turmoil he is causing in the family. He is not a spirit. He is a 240-pound hulk who says what he thinks and does what he wants, when he wants. Because of this, every family gathering is a predictable disaster."

Let Paul finish. He clearly defines who is behind the brother-in-law's behavior: "But [our struggles are] against the rulers, against the powers, against the world forces of this darkness, against the spiritual forces of wickedness in the heavenly places." But you may further object, "My brother-in-law is not in 'heavenly places' causing turmoil in our family. He is right here on the terra firma." True. But the energy for his behavior is not coming just from himself. He is energized by the evil spirit behind this world system—Satan. Paul spelled this out to the church in Ephesus: "And you were dead in your trespasses and sins, in which you formerly walked according to the course of this world, according to the prince of the power of the air, of the spirit that is now working in the sons of disobedience" (Eph. 2:1–2). What appears to be a conflict with your brother-in-law may be in reality a conflict with the evil one. Jesus experienced this very conflict with His own disciple, Peter.

Horns and a Tail?

One day Jesus began to explain in detail to His disciples how He must go to Jerusalem to suffer at the hands of the elders, chief priests, and scribes and ultimately be executed on a Roman cross. That was not the end, however. It was just a prelude to a glorious resurrection in three days. But this bleak prospect went over like a lead balloon with the disciples, especially Peter.

Taking Jesus aside, Peter began to rebuke the Lord sharply, saying, "God forbid it, Lord! This shall never happen to You." Sense the friction? Feel the intensity of the confrontation? Consider the Lord's firm response: "Get behind Me, Satan! You are a stumbling block to Me; for you are not setting your mind on God's interests, but man's" (Matt. 16:22–23).

Did Peter suddenly sprout horns and a tail and grasp a pitchfork as he spoke these words? Of course not. I suspect Peter quickly glanced over his shoulder to see whom Jesus was correcting. In fact, Peter would have declared that it was he, not Satan, who was engaged in this verbal interplay. Yet Jesus knew that it was the strategy of Satan to use His own disciples to attempt to thwart His single purpose of going to the cross to die for the sins of the world.

Consider Judas's treacherous betrayal of our Savior. At first glance it appears that an ambitious disciple desires to fatten his personal coffers by betraying Jesus to the religious leaders. It looks like greed, pure and simple. But Dr. Luke enlightens us to the real scheme of things. "And Satan entered into Judas who was called Iscariot, belonging to the number of the twelve. And he went away and discussed with the chief priests and officers how he might betray Him to them" (Luke 22:3–4). Was Jesus wrestling against flesh-and-blood Judas, or against the evil one, Satan?

Jesus did combat on both levels—flesh-and-blood people and the demonic spirits who were actually behind the human pawns of history. In reality, we do too. But at least we have the insight to know who may be *ultimately* behind the confusing and complicated problems we face with others.

Will these biblical tools be effective to unravel difficult problems? Yes! They will because they are of God and He declares that they have divine power to destroy arguments and every pretension that sets itself up against the knowledge of God (2 Cor. 10:4–5). What, essentially, are these tools?

TOOLS DEFINED

Rarely am I confronted with a home-repair project that does not involve the use of more than one tool. The use of the proper tools makes the completion of the task possible, not to mention easier. Likewise, in dealing with "scrambled egg" relationship problems that seemingly defy solution, one may be called upon to use more than one tool.

Just as tools for the repair of houses and machines come in different sizes and shapes, so do God's tools for the repair of human relationships. On one hand, they are not complicated and do not require much training or job skill. Like workshop tools, these principles become more effective with experienced use. On the other hand, they are hard to use because of pride, fear, anger, rejection, revenge, criticism, and the ever-present possibility of misunderstanding.

Remember, Jesus utilized the same godly tools we are going to discuss, and He was killed—but not without first leaving us an example to follow in His steps (1 Pet. 2:21). Again, I have found in my own life and in the lives of those we have served that these tools for resolving problems become more effective with use.

There are four tools. The first tool is *truth*. Truth can be viewed as a weapon as well as a tool. In Ephesians 6:14, we see truth listed as the first weapon in our spiritual arsenal. Denial—minimizing conflict and wrongdoing—is the evil one's strategy to prevent godly closure to difficult situations. Many conflicts are not resolved because truth is not applied or acknowledged.

Folks often reach a major impasse because they don't apply the truth of Scripture or admit the reality of the situation. Truths from God's Word are essential tools as we tackle various complicated problems in this book. Christian denial basically blocks God's access to a hurt or conflict that He wants to heal for our benefit and His glory.

The second tool is *action*. God clearly defines what actions should or should not be taken in many difficult situations. We will see that when certain precise actions are not taken, resolution escapes our grasp. Conversely, when certain actions or behaviors are consistently applied, restoration and closure can result. Closure may not become a reality for everyone involved in the conflict, but at least *you* can experience it.

The third tool is *attitude*, which can make or break the resolution of a conflict. Our attitudes control how we use the other tools as well as how effective they are. For example, pride results in strife and further conflict, but an attitude of gentleness, genuinely expressed, may open the door of the hardest heart (Gal. 6:1).

The fourth tool is actually the primary tool we will learn how to use. It is woven all through Scripture. The very first chapter of Genesis barely concludes before this tool is disclosed: God said, "Let Us make man in Our image, according to Our likeness; and let them rule over the fish of the sea and over the birds of the sky and over the cattle and over all the earth, and over every creeping thing that creeps on the earth." God expands the concept of mankind's rule by placing His creatures in the Garden of Eden "to cultivate it and keep it" (Gen. 1:26; 2:15).

You may ask, "Where's the tool?" Look at the words *keep, cultivate,* and *rule.* These tasks imply personal responsibility. "Adam and Eve," God declared, "I am giving you rule (power) over these things and you are to keep and cultivate this garden. This is your responsibility."

Then God introduced a new concept to Adam and Eve. It was not vague or ambiguous. It was clear and forthright. "And the LORD God commanded the man, saying, 'From any tree of the garden you may eat freely; but from the tree of the knowledge of good and evil you shall not eat, for in the day that you eat from it you shall surely die'" (Gen. 2:16–17). God established a boundary. "You may eat freely and enjoy to your heart's content the fruit from any tree. But I am establishing a boundary or limitation. Do not cross over it by eating from this one tree. It will be a transgression."

The word *transgression* is made up of two words, *trans,* meaning "across," and *gression,* meaning "to walk." Therefore this word means "to walk across" a boundary, border, limit, or truth.

God gave Adam and Eve the responsibility not to do something. Within their sphere or circle of responsibility, they were to rule, cultivate, keep, and enjoy the abundance of the earth. They had the full power of God behind them. But they were not to step across or out of their circle and eat from the tree of the knowledge of good and evil. It was Adam and Eve's violation of God's boundary that laid the foundation for human conflict. And since they violated God's boundary first, we now violate each other's boundaries, and conflict ensues.

In their classic book *Boundaries,* Drs. Henry Cloud and John Townsend clearly assert that the inability to set appropriate personal boundaries at appropriate times with appropriate people is one of the most serious problems facing Christians today. They have been able to trace many clinical psychological symptoms, such as depression, anxiety disorders, eating disorders, addictions, impulsive disorders, guilt problems, shame issues, panic disorders, and marital and relational struggles, to conflicts connected with boundaries. As a source of conflict and pain, I would add to boundary violation the failure to identify, assume, and fulfill one's circle of responsibilities. Again, these evil roots of conflict began in the Garden of Eden.

ENTER EVIL AND CONFLICT

Our first introduction to evil in the Bible is in Genesis 3: "Now the serpent was more crafty than any beast of the field which the LORD God had made. And he said to the woman, 'Indeed, has God said, "You shall not eat from any tree of the garden"?'" She replied that there was one thing they were not to eat or touch (she added the word *touch*). The serpent, the father of lies, launched a frontal attack with his favorite weapon—a lie: "You surely shall not die!" He further offered her a personal elevation to Godhood and power. By crossing over this barrier or boundary and leaving their circle of responsibility, Satan promised, Adam and Eve would be like God, knowing good and evil. Eve looked, she took, and she ate. Then she turned to Adam, who was standing by, and he took from her hand the forbidden fruit and ate.

How do we know that this was the first introduction of evil into the human arena? The apostle Paul was concerned that the Corinthian believers could fall into the very same trap of deception: "But I am afraid, lest as the serpent deceived Eve by his craftiness, your minds should be led astray from the simplicity and purity of devotion to Christ" (2 Cor. 11:3). Then the elderly apostle John, who had been banished to the Island of Patmos, was told by God's

Spirit the future and identity of this serpent, which he reported in his book: "And the great dragon was thrown down, the serpent of old who is called the devil and Satan, who deceives the whole world" (Rev. 12:9).

If we were able to interview Eve regarding that deceptive experience, just at the moment before she ate the fruit, we might ask, "Whom do you think you are talking to there in the garden?" Her likely reply would be, "Why, a snake, of course." Yet we know from the inspired Word of God that the snake was a disguise for Satan. Was Eve confronted by a flesh-and-blood reptile or was there a ruler, a power, and a spiritual force of wickedness behind it?

WHERE ARE YOU, ADAM?

Instantly, something did not happen. Though Adam and Eve crossed the boundary and ate, neither of them collapsed in death. But something else happened. With sin entered something else devastating to the first family and ultimately to us—shame. Yes, shame. Instantly they knew they were naked. That problem was quickly fixed. They created the first fashion statement with fig leaves sewn together and made themselves coverings to hide their naked bodies (Gen. 3:7).

That solved their immediate problem. Then it happened. They heard something—a sound. Not just any sound—it was the Lord God walking in the garden in the cool of the day. Big deal. So what? But fear shot through the hearts of the first family. *Run! Hide! Here comes God!* they must have thought. *Quick, hide among the trees. Safe! God will never know.*

Then they heard a deep voice. "Where are you?" Does an omniscient God need to ask the location of a man in hiding? The call was for Adam's benefit, not God's.

Adam spoke. He did not answer the moot "where" question. God had found him out. *God knew.* So Adam answered "what" and "why" questions: "I heard the sound of Thee in the garden, and I was afraid because I was naked; so I hid myself."

God then asked two pointed questions: "Who told you that you were naked?" Not waiting for an answer, He added, "Have you eaten from the tree of which I commanded you not to eat?" Or "Have you failed in your responsibility? Have you left your circle and crossed into Mine?"

One of the most crucial hindrances to solving complicated problems took place right there: blame shifting. The woman was the first target. Said Adam, "If it were not for her, this mess would have never transpired. She gave me the fruit and I had no choice but to eat it." Adam was bold enough to confront God: "The woman whom *Thou* gavest to be with me, *she* gave me from the tree, and I ate" (Gen. 3:12, italics mine).

In other words, "This whole problem is *Your* fault, God, and *her* fault." Adam's response was a total abdication of personal responsibility. Then and now, nearly all complicated problems or conflicts can be traced back to each person failing to fulfill personal responsibility. From this point on, the number one issue mankind must face is just that—personal responsibility. Fulfilling, or failing to fulfill, one's own responsibility will determine one's quality of life, quality of relationships, and level of inner peace.

Eve's quality of life deteriorated immediately. She could not handle the burden of her personal guilt or the projected guilt from her blame-shifting husband. She did the only thing she could see to do, which she learned from her husband—she shifted the blame: "The serpent deceived me, and I ate" (Gen. 3:13). She could not plead entrapment. God knew.

New Responsibilities

Eve suffered two major consequences. She would still bear children. That was in the original plan. But now, God said, she would expe-

16

rience significant pain in childbirth. Women through the ages will declare this is true. I have seen it firsthand in the births of both of our daughters, DeeDee and Michelle, and those of our two grandchildren, Taylor and Brittany.

The second consequence of Eve's sin is perhaps the hardest. "Yet your desire shall be for your husband, and he shall rule over you" (Gen. 3:16). One can almost feel the marital battle lines being drawn up.

The Hebrew word translated "desire" is the same word used in Genesis 4:7. In this passage God spoke to Cain, who had just failed to carry out his responsibility to present a prescribed offering to God: "Sin is crouching at the door; and its desire is for you, but you must master it." To Eve God seemed to be saying, "The way sin desires to rule you, Eve, so you will desire to control your husband, but he will have the ultimate responsibility to rule over you."

God was not ambiguous about what He meant by "rule." He revealed to the apostle Paul what "rule" should look like: "Husbands, love your wives, just as Christ also loved the church and gave Himself up for her"(Eph. 5:25). Like Christ, a husband in leadership over a wife should exemplify personal sacrifice, not dominant control. Jesus came to serve, not to be served (Mark 10:45). So too the husband is to serve each member of his family in sacrificial love.

On Adam's part, failure to fulfill his personal responsibility resulted in the ground being cursed. Now his focus would be on work—hard work (Gen. 3:17–19). Eve would want a relationship with her husband, and she would be tempted to control him to get it. Adam would become work focused, which would drain his time and energies from a relationship with his wife and his children. And the first couple passed down to us a combustible mixture ready to explode with the smallest spark of conflict.

Adam and Eve's failing to fulfill their responsibility did not end in their physical death. Instead, it resulted in a spiritual death or separation from a holy God. The apostle Paul commented on the generational consequences of this first selfish act: "Just as through one man sin entered into the world, and death through sin, and so death spread to all men, because all sinned" (Rom. 5:12).

But physical death did knock at the door of the first family through their children. How? Again, it occurred in a failure to fulfill personal responsibility. Because God accepted Abel's animal sacrifice and rejected Cain's bloodless sacrifice of agricultural produce, Cain became angry. God could not talk Cain into offering an acceptable sacrifice. God explained to Cain how his dejected countenance could be lifted up. He also warned him that sin was crouching like a hungry lion ready to pounce on him and destroy him. But there was still hope. He could work it out. By taking personal responsibility, he would have the power to master it (Gen. 4:7). Yes, Cain, it is possible!

Cain chose to remain angry and disobedient. He did not want to change. He became bitter and hateful. This reflected who was controlling him. The apostle John exposed this control source: "Cain, who was of the evil one, . . . slew his brother. And for what reason did he slay him? Because his deeds were evil, and his brother's were righteous" (1 John 3:12).

Cain would not assume and fulfill his own responsibility to change, perhaps because he was too jealous of Abel. No doubt Cain's anger escalated into rage as he talked to Abel about God's rejection of his sacrifice. His anger erupted, found a target, and Abel died.

Where's Your Brother?

Just as God questioned Adam and Eve, He pricked Cain's conscience with the question, "Where is Abel your brother?" Cain's answer was an outright lie, "I do not know," followed by defensiveness, "Am I my brother's keeper?" (Gen. 4:9). In other words, "Do I have a responsibility to watch over the general welfare of my brother? He is not my responsibility." As we've seen with Adam and Eve, the act of abdicating one's personal responsibility is rooted in a heart manipulated by the evil one, Satan. Jude describes deep anger, rebellion against God, and the rejection of personal responsibilities as "the way of Cain" (Jude 11).

Cain may have felt he was not his brother's keeper, but he was his brother's killer. Therefore God brought closure to this conflict through the tool of human responsibility and accountability. God judged Cain and imposed a sentence: "You shall be a vagrant and a wanderer on the earth" (Gen. 4:12). But God also granted him mercy, "appointing" him a sign that protected him from those angered by his actions.

As with Cain, God does not deal with us by a formula, but by precept or principle from His Word. God's tools for conflict resolution are not formula driven; they are principle directed.

TOOLS ARE NOT FORMULAS

It is my personal discipline of life to read through a new Bible each year. But every year I get bogged down in a different exciting section. One of the things I enjoy doing, especially as I read the synoptic Gospels (Matthew, Mark, Luke) and the general gospel, John, is to observe how Jesus helped people. His was no assembly-line approach to people's needs. He never treated two encounters alike.

On one occasion, He merely touched the eyes of two blind men and they were healed (Matt. 9:27–30). On another occasion, Jesus saw a man who had been blind from birth and He spat on the ground, made clay of the spittle, and commenced to rub the clay in the man's eyes. He then instructed the man to wash the clay off at the pool of Siloam. Upon doing so, he was healed (John 9:1–7). Finally, John Mark records an occasion when Jesus led a blind man out of the village of Bethsaida, then spit on his eyes and laid hands on him. After the second time the Lord Jesus laid His hands on the man's eyes, the man could see everything clearly (Mark 8:22–25).

What formula can we learn from these three miracles? Do we touch people's eyes, spit on the ground, or spit on their eyes? I can see you shaking your head. That's how I feel. Jesus did not stress formulas as much as faith: faith in Him, faith in His Word. There are no six steps to do this, seven steps to accomplish that, or nine important steps to guarantee these results; not even in the important area of prayer.

Jesus' disciples asked Him to teach them to pray. He did so. He gave them what we call the Lord's Prayer (Matt. 6:9–13). In actuality, it was the disciples' prayer. Yet Jesus never intended it to be a formula—the first or last word on prayer. It is very insightful, but it is not an exhaustive treatise on the subject.

In the same way, the power of responsibility, and how to implement it in working through a difficult situation, is not a formula. It is a principle of Scripture that is an outgrowth of the character of God. It is a way of God. Yet be clear on this: implementing His ways may or may not bring peace, even though we may strongly desire peace, especially with someone dear to us.

PEACE ON EARTH

We are faced with two realities in Scripture that if placed side by side, appear to be contradictory. The first is peace. Our Lord is the Prince of Peace (Isa. 9:6). Peace reflects His character. Peace is God's ultimate goal in all relationships, for He has "called us to peace" (1 Cor. 7:15). We are to proactively seek and pursue peace with everyone (Heb. 12:14; 1 Pet. 3:11). There is personal accountability in working toward peace. The apostle Paul strongly urged, "If possible, so far as it depends on you, be at peace with all men" (Rom. 12:18).

But the words "if possible" hint at the second reality. Jesus said plainly, "Do not think that I came to bring peace on the earth; I did not come to bring peace, but a sword" (Matt. 10:34). But notice what kind of relationships may be affected by His presence: "I came to set a man against his father, and a daughter against her mother" (v. 35). How does this statement mesh with the commandment that sons and daughters should honor their parents, that their lives may go well and last long (Eph. 6:2–3)?

The extended family is also included in this "sword." A daughter-in-law will be set against her mother-in-law. And Jesus concluded with a drastic statement from the prophet Micah that strikes at the very foundation of society—the family: "A man's enemies will be the members of his household" (Micah 7:6). Why? The answer is simple. When a man makes peace with God, he may be expelled from the family: disinherited, disenfranchised, ostracized, shunned, disowned, rejected, and even declared dead. Yet salvation is only one "sword." Obedience to God, even in a Christian family, can result in some of the same hostile reactions.

An overprotective mother may not let her married daughter go. She may still want to control her in the marriage. If that daughter would indeed "leave and cleave" to her husband and respectfully refuse to be controlled by her mother, more than a sword of separation could fly between the daughter and mother. Obedience to God can bring a sword of separation. What is a married son or daughter to do in a case like this? What is his or her circle of responsibility toward the mother-in-law? This may be what the apostle Paul had in mind with the phrase "if possible." It may mean that you can do all that you are responsible for before the Lord and peace may still elude the relationship. But peace doesn't elude your own heart. You have worked it out—for you.

Identifying, assuming, and fulfilling personal responsibility remains the key ingredient in resolving relationships. Fulfilling one's circle of responsibility brings personal peace with God, although doing so may cause conflict in other significant relationships. It is sobering to recall that Jesus said, "If the world hates you, you know that it has hated Me before it hated you" (John 15:18).

Where Do You Begin?

With close to forty years of helping people work through conflicts in interpersonal relationships, the most powerful tool I have used is that of circles of responsibility. It is not a formula. It is a way of God that has practical ramifications. With the family Pastor Tim was working with, we used this same tool. It is the purpose of this book to help you learn how to use the biblical tool of circles of personal responsibility as a powerful means to reduce, and even in many cases end, serious conflict in current or former relationships.

Think of a conflict or problem you have with someone—the more complicated and difficult, the better. Gather all of the pieces. Write each aspect down as best you can. Ask our heavenly Father to use what you learn from His Word and His ways to empower you to work through this difficult challenge.

You may have many practical questions. I pray that experience has taught us enough to answer many of them. Honestly, some questions baffle me to this day. Take heart. God is not stingy with His wisdom. Ask and you will receive (Matt. 7:7). He will not make you feel stupid or silly to ask for it (James 1:5). Get ready, for you are in store for an awesome adventure. You are going to see God release the power of personal responsibility in restoring relationships in your own life. Yes, it is possible!

TWO

WHAT REALLY HAPPENED?

time + effort

My pastor-friend, Tim, was overwhelmed. Remember the couple he called me about in the last chapter? An alcoholic husband and father, critical and angry wife and mother, and kids—they all spelled disaster. Where would you start, Tim wondered, to restore such a fractured home? I suggested that Tim and I meet with the family at his church. When I got there, the look of relief on Pastor Tim's face said it all: "Man, am I glad you are here."

Tim introduced me to Kari and Mark. None of their children would come. I had requested the use of either a chalkboard or marking board, so after brief introductions we left the pastor's study and went into one of the classrooms of the Christian school.

Kari and Mark were fashionably dressed. I think they wanted the best to be seen before the worst was heard. Pastor Tim nodded for me to begin. In my introductory remarks, I thanked them for the investment of time and energy they were making in their marriage. Then I summarized two important principles, ones we live and work by in our ministry. First, we were there not to just fix problems but to learn how to work them out using the principles of the Word of God. Second, we were there to learn how to do this so we could help others.

No Vacuum

These two principles are also a reflection of the character and plan of God for our lives. The apostle Paul stated it this way: "Blessed be the God and Father of our Lord Jesus Christ, the Father of mercies and God of all comfort; who comforts us in all our affliction so that we may be able to comfort those who are in any affliction with the comfort with which we ourselves are comforted by God" (2 Cor. 1:3–4). God comforts us for both our personal benefit and for that of others who need our comfort. God gives hope when we feel hopeless and strength when we feel weak—and we share these with others.

The word *able* in the passage implies two things—ability and resource. God uses what we go through to equip us with the ability to help someone else. The Holy Spirit within us is our always available resource. But God's indwelling presence does not give us experience. When we experience God's Word firsthand in our own lives, it equips us to comfort others in their shattered and scrambled lives. That is the reason the apostle Paul directed the spiritual ones to go to those who are trapped in any sin or trespass for the purpose of restoring them (Gal. 6:1). The spiritually attuned have not just gone through the Word of God, but the Word of God has gone through them. It is often our own pain that lays the foundation for preparation to minister to someone else. No problem that we encounter happens in a vacuum—without a purpose.

But that day, Mark and Kari were not there to learn how to help others. Their lives were a mess. Their kids' lives were a disaster. Nothing was working for any of them. They were there to help themselves—which is where healing begins.

24

THE A'S AND B'S OF COMMUNICATION

We felt dwarfed in the large, empty classroom. Each of us selected a front-row desk. I suggested we turn them into a half circle, facing the green chalkboard. I asked Pastor Tim to commit our time to the Lord in prayer. Nervous but hopeful, he graciously thanked the Father for what He was going to do that afternoon.

I slipped out of the rather snug school desk and walked to the board. Picking up a piece of chalk, I drew an *A* on the left side of the board and a *B* on the right side. Then I asked, "What are the two letters that I have printed on the board?"

"A and B," Kari offered, sounding bewildered.

"Right. Now, if I put a *t* behind the *A* and an *e* behind the *B*, what do I have?"

"At and Be," nervously responded Pastor Tim, perhaps hoping not to embarrass Mark and Kari with my juvenile simplicity.

"Good. What we are going to do is very simple. First, we will try to determine what is really going on in the family. We will list under *At* what you think the problems are in the family. Then we will list under *Be* where you want to go. Finally, we will list between *At* and *Be* the hindrances to going from where you are at to where you want to be. If you do not know clearly where you are at, you will not be able to determine with any certainty where you want to be, nor be able to identify the obstacles impeding progress to that goal. If nothing else today, let's determine where we are. Let's look at the things that are not working for you."

This approach is one I have used for years to assist families or individuals to work through difficult problems. I observe this pattern throughout Scripture.

The apostle Paul dealt with many complicated problems, not just with the unsaved but with those in the church. He usually identified the wrong that people were doing before he launched into corrective measures. The church at Corinth was just one classic example of this procedure.

Corinth was a well-established church by New Testament standards. The apostle affirmed, "In everything you were enriched in Him, in all speech and all knowledge, even as the testimony concerning Christ was confirmed in you, so that you are not lacking in any gift, awaiting eagerly the revelation of our Lord Jesus Christ" (1 Cor. 1:5–7). A church does not get much better.

Though as a whole the church had its strong points, there were roots of instability and potential destruction. In dealing with these issues, Paul clearly described where they were at on each issue, then what needed to be corrected. He learned through friends at Corinth that there was a power struggle causing a great deal of friction. He cut to the quick and hit the issue head-on (1 Cor. 1:11). He then picked up this theme of jealousy and strife again in chapter 3.

Chapter 5 opens soberly: "It is actually reported that there is immorality among you, an immorality of such a kind as does not exist even among the Gentiles." A Corinthian believer was having an incestuous affair with his stepmother. This was explicitly prohibited by both the Old Testament law (Lev. 18:6; Deut. 22:22) and Roman law. Paul knew that if the sin or offense was not clearly stated up front (under the *At* position), the church would not take decisive steps to correct it. Sexual issues are usually the most covered-up, ignored, and denied issues in the church. But not with Paul. He had to make clear where the church of Corinth was at, even if it meant dealing with some heinous issues.

Chapter 6 opens with another tidal wave of major sin and conflict crashing upon the shores of this early church. "Does any one of you, when he has a case against his neighbor, dare to go to law before the unrighteous, and not before the saints?" Paul asked. Again, right up front, he named the actions before suggesting solutions. "Look where you are at!" was the apostle's cry. It was like he took an x-ray before proceeding with the corrective surgery.

THE FAMILY X-RAY

Before any orthopedic physician will set a broken bone or perform corrective surgery, he wants to see a clear set of x-rays. He wants to evaluate the extent of the damage and determine what needs to be done. Then, through follow-up x-rays, he is able to monitor the progress of the healing. For these same reasons, we attempt to take an x-ray of the conflicts that are causing pain and damage in people's lives.

Solomon underscored the wisdom of first determining where a person is "at" before proposing a solution: "He who gives an answer before he hears, it is folly and shame to him" (Prov. 18:13).

At Tim's church that day, I asked Kari and Mark to name what they saw happening in their marriage. I explained that we wanted to take a family x-ray, and I offered a few communication tools.

First, the goal of this phase was fact finding, not fault finding. When Mark blurted out that Kari was always criticizing him, I told them I was not interested right now in who was doing what. If our first step was to assign blame, one or both of them might shut down and refuse to cooperate. Once that happened, the spouse would become defensive instead of informative. Then he or she might revert to issue hopping and even name-calling, which never result in a righteous end or bring clarity, correction, and closure.

Second, I strongly suggested that one person speak at a time. This may seem relatively juvenile, but remember, whatever Mark and Kari had been doing was not working. They may still have been children emotionally, so they acted and fought that way. Personally, I believe that by allowing each person time to speak, we display mutual honor and respect. Paul urges us to outdo one another in showing honor (Rom. 12:10), and the apostle Peter simply says, "Honor all men" (1 Pet. 2:17). Letting another talk without interference exemplifies that honor.

27

There is also a very practical reason for this one-at-a-time communication tool: talking is not listening. Think about it. Am I listening with understanding if I am formulating my defense? Am I noting the other person's tone of voice or evaluating his/her body language if I am planning my response?

Jesus perceived that many of His hearers were not listening. He often preceded or concluded His teaching by saying, "He who has ears to hear, let him hear" (Matt. 11:15). Jesus knew that though His audience had physical ears, that did not mean they were listening. One way to help facilitate listening is by allowing one person to talk at a time. This also prevents one person from monopolizing the conversation with speeches, lectures, or angry interruptions. Monopolizing the conversation usually is a control technique a person uses to prevent a loss of pride or to get attention.

Listening must be harder than talking. That is the reason God's Spirit directed James to write, "Let everyone be quick to hear, slow to speak and slow to anger" (James 1:19). Some have said that since God gave us one mouth and two ears, He must have wanted us to listen twice as much as we talk. The fact is, listening is usually the first necessary ingredient in working out any conflict. Repeatedly I hear husbands and wives or parents and teens who have genuinely listened for the first time say, "Oh, I didn't know you felt that way!"

The response? "I've been trying to tell you this for years, but you just wouldn't listen!"

Listening first and talking second works even with teenagers and their parents. Colleen was a popular high school senior. She lettered in varsity swimming and had been a cheerleader three of her four years of high school. Her home life wasn't as successful. She wanted out. She ran from the house during a recent argument with her parents. All three consented to family counseling. When I asked Colleen to share where she was at, I quickly noticed that both parents repeatedly interrupted Colleen to tell her where they thought she was in her life. I graciously asked her father to let her finish—we all desire this honor and respect. He got the message. Less than a minute later Mom interjected. I turned to her and gently requested that she, too, allow her daughter to finish.

It was amazing to all concerned. Colleen felt heard. Dad was pleasantly surprised to learn his daughter had both positive and corrective things to say. Mom looked totally relieved that she did not have to defend, explain, or translate for anyone. It was absolutely the first time all respectfully listened to one another. The phrase I kept hearing was, "I didn't know you felt that way." Of course they didn't. How can you listen if you are talking, formulating a defense, blame shifting, name-calling, yelling, or screaming? With a new rule set to let one person talk at a time, I then introduced the third communication tool: seek to understand what is said. Jesus often appealed to His listeners to do this.

HEAR AND UNDERSTAND

On one occasion the Pharisees and scribes challenged Jesus regarding His disciples' not washing their hands before they ate bread. It was not a hygiene issue. The religious leaders accused the disciples of failing to observe the tradition of the elders regarding the ceremonial washing of hands. This was a rabbinic tradition, not a Mosaic law. It involved an elaborate ritual that included not only hands but also cups, pitchers, and cooking utensils.

After firmly rebuking the hypocritical leaders, Jesus turned to the multitude and said, "Hear, and understand" (Matt. 15:10). He then quickly clarified that it was not what goes into the mouth that defiles a person but what comes out. The Pharisees were wrong in thinking their laborious washing kept them spiritually clean. But before He gave this clarification they were urged to "hear, and understand." The third tool is just that—hear and understand.

In his book *Caring Enough to Confront,* David Augsburger

vividly describes the heart of a husband who wants to hear and understand his beloved wife.

> I want to hear you accurately, so I'll need to check out what I hear at crucial points to be as sure as I can that my meanings match your meanings. I get an inkling of what your meanings are from your words, your tone of voice, your face, gestures, and body movements. But it is only an inkling. I must check it out at times by replaying what I heard for your approval, until you agree that you have been heard. I want to hear deeply, clearly, accurately enough that I am able—to some real extent—to feel what you feel, hurt a bit where you hurt, and want for you the freedom to be all you are becoming.

How did the husband confirm what he heard to see if it was what she meant? Simple; listen to him again: "I must check it out at times by replaying what I heard for your approval, until you agree that you have been heard." This is an excellent practical tool.

Dr. Gary Smalley, speaker, best-selling author, and seminar teacher, has mastered this tool. I have seen him in action as he invites people from his seminar audience to use this tool as we all eagerly look on. He will ask a wife to share a thought with her husband and then have him repeat back what he heard. Often we hear what we want to hear or what we think we heard. We may even reject it because we do not like what we heard. We may not listen because of a sharp tone of voice or rejecting body language. One friend commented to me, "I am especially bad about not listening to my husband when his voice sounds a certain way. Anything he says in that way I do not hear."

Smalley will not let the couple explore a solution to the problem until both the husband and wife can honestly acknowledge they heard *and* understood what was said.

All of these tools would be useful for Mark and Kari. We would use them to gain an objective, forthright description of what was happening in their home.

WHERE ARE WE "AT"?

"Kari," I began, "would you briefly share what you see happening in the marriage?"

"Well," she started hesitantly, "he lies all the time."

I reminded her to just name the offensive actions and attitudes, instead of blaming or assigning responsibility. I then wrote the word *lying* under the word *At*. Seeing it was safe to share honestly, she abandoned any reservation and quickly listed the following:

At
Lying
Unfaithful
Distrustful
Vengeful
Dishonoring
Cursing
Undisciplined
Alcoholic
Abusive
Abandoning
Unloving
Uncaring
Selfish
Thoughtless
Sarcastic

She paused, then said, "I guess this will do for starters."

I turned to Mark and thanked him for his patience. I asked him to do the same thing. His list included

At
Fighting
Withdrawing
Critical
Perfectionistic
Yelling/Screaming
Dominating
Controlling
Overprotective
Disrespectful
Unsubmissive
Angry/Raging
Taking sides

"That about says it all," he concluded.

Kari and Mark stared at the lists. It was a Kodak moment. For twenty-seven years they both were involved in doing these things. This was the first time they looked at the family x-ray to see what had really happened; for once they didn't use the volatile mixture of yelling, outbursts of anger, name-calling, and other destructive ways of communicating.

Where Do We Want to "Be"?

I asked Mark and Kari to tell me how they felt about what was written on the board. Their shame and embarrassment were apparent. But it was important for them to go on record with how they felt. An emotional response helps acknowledge the reality of what has for years been denied. A deep sense of sadness poured over their countenances as if to ask, "So this is all we have to show for almost thirty years of marriage?" Both expressed that it did not look good.

I asked if we could go over the list and determine each word's opposite.

"Why? This is a mess. This can't be fixed," Kari said in a voice overwhelmed with despair.

"Would you do it anyway?" I urged.

They needed a great deal of encouragement and support at this point. It was important to give them hope. Hope for Kari and Mark included honestly understanding and agreeing where they were at and visualizing where they wanted to be; it involved affirming that their goals *were* achievable. After all, they could do anything God expected of them through Jesus Christ, who would give them the strength (Phil. 4:13). Then we could determine a workable plan, *how* to go from where they were at to where they wanted to be.

The list on the chalkboard looked like a human impossibility. I have never met an impossible marriage, but I have met some impossible people. People who are willing to work hard are winners. I assured them, "We can work it out."

Then it was time to finish an honest x-ray of the marriage and family. We began to determine where Kari and Mark wanted to be. This list is usually the opposite of what estranged spouses are doing.

"What is the opposite of lying?" I inquired matter-of-factly.

"Truthful," Mark asserted.

"Good." I wrote truthful under the *Be* column.

"What is the opposite of unfaithful?"

"Faithful," Kari blurted out with an angry edge to her voice.

We continued down the list. Pastor Tim was helpful in getting through an impasse when they had difficulty determining the opposite word. Their lists looked something like this:

At	*Be*
Lying	Truthful
Unfaithful	Faithful
Distrustful	Trustful
Vengeful	Forgiving
Dishonoring	Honoring

Cursing	Blessing
Undisciplined	Self-controlled
Alcoholic	Sober
Abusive	Kind
Abandoning	Loyal
Unloving	Loving
Uncaring	Caring
Selfish	Sacrificial
Thoughtless	Considerate
Sarcastic	Complimentary
Fighting	Harmony
Withdrawing	Sharing
Critical	Affirming
Perfectionistic	Balanced
Yelling/Screaming	Soft voice
Dominating	Serving
Controlling	Interdependent
Overprotective	Healthy independence
Disrespectful	Respectful
Unsubmissive	Submissive
Angry/Raging	Forgiving
Taking sides	Impartial

How would you know what to suggest on the *Be* side? I keep in mind the nine fruit of the Spirit (love, joy, peace, patience, kindness, goodness, faithfulness, gentleness, and self-control—Gal. 5:22–23). Most of the items listed under the *At* column are the negatives of these nine positive qualities.

COMMITMENT TO ACTION

There are important reasons for filling out both the *At* and *Be* columns. Once people clearly see where they are at and where they want to be, they can decide where to go from there. I put it to Mark and Kari this way: "You both agree where you are *At* right now and where you should *Be* in your relationship. But is this where you *want* to be?" That may sound like a dumb question. Presumably counseling was where they wanted to be or they would not have come. But that is often not the case.

Hundreds of people have come to me for pastoral counseling at great expense to both their time and resources. I used to naively believe that if they made this extra effort, they naturally wanted help and were willing to make changes. This wasn't always so. A spouse may want me to help change his mate but remain unwilling to change himself, let alone make adjustments. Such a couple will describe where they are *At*, agree where they want to *Be*, and even head in that direction, but they will end up back where they started.

When pressed for the reason they do not want to change, they rarely give a reason. Instead I hear excuses, along with blame-shifting statements like, "It's her fault."

Another reason I ask people to identify where they are *At* and where they want to *Be* is to serve as a point of commitment—to set a basic goal. Then they can practice accountability and measure progress; they can see how far they have come and where progress is still needed. This is one of the ways of God.

Jesus saw the need for commitment to a goal in His potential disciples. As our Lord set out on another preaching-teaching mission toward Jerusalem, a wealthy, influential young man ran up to Him, dropped to his knees, and asked, "Good Teacher, what shall I do to inherit eternal life?" (Mark 10:17). Talk about sincerity! This man ran up to Jesus, assumed a submissive posture, and called Him "Good Teacher." Honestly, I would have been more than willing to help a person so gripped with urgency and eagerness for spiritual guidance.

The young man knew where he was *At*. He was insecure about his future destiny, but he believed he could change this. That was where he wanted to *Be*. All he needed to know was what good deed to do to achieve eternal life. To his satisfaction, he explained, he had kept the Commandments, going back perhaps as far as age twelve, when he became a "son of the law" at his bar mitzvah. His challenge to Jesus was, "Name the requirement and I will fulfill it."

The penetrating eyes of the Savior pierced to the depths of his heart. "Sell your assets and give them to the poor." It must have felt like a powerful blow to the stomach. The young man emotionally doubled up in pain and his "face fell, and he went away grieved" (v. 22). What went wrong? What happened to his urgent sincerity? Jesus knew. Jesus saw that under his religious veneer, wealth was his real god. He was unswervingly devoted to it. It represented everything important to him. He had already violated the first commandment to have no other gods before Him (Exod. 20:3). Jesus knew the young man wanted security on his own terms, instead of on our Lord's terms of sacrifice and service. The Greek verb translated "Come, follow Me" is a command, not a suggestion. Where was Jesus going? To Jerusalem and to the cross.

For me, the poignant part of this story is in the words "and looking at him, Jesus felt a love for him" (v. 21). There are only five people singled out by name in the New Testament as those whom Jesus loved: Mary, Martha, Lazarus, the apostle John, and the rich, young politician. He personally experienced the love of Jesus and then walked away from it. What an eternal loss!

The young man knew where he was *At*. He sincerely knew where he wanted to *Be*. His life was headed in that direction. But the cost and commitment were too much and revealed his core belief system that wealth, position, prestige, and power were in reality everything.

Addicted to Misery

The cost of change strikes to the core of people helping. Many will acknowledge where they are *At* and even give mental assent to

36

where they need to *Be*. They go through all kinds of effort to convince others that they are going to change. Then at some point, they go right back to where they were.

Dr. Robert Becker wrote a book entitled *Addicted to Misery: The Other Side of Co-Dependency*. Interestingly, this book underscores the idea that the unstable desire to change occurs in the non-Christian arena as well. I have read this paragraph to many:

> For years, I have worked with co-dependents and adult children of alcoholics. Many were recovering chemical dependents themselves or living in dependent relationships. The most striking phenomenon I saw was those people who, after working hard to alleviate many life stresses or at least to regain some manageability in their lives, then returned to the state of misery they were in before coming to therapy. Time and time again, they attained a level of successful emotional functioning, working through the obstacles and conflicts and then, with full awareness, they would march right back to unhappiness and emotional distress.

It is the bent of human nature to return to dysfunction or sin-function. It takes active, volitional decision to do otherwise. God uses the Book of Judges to illustrate through Israel this human bent to return to the sin-functional *At* position in relationships, whether it is with God or with man.

Judges 2 and 3 reveal the simple pattern. First, during the life of Joshua and his generation, God's people lived a life of relative obedience. That was where they were supposed to *Be*. Then, when that generation died out, the nation plunged into idolatrous practices and deep sin, returning to stage *At*. God could not let life work for them in the place of sin they were *At*, so He initiated servitude. He raised up various groups to enslave His people. The pain got worse. So, Israel cried out to God for deliverance. As a nation they acknowledged their failure to be obedient to God's laws. They knew where they were *At* and did not like it; they knew where they wanted to *Be* and needed God to deliver them. So then God raised up a judge, a deliverer, to regain the freedom Israel had lost through its sin-functional lifestyle. God faithfully delivered them and gave them rest. The fruit of obedience was peace. But then a new generation grew up and forgot the apostasy and judgment of the past; these men and women turned right around and repeated it. They fulfilled the prophetic words of Santayana, "Those who cannot remember the past are condemned to repeat it." This cycle replays seven times in the Book of Judges alone. It was as if Israel were addicted to misery.

This cycle is a downward spiral. It is these downward spirals that ultimately cause the deep relational pain that finally drives people to a trusted friend, a godly pastor, or a competent counselor for relief. But the cry for relief may not include a desire to change a sin-functional lifestyle. It may be just a plea for relief from the consequences of wrong behavior.

For genuine, lasting healing to take place, the cycle must be broken, the downward spiral stopped. A new pattern of obedience must be instituted, if peace, restoration, and resolution are to be practically realized.

If people can grasp where they are in this cycle, as illustrated by Israel, and where they could be, and even achieve a small portion of it, it could serve as a motivation to return to their continued growth in Christ. This would stop the downward spiral of personal and relational destruction.

Break the Cycle

This is exactly what God was attempting to communicate to the church of Ephesus: "I know your deeds and your toil and perseverance. . . . [You] have not grown weary. But I have this against you, that you have left your first love. Remember therefore from where you have fallen, and repent and do the deeds you did at first" (Rev. 2:2–5).

"Remember from where you have fallen"—"Look what has happened." This statement implies that the church at Ephesus knew where it had been (the *Be* position) and then fell away (back to the *At* position). The believers were in a downward spiral. Then God firmly directed them to "repent [reverse directions] and do the deeds you did at first." In other words, "Break the cycle. Return to the *Be* column of positive, healthy, obedient living."

If the Ephesian church had not had a clear picture of where it used to be, it would have been futile for God's Spirit to urge a return. Knowing where you are *At* and where you should *Be* clarifies the direction in which you want to go. Can you make a commitment to that direction? Does each spouse agree on that goal? Do they believe the family x-ray?

Marilyn and Bruce had been through extensive counseling before they came to us at Living Foundation Ministries. As a matter of course, I inquired what previous counseling they had had, what issues they covered, and what closure or correction they accomplished. To my dismay, counselees sometimes tell me that for all the time, effort, and expense they put into counseling, they accomplished little. For that reason I ask them to tell me where they are *At* and where they want to *Be* and to make a commitment to move in that direction.

At the end of our first session, Bruce looked at Marilyn, then turned to me and said, "We have learned more in this one session than we did in months of counseling with others." Many people object to counseling, saying that it does not seem to go anywhere. They meet and meet and dread another meeting. If the time drain is not bad enough, the lack of accomplishment, change, or identifiable progress is downright discouraging.

When counselees ask me if I feel they are making progress, I can refer them to their own *At* and *Be* lists. Have they moved from one list to the other on any issues? Have they learned new tools of relating? Are they using their tools? Have they brought closure to any longstanding hurts?

Another benefit of the *At* and *Be* principle is to give all concerned an ability to monitor progress. With every journey there are points of departure and a destination, but also mileposts of evaluation along the way. I explained to Marilyn and Bruce the benefits of this procedure: you will always know where you are and where you are going, and you will be able to monitor your progress. You will experience accomplishment. You will experience closure. You will be able to move on and break the cycle not by trying to forget the past but by working out each issue of the past and present, using the tools of Scripture.

Yes, this is a painful journey. The apostle Paul called the churches of Galatia "my children, with whom I am again in labor until Christ is formed in you" (Gal. 4:19). Paul went through the throes of birth pains, as it were, to bring the Galatians to salvation. Then it was as if he had to endure painful labor again as he struggled to deliver them from the false teachers ravaging the church body.

Paul knew the Galatians were delivered from the control of the current evil age by God's will (Gal. 1:4). But instead of being conformed to the image of Christ, they had deserted Him for a different gospel (Gal. 1:6). This apostasy could crush the heart of the staunchest discipler. It is a replay of the downward spiral patterned in the Book of Judges. But Paul also knew the Galatians could rebuild for the future by breaking the cycle of the past. The journey would begin with truth.

NOTHING BUT THE TRUTH

Marvin and Betty had been married nineteen years. He was a pastor who had been asked to leave his church. One of the unconfirmed reasons was "moral indiscretion," a church euphemism for adultery.

40

He would disappear for hours on end. Even as an evangelical, he secretly enjoyed visiting upscale taverns late into the night.

I asked Betty to describe what had happened in the family relationship. It was not easy for her. In less than fifteen minutes, she described their family life. Then I turned to Marvin and asked him to follow suit. Out of my peripheral vision, I caught Betty's look of surprise. No detail came near to matching. If I did not know better, I would guess that they were living in two separate houses with different mates and kids. This puts a people helper in an awkward position. Both could not be telling the truth.

When faced with conflicting stories, I make it clear that since I was not there, it is not my place to verify or investigate the facts. Experience has taught me to ask certain questions that in time reveal much of the truth. If there is no agreement on the facts, how can you help determine where people are *At* and where they should *Be* and coach them in how to get there?

First, I prayed. I acknowledged our dependency on God to direct us. It is incredible how the Holy Spirit exposes a direct lie— sometimes through the lying party, sometimes through another source.

During one of our sessions, while still determining where she was *At*, Betty announced that her doctor had just confirmed she had a sexually transmitted disease. She paused, looked at Marvin, then me, and said, "I have never known another man sexually but my husband. I was a virgin when we married." Marvin stammered that she could have gotten it any number of ways. She glanced at the floor, then to him, then to me, and said, "The Lord knows the truth." Marvin abruptly stated that the counseling was not going anywhere and that he was done.

Betty and Marvin divorced. Many sad truths came out in court. But God has not called many of us to spend our time and energy investigating the truthfulness of people's stories. Instead we are to look for the broken pieces and be used of God to bring healing.

We often have to work with the pieces they give us. We have to collect the bits of Humpty Dumpty's shattered life the best we can. God does not normally strike down people who lie to us as He did Ananias and Sapphira when they lied to Peter about their property (Acts 5:1–11). We do not have the adultery test to perform on a woman if a spirit of jealousy comes over her husband, as Moses was instructed to conduct (Num. 5). We are not able to cast lots to determine who has sinned in our group as Joshua was able to do regarding the sin of Achan (Josh. 7:14). But we have the witness of God's Spirit in our hearts. Often He tells me that there is something important missing in what I am being told. In such cases I leave the responsibility of revealing the truth of what happened with God.

When a person tells me something has happened in his past that makes him uneasy, but he does not know what it is, I *do not* guess or suggest what it may be. I have led hundreds of people in King David's prayer:

Search me, O God, and know my heart;
Try me and know my anxious thoughts;
And see if there be any hurtful way in me,
And lead me in the everlasting way.

(Ps. 139:23–24)

David was asking God to test and prove his loyalty to Him. He asked God to investigate if there was any "offensive way" or "way of pain" (literally) in his life. We can ask God to look for those ways of pain in our lives that may have been caused by others.

More times than not, a name, place, face, or situation will come to a person's mind in bits and pieces. Sometimes the counselee does not want to think about it or look at it. I respect that request. Yet I do ask if they would at least share with me the fear they have about looking at it. With rarely an exception, when the fear is adequately addressed, the person is more than willing to look at the memories that God brings to the surface.

God is more desirous for us to use His tools, truths, commands, and insights than we are, especially if we go on record that we are doing it for His glory. This underscores another reason it is important to get the truth out in the open. It brings glory to God.

TRUTH AND GLORY

The retreating warriors were struck down one by one. Thirty-six men lay slain. Joshua ripped his robes in grief, shock, and shame. "Alas, O LORD God, why didst Thou ever bring this people over the Jordan, only to deliver us into the hand of the Amorites, to destroy us?" (Josh. 7:7). The answer was sin. But whose?

Through the process of elimination, Joshua pinpointed Achan as the thief. Perhaps the most unusual aspect of Joshua's confrontation is what he requested: "My son, I implore you, give glory to the LORD, the God of Israel, and give praise to Him; and tell me now what you have done. Do not hide it from me" (Josh. 7:19).

Note the connection Joshua made between truth and glory. It gives glory to God to honestly declare the truth of what happened. It is a time of glory and praise to God to honestly and truthfully declare where one is *At,* what he has done, because that serves as a foundation for rebuilding and gives direction to begin. A detailed description may not be necessary, but naming the offense is (Eph. 5:11–13).

The apostle John expressed the need for an honest disclosure this way:

> If we say that we have fellowship with Him and yet walk in the darkness, we lie and do not practice the truth; but if we walk in the light as He Himself is in the light, we have fellowship with one another, and the blood of Jesus His Son cleanses us from all sin. If we say that we have no sin, we are deceiving ourselves, and

the truth is not in us. If we confess our sins, He is faithful and righteous to forgive us our sins and to cleanse us from all unrighteousness.

(1 John 1:6–9)

Note what exciting benefits we experience when we walk in the light of His truth—fellowship with God and each other. What if we fail? "If we confess" or acknowledge our failure or sin, this brings glory to God and the peace of God.

Honest appraisal of what has happened and where we ought to be in the light of God's Word and His Spirit lays the foundation for rebuilding broken relationships.

It is easy to get bogged down in the paralysis of analysis in identifying the pieces. We need to do something with them. It is time to go to the next step with Kari and Mark. We have taken a relationship x-ray, assessing where they are *At* and where they want to *Be*. We know what happened. Now it is time to do what we have been putting off so far. It will be painful. But it is one of the important keys to working it out.

THREE

WHO WAS REALLY RESPONSIBLE?

So far, so good. Kari and Mark agreed on what was happening in their marriage. At that point, no one was at fault and no one was to blame. No one was responsible for anything. This picture was about to change.

Mark and Kari had listed where they were *At* and agreed where they wanted to *Be*. Now the real work began. Now it was time to separate and assign personal responsibilities for the actions and attitudes that had put the marriage on a collision course. Why is this step important? Because it is God's way of restoring relationships. God designed the need to identify and separate out each person's circle of responsibility. Doug was a case in point. "Doug's on the phone. Would you talk to him for a minute?" asked my wife, Linda. I knew it was long distance. After a few pleasantries, Doug reluctantly acknowledged that he and his estranged wife had not followed through with a project I had suggested months before. The request had been basic: list where each one was *At* in the marriage and where they wanted to *Be*. The *At* side was most important. Doug and his wife lived three hours away, and I wanted them to come to my office prepared to work with some awareness of what their problems were.

"Well, Chuck, I just can't get past the fact that my wife has a spending problem. She has racked up $45,000 worth of debt and I'm working three agricultural-based jobs to pay it off." In our brief conversation, I tried to learn more about his relationship with her. He sheepishly admitted he currently had no relationship with her, never had one, and didn't know what one was like. Then the bombshell: he was not even interested in a relationship. No amount of urging could persuade Doug that his wife wanted a relationship with him. If she couldn't have him, I explained, she would spend to deaden her own emptiness and to punish him where it hurt him the most, the pocketbook. What I said seemed to shoot past Doug with the speed of an arrow. He responded, "But I still can't get past the $45,000 debt hanging over my head." I was reminded of Jesus' familiar beam-and-speck analogy.

THE BEAM AND SPECK OF PERSONAL RESPONSIBILITY

On a mountainside in Galilee near Capernaum, Jesus taught what is commonly called the Sermon on the Mount. Near the end, He zeroed in on a practice very common to the Pharisees—judging others while ignoring their own faults. "Do not judge lest you be judged," He told them. Then Jesus posed a rhetorical but penetrating question: "Why do you look at the speck that is in your brother's [or wife's] eye, but do not notice the log that is in your own eye?" How could they help others and fail to see their own glaring needs? "How can you say to your brother [or wife], 'Let me take the speck out of your eye,' and behold, the log is in your own eye?" Conclusion? "You hypocrite, first take the log out of your own eye, and then you will see clearly to take the speck out of your brother's eye" (Matt. 7:1, 3–5).

I paraphrased this passage with Doug. "Why don't you identify, assume, and fulfill your own circle of responsibilities first? Then you will see clearly how to deal with your wife's responsibility." What was Doug doing? Just the reverse. He was focusing on his wife's alleged wrongs as a subtle deflection away from his own responsibilities.

Two very dear friends came to me with the same core issues that plagued Doug and his wife. John admitted that it was his goal to shrink his circle of responsibility down to a size of a pea and inflate Alice's circle to the size of a basketball. John had a reason for this. He wanted Alice to feel she carried the total blame for any family difficulty. John was a skilled blame shifter and controller. Alice was a classic pleaser. Compliant pleasers will assume fault in order to pacify angry controllers. John majored on splinters and totally ignored the beams. For years he saw Alice's splinters as beams. She believed his lies about her.

The sizes of the speck and the beam emphasize the importance of personal responsibility. Doug's log was a primary beam that would fully support the roof of a building. His wife's speck was a small, dry bit of wood, such as a speck of sawdust. The large beam is God's perspective of our own responsibility. The speck is the other person's responsibility. Our personal responsibility is always greater because it is usually the only responsibility over which we have control. But our selfish mind reverses it. We may admit to a small speck of our own, but it is in no way as large as the massive beam grotesquely protruding out of the other person's eye.

Jesus' teaching on the beam and speck does not alleviate Doug's wife's responsibility to control her spending. But it does teach the necessity of seeing and assuming one's own responsibility first, which will clear up perspective to see clearly the other's needs and viewpoint. What Doug could not understand was that he was operating with a handicap. The "log" in his eye was obstructing his vision of both his and her needs.

"Shouldn't you talk to her about her compulsive spending?" you may ask. She did not call me. Doug did. It is important to deal

deal
with the person who comes to you, not the one who is not there. Jesus frequently did this.

Out of a bustling crowd came a strong appeal to Jesus: "Teacher, tell my brother to divide the family inheritance with me." The text is not clear whether the brother was present or not. But Jesus responded to the one who made the appeal on the basis of personal responsibility. "Man, who appointed Me a judge or arbiter over you?" That was not Jesus' circle of responsibility. He then addressed the crowd, pinpointing the offended brother's need: "Beware, and be on your guard against every form of greed; for not even when one has an abundance does his life consist of his possessions" (Luke 12:13–15). Jesus focused on the man's greed problem rather than the brother's alleged unfairness. He was not implying it should never be addressed. But He was focusing on the need of the one present.

Quite often only one spouse will come for counseling. His or her motive is usually to get some advice on how to change, fix, or manipulate the other spouse into a desired behavior. I normally draw three circles, designating one for the absent spouse, one for the present spouse, and one for the marriage. Even the most gifted marriage counselor is able to help only the one that is there.

I draw these three circles for a very practical reason. I ask the spouse who is present to write in her own circle what she is responsible to do, what she can or cannot do. Then I have her fill in her mate's circle—what he is responsible to do. Now we have her issues in her circle, his issues in his circle. The third circle is reserved for *their* issues. Doug has to deal with the fear of failure and intimacy that fuels his avoidance of a relationship. His wife has to deal with her bitterness for his abandonment and failure to build a relationship with her. The third circle would include the need to mutually decide on a budget that would bring the family's expenses back into balance. It is important to separate out his issues, her issues, and their issues. Most problems defy solution because of a failure to identify and separate out each person's circle of responsibility.

Then there is the other scenario: a mate comes for counseling to learn what he can do *himself* to fix his mate. He fails to understand that if his spouse had cancer, he could not take the cobalt treatment for it. His behavior can influence his spouse, but he cannot fix her. The principle Jesus worked from was that you help the one who is present to identify, assign, and assume his or her own circle of responsibilities.

The apostle Peter struggled with this concept of personal responsibility. We see this illustrated again at Jesus' third appearance following His resurrection as He was standing along the shore of the Sea of Tiberias. Seven of the disciples had returned to their vocation of fishing and had caught nothing all night. A stranger instructed them to cast their nets on the right side of the boat. They did, and the catch was so huge they could not haul it in. Instantly, John recognized the stranger as Jesus, and Peter impulsively plunged in and swam to shore.

As they sat around the glowing coals, eating the baked fish and bread Jesus had provided, He recommissioned Peter to tend and feed His lambs, those who would become believers in Christ. Three times Peter betrayed Jesus, three times Jesus inquired of Peter's love for Him, followed by clear instructions to shepherd His sheep (John 21:1–17).

Jesus then turned the conversation to inform Peter how he was to die. This had to be hard to hear. Glancing at John, Peter said, "Lord, and what about this man?" Jesus utilized the circle of responsibility principle to convey an important truth to Peter: "If I want him to remain until I come, what is that to you? [That is John's circle of responsibility] You follow Me! [That is your circle]" (vv. 21–22).

The apostle Paul explained to the Christians in Rome the same need to identify and separate their own circles of responsibilities in order to reduce conflict and increase peace. "If possible, so far as it depends on you, be at peace with all men" (Rom. 12:18). The phrase "so far as it depends on you" is the same phrase Paul used in

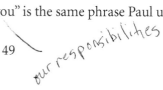

our responsibilities

explaining his responsibility in proclaiming the gospel. "Thus, *for my part,* I am eager to preach the gospel to you also who are in Rome" (Rom. 1:15, italics mine). The phrase in the original language means "so far as proceeds out from you." Paul emphasized that he had done, was doing, and would do everything he humanly could to accomplish the spread of the Good News. In like manner, he encouraged the church members in Rome to do everything within their power to be at peace with each other. This was the same attitude we encouraged with Mark and Kari.

BACK TO THE DRAWING BOARD

Cooperation was the order of the day as Mark and Kari completed their *At* and *Be* lists. Then came the stressful part. I drew two circles, about two feet in diameter, on the board. I put Mark's name under the left circle and Kari's name under the right one. Surveying the *At* list on the board, I said, "Who has been doing the lying?"

As if on cue they replied at the same time: "He/she does."

No problem. I wrote "lying" in both circles. "What about cursing?" She eyed him with an I-dare-you-not-to-admit-this look. Mark shrugged his shoulders to indicate his guilt. "How about withdrawing?" The vote went to Mark again. "Who is critical?" Kari's eyes dropped as she nodded her head. I added that to her circle.

We went down both of their lists. Sometimes both were guilty. There were occasional flair ups: "Yeah, but he [or she] . . ." I knew we were right on target when the blame shifting surfaced. Facing responsibility does not feel good because it brings with it conviction. Blame shifting is the detour of personal responsibility.

As I have used this tool of assigning personal responsibility through the years, I have heard a husband or wife frequently say, "I feel you are picking on me." I used to launch into a long, defensive explanation of what I was doing. But in recent years it dawned on me: *This is probably the first time these people have had to face a per-*

sonal x-ray of who they are and what they have done. I also realized that to attack is to distract. It is issue hopping in its purest form. So now I merely say, "We can discuss fairness at a later time if you wish; however, now we are talking about your sarcasm. Is this part of your lifestyle?" Their exasperated looks convey the reality that their strategy to distract from the issues does not work.

From time to time a people helper has to evaluate if, in fact, he has been balanced or has focused on one person more than the other. The visualized circles help keep the focus. Also it is appropriate to simply ask if anything has been overlooked in either spouse's circle. When one of them has had a basically healthy Christian lifestyle, their circle may indeed contain less than the habitually offending spouse's circle.

ADD A CIRCLE

Although Kari and Mark's children were not present, their names and behaviors frequently came into the conversation. Every time another person is mentioned while addressing a conflict, be it children, in-laws, parents, or relatives, add a circle for them. It will add some value to the family x-ray.

We often hear that a particular problem is so complicated that it defies solution. We are back to the dilemma that all the king's horses and all the king's men had with Humpty Dumpty. Yet the answer may not be as complicated as it appears. By adding a circle for each person relevant to the conflict, we answer two questions. First, *who* is responsible for *what?* Identifying and clarifying personal responsibility for each offense will quickly tell you what should be done and who should do it. Second, it will answer who is *not* responsible for *what.* It is as important to know what one is *not* responsible for as what one *is* responsible for.

King Solomon's insight in Proverbs 26:17 is revealed through a curious comparison: "Like one who takes a dog by the ears is he who passes by and meddles with strife not belonging to him." The word *meddle* literally means "infuriates him, or excites himself over." If one grabs a dog by the ears, he can expect to be bitten. In like manner, if he "excites himself over" a quarrel that is not his responsibility, he can expect trouble for himself by interfering in a conflict he knows little or nothing about. Earlier Solomon urged, "Do not contend with a man without cause, if he has done you no harm" (Prov. 3:30).

Afraid to Look

But what do you do when someone involved in a conflict does not see or even want to see his responsibility? There are reasons for this avoidance. First, he may have been shamed as a child for making any mistakes and grew up afraid of failure. A mature person has learned through the years that it is all right to fail. It is a part of life and one will recuperate. Some people, however, enter adulthood never having heard the important persons in their lives say, "I was wrong. Would you forgive me?" They have no role models to follow in how to correct a mistake. They feel they will lose their worth if they own up to a failure in personal responsibility. Some would call it pride.

Instead of being devalued in others' eyes, people who make mistakes and humbly own up to them are admired and respected for their character (Prov. 29:23). Those who are controlled by their fear of rejection, abandonment, and pride cannot admit their mistakes, and they are not respected.

A second reason people may not want to see their circle of responsibility is that it is a new idea. If one was raised in an environment of blame shifting, to assume personal responsibility is totally foreign to his/her experience and scary. If parents do not acknowledge personal wrongs to their children, the children quickly learn it is not necessary to admit wrong. It would be a source of shame to do so.

꙳⁷⟩ The third reason people may avoid looking at their circle of responsibility is that they may feel that someone else is always responsible. The person who believes this avoids all personal *accountability.* This was exactly what John was doing to Alice and what Doug was doing to his wife. To acknowledge personal responsibility implies accountability to change, adjust, admit a need, or even confess being wrong. Hell would freeze over before either John or Doug would do this. Even people in the ministry get caught in this fear-of-disclosure trap.

A pastor from a small, rural church requested I meet with him, his wife, and his teenage daughter. Pastor Martin told me, "She's a rebel, resisting God, making poor choices, hanging around with older men, and lying through her teeth." A mutual pastor-friend who referred them to me had called and alerted me to the situation and filled me in on the daughter's perspective.

I gently asked the daughter if she would share what was going on in her life and where she was hurting. Personally I was taken aback that she would be so honest with her parents present. She had been hit and slapped, cussed at, criticized, shamed, betrayed, and not protected. Dad was never home, and Mom would not come to her aid even when she later acknowledged her husband's harsh treatment of their daughter and favoritism of their younger son.

Ironically, the teenager's pastor-father did not dispute her claims. What jolted me was when he declared, "I will not take any responsibility for her behavior. She can't blame me for her poor choices." I did a double take. I glanced at his shy wife, who immediately dropped her eyes as if to say, "Please, don't bring me into this." She, like Alice, was a compliant pleaser. He, like John, was an angry controller.

Many parents bring their rebellious teens to me to fix. Yes, they do need "fixing." But so do their parents. I am often frankly told, "We did not come here to discuss us. We're here to fix them." When I hear this, two Scriptures come to mind. In the last verse of the last book in the Old Testament, Malachi declares, "He will restore the hearts of the fathers to their children, and the hearts of the children to their fathers" (4:6). Most inappropriate behavior by adolescents is their way of crying out for help and of getting their needs met. Often the cure is to restore or develop the emotional bond between parents and their children.

The second verse is the apostle Paul's instruction to the churches in Galatia, "Do not be deceived, God is not mocked; for whatever a man sows, this he will also reap" (Gal. 6:7). Although the apostle was primarily dealing with the question of financial support of Christian workers in the Galatian churches, the broader principle remains. The sower must decide what kind and size of crop he wants. Then he has to select the type of seed that will accomplish those goals. If you plant wheat and want corn, wheat is what you will get. A common definition of insanity is "doing the same thing over and over again, expecting different results." If you keep planting wheat year after year but expect to harvest corn, you need an agricultural refresher course. You may curse the ground or God, but the farmer is the one with the problem.

This pastor-father sowed devastating seeds of anger, rage, and shame but expected godliness. The Scripture makes it abundantly clear this is mocking God and He will not tolerate it. Corn will beget corn, not wheat. Therefore, the third reason one may fail to see his circle of responsibility is that he feels that someone else is responsible.

The fourth reason one does not want to see his circle of responsibility is a fear of dealing with conflict. This is not an accountability issue but a fear of not knowing what to do. Most of their lives these people have tried to escape from conflict in one of several ways. The exploder erupts with anger in a conflict. The imploder swallows his anger. ("Peace at any cost" is his motto.) The runner escapes into alcohol, drugs, sex, TV, work, hobbies, soap operas, civic involvement, reading, computers, or religious activities. (Some of these activities are not wrong in themselves. Yet all of them can be used as an escape from the fear of what could happen if they saw something they had to deal with.)

#5   The fifth reason one cannot see his circle of responsibility is outright denial. "What problem?" he asks.

DENYING GOD ACCESS

Denial is not a river in Egypt. Having crossed the Nile several times, I wished I could have found a sign in English with the Nile in the background—and for good reason. When people don't want to believe that a problem, a difficult issue, or a responsibility even exists, I wanted to point to the picture and remind them that denial is not a river in Egypt. It is what they are doing now.

What is denial? According to Drs. John and Linda Friel, authors of *Adult Children: The Secrets of Dysfunctional Families,* it is one way we protect ourselves from a reality that is too painful to let into our conscious thinking. A working definition of Christian denial that I have used for many years describes the seriousness of what denial does: *It denies God access to a problem that He wants to heal for our benefit and His glory.*

Note four sobering aspects of this definition. First, denial factors God out of the process. That in itself can be personally devastating. Why? Because one of the common features of a problem is worry. Worry is facing a present or future situation with God factored out. It is hard to look our Savior in the face with a determined focus and worry at the same time. In reality, a trial may be God's loving wake-up call that He wants to be more intimately involved in our lives.

Second, with God factored out, we have denied Him access to our problem. God is wise enough to let us sweat, stew, fret, and worry until we are willing to turn to Him. We are not to be anxious for anything, but we are to factor God into the process by prayer,

be concerned — not worry [handwritten marginal note]

#1 [handwritten marginal note]

#2 [handwritten marginal note]

supplication, and thanksgiving, and spell out our requests to Him. The net result is peace (Phil. 4:6–7).

Third, denial blocks access to the very solution and relief of our pain. God could comfort, heal, restore, encourage, and give us some badly needed hope (2 Cor. 1:4). This may have been the reason He allowed the problem in the first place, to develop our faith and increase our endurance under trials (James 1:3). The net result is that we do not get healed or helped; in fact, we stay stuck.

Finally, denial robs God of His glory. Jesus said it this way: "Let your light [life] shine before men in such a way that they may see your good works, and glorify your Father who is in heaven" (Matt. 5:16). Paul summarized it best: "Whatever you do, do all to the glory of God" (1 Cor. 10:31). And through God's mercy, if we suffer with Him we will be glorified with Him (Rom. 8:17).

People therefore may fail to see their circles of responsibilities for lots of reasons. Some try to avoid conflict by running while others just deny a problem exists. But Traci and Nick had a more difficult problem. It was not a matter of assigning responsibilities but experiencing blurred circles.

BLURRED CIRCLES

"Chuck, I feel I have my mother-in-law in my bedroom," said Nick, a very frustrated young husband. I could not help but think this was going to be interesting. I asked Nick if he would explain what he meant. He related this story.

It started before they were married. The blinders of love and the intoxication of romance obscured what was taking place. Nick described his wedding day. Before Nick and Traci left for their Hawaiian honeymoon, Traci called her mom from the airport. She called her mother upon arriving in Honolulu. Each morning and evening she called Mom. There would have been intermittent calls during the day if it were not for their packed schedule of swimming, snorkeling, bike riding, hiking, and surfing. "In fact, she talked to her mom before we came here tonight and her mother will expect a call from Traci when we get home. She is going to grill her about what we said to you and what you said to us."

I looked at Traci, and her chagrined countenance conveyed that Nick was telling the truth. Gently I inquired if her mother was ill or needed close supervision due to her age or for health reasons. Traci said no, she was in good health and held a very responsible job.

Then I asked Traci if she would give me a brief summary of her growing up and any particular issues or problems her parents had. Her brief answer told it all. Her dad was an alcoholic and died when she was ten. Though the marriage hadn't been good, it had met some of the mother's physical and emotional needs. After the death, Traci's mother turned to Traci for comfort, security, and companionship to fill her own void.

"Did you feel you became your father's replacement?" I asked her.

"No question. Mom often told me I was all she had. She needed me to take Dad's place. I became her confidant, counselor, nurturer, encourager. Sometimes I felt like I was the mother. But Mom needed me to do that for her. I love my mom, and I don't see Nick's problem. Yes, she is a little nosy, but that's Mom."

Most people who leave their circles of responsibility and cross over into others' circles do so ignorantly, impulsively, and naturally, and they rarely intend to hurt anyone. They create blurred circles.

Traci and her widowed mother's relationship reminded me of an old fishing reel I had as a boy. It tangled quite easily. The more I attempted to untangle it, the worse it got. I recall staring in bewilderment at my Mylar fishing line–filled hands, totally at a loss. I ultimately did the only thing I could. I took my fishing knife and cut it all loose from the reel. Each strand of fishing line fell to the old wooden dock in a snarled mess. You can do that with fishing lines, but it's not the best solution for family conflicts.

This tangling of lives is often referred to as *enmeshment*. God affirmed that the establishment of each new home through marriage would be characterized by the "leave and cleave" principle. Right from the beginning God established marital boundaries by declaring, "For this cause a man shall leave his father and his mother, and shall cleave to his wife." The natural outgrowth of that union was that "they shall become one flesh" (Gen. 2:24). What does a relationship look like if that does not happen?

ENMESHED CIRCLES

The problem is, neither person in a blurred, enmeshed relationship can tell where his/her own identity ends and the other's begins. These people do not have identities of their own and therefore do not have clear circles of responsibility. Their reasoning is, "My problems are your problems, and vice versa."

Traci's mother had no identity of her own. She lived for and unintentionally through her daughter. It was logical for her to call and ask intrusive questions. It was as if she were going on the honeymoon and to marriage counseling, in fact, as if she were the one who married Nick.

What happened if Traci did not call her mother? At their next conversation she would hear, "It's about time you called"—sarcasm that pierced Traci's oversensitive conscience. Her mother would continue, "I thought you died! I know you're busy with your new life and don't have time for me. After all, I have been there for you only all your life."

An enmeshed relationship builds a relational bookkeeping system. It is designed to keep track of all the overinvestment, cloaked in sacrificial terms, so that as the child reaches adulthood, she is so "in debt" she will not even think of reducing or ending this unhealthy relationship. Insecurity is the issue. The child serves as the adult's insurance against ever being alone. Again, God is virtually factored out, if not outright replaced. But He alone has guaranteed, "I will never desert you, nor will I ever forsake you" (Heb. 13:5).

Enmeshed adult children feel totally responsible for preventing their overdependent parents from experiencing loneliness. Despite all the overprotection that such children provide, the parents' loneliness does not abate. Why? Because loneliness is God's call to our heart for fellowship with Him, not our call for another person to fill the God-shaped void in our hearts.

Our deepest needs are never filled with human relationships. *true*
King David's choir director, Asaph, struggled personally to the conclusion, "Whom have I in heaven but Thee? And besides Thee, I desire nothing on earth" (Ps. 73:25). Still, we still tend to exchange earthly position, power, and possessions for contentment with the true God.

Another characteristic of an unhealthy relationship is that one person blames the other for her own unhappiness. This was evident in Shelia's relationship with her mother, Ann. Ann repeatedly told Shelia that she had never done anything she would need to apologize for and she could be happy if it were not for other people. She criticized Shelia for any conflict they experienced because it couldn't be Ann's fault. Ann would not take any responsibility for her own life. Again, this is the same tactic John and Doug used to avoid personal responsibility in their respective marriages.

The trouble is, people like Shelia's mother assume that if others are responsible for their unhappiness, others are also responsible for their happiness. Yet here it takes a strange twist. If one is happy, the other one feels she needs to be moody and even depressed. Why? Each one feels responsible to maintain a balanced emotional environment. And just to confuse things more, if one person gets depressed, soon either both will get depressed or one will try to overcompensate for it with ecstatic behavior. It is crucial to note that in such cases, no one is being led by or responding to God's Spirit; each is responding to the other's emotions. True, we are to "rejoice with those who rejoice, and weep with those who weep" (Rom. 12:15), but that is totally different from being depressed with those who are depressed or overcompensating with other extreme emotions.

In enmeshed relationships, peace is not allowed. Why? Each one's energy comes from turmoil. Chaos creates excitement, and excited emotions result in adrenaline highs. This is totally contrary to the goal of the indwelling of the Holy Spirit, whose fruit is joy, peace, and self-control. God's Spirit does not control enmeshed believers. Happiness, which depends on circumstance, replaces joy. Peace does not feel normal, so each one seeks turmoil. Emotional control replaces self-control. Such people become thermometers reflecting the family's atmospheric temperature, instead of thermostats that set the temperature through God's Spirit.

Enmeshed people also identify with each other's pain abnormally. No one is allowed to make a mistake and learn by it without shame. The enmeshed hate those who make mistakes, because enmeshed people suffer concurrently. I saw this vividly with Eric.

While a youth pastor in Southern California, I had a sophomore in high school come into my office rather upset by a decision his mother had made for him. Eric's complaint was simple: his mother would not let him play football. I quizzed him regarding his attitude at home, family conflicts, and fulfilling responsibilities, and I came up bone-dry.

After gaining permission from Eric, I called his mother. She was a dear Christian woman. I asked if she had some particular reason she did not want Eric to play football. If it was an obedience issue or character deficiency, perhaps I could help. Surprisingly, it was neither. She reassured me that Eric was a terrific, responsible kid. After a pause she confided that she just did not want to see him get hurt. Hurt? I played football. Football is all about getting hurt. But God's Spirit prompted me to ask, "Are you concerned you will feel his pain, and it may be too much for you to bear?"

Another pause. "I know I should not feel this way, but I can't help it."

"I can see it would be hard. Could we talk about this together next week here at the church?" To her credit, in a short time, Eric's mother was able to locate and understand where her real pain was coming from. She had experienced many childhood losses. Eric's potential pain got her in touch with her own past pain. She allowed the healing grace of the Lord Jesus to touch her and heal her. As for Eric, his coach was grateful I had the talk with his mom. Eric had an outstanding three years, and so did Mom.

Unfortunately, some blurred circles are harder to clarify and resolve.

EMOTIONAL INCEST

Further probing of Traci's home life revealed the darker side of enmeshment. As I learned more about Traci's home life, a strange feeling crept over me. I honestly believe that the intention of her mother was pure. Yet something happened that turned out to be devastating to Traci emotionally.

Physical incest is an adult using a child to meet the adult's sexual needs. Emotional incest, on the other hand, is an adult using a child to meet their adult emotional and psychological needs. The Hebrew word for incest is translated "confusion." This is exactly what happens in the child's mind when he or she is physically or emotionally called upon to meet adult needs.

When Traci's mother lost her alcoholic husband, she was left with her own needs unmet. They had had a codependent relationship, in which he was dependent on the alcohol, and she was dependent on the relationship. Neither was satisfied. In an extreme codependent relationship, one adult expects another adult to act in the place of God on his/her behalf. I call it relational idolatry.

[handwritten note: look to another person (not God) to fill any void]

61

This can take many forms. Once I attempted to help a Christian woman out of a physically abusive relationship. I saw the actual pictures of her bruised and battered face. Yet she told me that she would rather be killed by her husband than live life without him. It was not a divorce issue. It was a fear-of-being-alone issue. Her husband, in actuality, took the place of God in her life. Fortunately for them both, he received some serious help that turned him around. Yes, she is still dependent, but she has made some major changes.

Not all dependent relationships are adult to adult. Unfortunately they can be adult to child. When Traci's father died, her mother turned to Traci instead of seeking adult help from her friends, her church, and her family. For hours on end, Traci had to listen to her mother bemoan how she missed her husband and all the "good" times they had. Mom looked for comfort and reassurance from Traci that things were going to be all right. Traci could not go anywhere without her mother's constant vigil. She would talk her out of playing with her friends, involvement in school activities, going to church camps—all on the basis that Mommy needed her or that Traci might get hurt. This was emotional incest.

Traci was her mother's total focus. Instead of a God-centered home, it was a child-centered home. Instead of God being factored in as the ultimate supplier of their needs, it was "us against the world."

The results were dysfunctional or sin-functional. It is never right to elevate another human being to the place of Almighty God. Traci became her mom's God-substitute. Their relationship was controlled by fear instead of faith. Traci felt totally responsible for her mom's needs. In fact, their emotional perversion caused her to feel overly responsible for everything and everybody. As a result, Traci lied to herself about her own feelings, wants, and needs. They were stuffed and forgotten. This was her foundation for blurred circles.

BACK TO BASICS

What is the beginning point of reducing conflicts in relationships? It is found in the principle of circles of responsibilities. First I suggested that these people in conflict start by honestly identifying what has happened and is happening in the relationship. They should make a list of actions that are taking place. This step would help them see the reality of the factors in the conflict. Then I asked them to assign the appropriate blame: who is responsible for what. They had to be sure to include what rightfully belongs in each circle.

⚬━⚬━⚬━⚬━⚬

Traci and Nick completed these steps and were ready for the rest. Today they have a growing, healthy relationship. And Traci's mom is doing great. How did they work it out?

FOUR

How Do
In-Laws Fit In?

This was Nick's second marriage and Traci's first. During the five years they had been married, they realized a number of mistakes they had made. So they began attending a church where the Bible was taught clearly. They were working to get their lives on track personally, spiritually, and maritally. But because they had reached an impasse regarding Traci's mother, they came for counseling.

Their story is very common. In-law conflicts are normal. Not only do newlywed couples have to adjust to each other, they have to adjust to the new extended family. Being an in-law myself, I know that even when we've given our full blessing to the marriage, there are still adjustments to make with the new "son" or "daughter." When these transitions are not made smoothly, conflict is inevitable.

New Circles for Old Families

I had the privilege of jointly performing the wedding ceremony for my oldest daughter, DeeDee, and her fiancé, Roger. His father was a pastor too, so we were able to tie a "double knot." Before the couple exchanged vows, Roger's dad gave a challenge to his son. Then it was my turn to do likewise to my daughter. I had written out word for word what I would say. It was going to be short and sweet—no tears. I stoically stood attired in my black tuxedo with my Bible in one hand and a microphone in the other. Admiring the beautiful bride, I began to read the opening line.

"DeeDee, today ends a relationship you and your mother and I have had for twenty-one years." Suddenly, tears began to pour down my face. I lost it! I had no handkerchief. Quickly glancing around, I could not find a box of tissue anywhere. I don't know if they ever got the sleeve of that tuxedo cleaned.

What happened? This was going to be a beautiful, smooth ceremony, then we would head off to the gala reception. But I now stood face-to-face with a new reality. I was giving my daughter to another man. In spite of all my denial up to that point, the new circles of responsibilities being formed glared at me.

I told myself to get a grip and get on with it. I glanced down to the next line of my notes, which read, "But today begins a new relationship that your mother and I look forward to enjoying together with you." A new relationship and new circles for both the newly formed family and the old family.

I have already mentioned Moses' account in Genesis 2:24, where God established the "leave and cleave" principle. A young wife once pointed out to me that Genesis 2:24 specifically states that it is the *man* who is to "leave and cleave." It does not say the woman has to also. I acknowledged her point, then asked if she was familiar with Ephesians 5:22: "Wives, be subject to your own husbands, as to the Lord." I asked her if she would see any difficulty with a wife who was still directed by her parents while attempting to be subject to her husband.

"Well, I know," she replied, "but I just think a woman doesn't have to act like her parents are dead." I suspected from that statement that a lot of confusion existed in her mind and that she, her husband, and even her parents were at odds over their new roles and their circles of responsibilities.

Parents Were Not Invited

Although Roger's father and I were performing the actual ceremony, we did not conduct the premarital counseling; DeeDee's pastor did. The young couple attended a number of sessions, covering the bases for building a godly marriage. But Linda and I had no formal training to be in-laws or grandparents.

It is taken for granted that we as parents will know how to act toward our married children. The truth is, we usually don't. Just look at the sick in-law jokes that permeate our society, especially about mothers-in-law. (I am married to one, and I think she is great.) The tasteless, shaming jokes only cover up an even sadder reality, that there may not have been a genuine "leave and cleave" by the adult child but instead a "leave and grieve" by the in-laws.

Some will attempt to ignore reality by saying, "I have not lost a son; I have gained a daughter." That sounds great. Many new daughters-in-law have added a great deal to the extended family. That is not the issue. Those parents did lose a certain kind of relationship with their son. Now they relate to him in a totally new, God-designed, healthy relationship—if the healthy transition occurs.

Parents can forget or refuse to acknowledge that their adult children have formed new circles of responsibilities. When their children were young and living at home, it was appropriate to tell them to clean up their rooms. Now that they are married or on their own, it is out of place to tell them to clean up their apartments. That is no longer within the parents' circle of responsibility. Failure to acknowledge this biblical reality results in unnecessary emotional pain for the adult children and their parents.

Often parents will do to their married kids what was done to them. They may think it is normal to be controlling or manipulative because that is how they were treated. Fortunately, most parents who recognize what happened to them purpose to act differently toward their children. But what if they don't? What can a young husband and wife do when extended family blurs the boundaries and circles of responsibilities and becomes painfully intrusive in their lives? This was the case with Nick and Traci.

HONOR VERSUS OBEY

It was time to suggest some practical steps for Nick and Traci to take with her mother. These were designed to take Traci's primary focus off of her mother—while still loving and honoring her—and redirect her energies toward her newly formed family. One suggestion was to begin limiting the frequency and length of the phone calls.

"I could never do that!" Traci objected. Her sudden panic was obvious. "Just talking about my mom this way makes me feel bad, like I'm disloyal. I love my mom, and I could never do anything to hurt her. Even God said we are to honor and obey our parents. I don't want to disobey God or my mom. Sorry!"

Assigning circles of responsibilities with parents and in-laws after marriage is not easy. Just a hint of it in this direction sent Traci into orbit. This is a common response because the extended family is a touchy area.

Perhaps the number one reason for adults' continuing conflicts with their parents is that they fail to distinguish between honoring and obeying their parents. Failure to make this crucial distinction prevents adult children from acting in a responsible, respectful, adult manner, as God designed. Traci's response made clear that she needed a fuller understanding of the concepts of honor and obedience.

Traci was right. God does command children to obey their parents: "Children, obey your parents in the Lord, for this is right" (Eph. 6:1). Not only are they to obey, but they are to honor their fathers and mothers. Paul affirmed this: "Honor your father and mother (which is the first commandment with a promise)" (Eph. 6:2).

Actually, this is the second commandment given by God that is coupled with a promise (Exod. 20:6). Paul was probably indicating that this is "first" in the sense of being of primary importance for children. It also includes a special promise for them—a stable and long life. I have never met a person with a biblically balanced quality of life who did not have at his or her core honor for parents and authority.

Obedience Ends; Honor Continues

This is where Traci was confused. When Traci and Nick married, they had a traditional wedding. Her brother walked her down the aisle in her father's absence. The pastor asked a simple question as they stood before him in the presence of family and friends. "Who gives this woman to be married to this man?"

"Her mother and I," came the brief reply. From that point on, the familial responsibilities were transferred from her mother and siblings to Nick. This is a traditional ceremonial rite that visualizes the biblical "leave and cleave" concept.

Instantly something changed. It was not physical. Traci was as beautiful as ever. Nick was still as handsome. There were no bells or whistles, lightning or thunder. Yet something happened inside—a severing, separating, a movement apart, not from Nick, but from Mom.

I asked Traci what she thought took place at that point. What had changed? What would be different? She paused, then said, "I guess I will not live at home but with Nick. We will start our own family and begin to live life together."

"Good. What changed with your mom?"

"I guess I will not be living in her house. We will pay our own bills. I don't know what else changed."

"What about 'honor and obey'?"

"Nothing. I still need to honor and obey my mom. She is still my mom. Getting married didn't change that."

"Do you really believe you should obey your mother as a married woman in the same manner as you did as a child?"

"No, I mean . . . Well, I have to obey God and not hurt my mother."

"Can you be subject to your husband and your mother at the same time?"

Traci's anxiety rose to a point that I believe if she could have, she would have bolted out of my office. She was stuck and confused. Confusion usually means there is a collision between what we know to be true and what we feel is true. Traci knew intellectually it was time to grow up and transfer her allegiance and loyalty to her husband. But her feelings screamed at her that she was abandoning her mother, who had been there for her all her life.

"Traci," I began, "you are commanded by God to honor your mother for life. That never changes. Yet now as an adult, you are not obligated to obey your mother, especially after marriage." I asked her to open the Bible laying on the coffee table and read to me 1 Corinthians 13:11.

Traci was familiar with the Love Chapter. But what did it have to do with these issues? She began to read, "When I was a child, I used to speak as a child, think as a child, reason as a child; when I became a man, I did away with childish things."

(You may be thinking, *Why can't she just get a grip? Grow up. Cut those apron strings. Get a life!* You may have negotiated the transition from being a single young adult to being married with little or no difficulty. Good. But for many it is not that easy.)

I looked Traci in the eye and reassured her that her mom would always hold a special place in her heart; in fact, God encourages her to honor her mother. After a pause I added, "But you are not commanded to obey your parents in adulthood. A new home establishes a new order of responsibility. Obedience ends; honor continues."

I asked her to read Ephesians 5:22: "Wives, be subject to your own husbands." A new order of accountability begins for the wife; a new role is designed for the husband. He is to be the chief servant and lay down his life for his wife as modeled by our Lord (Eph. 5:25; Matt. 20:28). He cannot serve his parents to the same degree and priority as he does his wife and children.

One practical illustration of this shift away from a parental focus to a marital focus is seen in the physical relationship between a husband and wife. The apostle Paul clarified this to the Corinthian believers: "The wife does not have authority over her own body, but the husband does; and likewise also the husband does not have authority over his own body, but the wife does" (1 Cor. 7:4). Authority and control are to remain within the bounds of the marriage and are not to be negatively exerted by in-laws from outside that bond. Paul further defined the new, established order when he said, "Christ is the head of every man, and the man is the head of a woman, and God is the head of Christ" (1 Cor. 11:3). Extended family is excluded from this order.

I posed a pointed question to Traci that tied these passages together. "Where are parents mentioned in the structure of the newly established home?" Her silence spoke volumes. I could tell she felt trapped. But a new understanding of the difference between honor and obedience was about to release her from that trap.

HONOR FROM THE HEART

This conflict was hard for Traci. She was trained as a child to follow her emotions as modeled by her mother. Now God was retraining her spirit to respond to His Spirit through His Word. She would learn something new about honor.

Honor is an attitude of the heart. Respect flows naturally from it. God designed His family system to include honor and respect for parents. This is to be a lifelong heart attitude. In adulthood, though, it is not a matter of obedience to their commands or demands.

Honor never ends—for parents or anyone else. As believers we are to give preference to one another in honor (Rom. 12:10). As we discussed earlier, the apostle Peter eliminated any room for dishonor of anyone when he wrote, "Honor all men" (1 Pet. 2:17).

One idea has been very freeing to adults who confuse obedience and honor: It is not dishonoring to graciously decline an invitation, a request, or even a command issued by their parents. Since honor is an attitude of the heart, one can decline an invitation in an honoring way.

How many couples dread the holidays because of the demanding expectations of the extended family? Thanksgiving and Christmas are times of expressing gratitude to God for His generous provisions. But that dreaded preholiday phone call can virtually rob the season of its joy. Let's go back to an earlier couple, Mark and Kari, for a moment. Such a phone call was an occasion for Mark and Kari to fight and for Mark to use as an excuse to stay drunk.

Mark came from a large family. His parents came from a tightly knit community. At Thanksgiving and Christmas, all the kids and grandkids were expected to be at his parents' home—no excused absences.

Kari wanted to start some of their own family traditions. She was even open to alternating holidays between the in-laws' homes and their own. Her parents had been very gracious, even though they would have enjoyed having them visit for a holiday dinner. But Mark's controlling parents made it clear that he belonged at their house, and Kari had better not cause any trouble.

I shared the same insights regarding "honor and obey" with Mark and Kari that I related to Nick and Traci. But I ran into the same logjam on both fronts—neither wanted to hurt their parents.

NOT RESPONSIBLE FOR OTHERS' HAPPINESS

Mark had the same sentiment for his controlling, demanding parents as Traci had for her widowed mother. Regardless of what their respective parents had done, neither Mark nor Traci wanted to hurt their feelings. That in itself is not wrong. It is important to be sensitive to our parents. But a deeper problem loomed. A core belief of many adult children is that they are responsible for the *ultimate* happiness of their parents. Neither Mark, Kari, Traci, nor Nick said this outright. It is a subtle (and sometimes not so subtle) message that insecure parents communicate to their children. Our missionary friend Evelynn strongly reinforced this to me.

It was our privilege to host Hugo and Evelynn at our home while they were on deputation, raising their missionary support. They accompanied us to a parenting seminar where I spoke on how to reduce anger in children. I shared that adults are not responsible for the ultimate happiness of their parents. While driving home, during a lull in the conversation, Evelynn quietly said, "I wish I had known this thirty years ago."

"Known what?" my wife inquired.

"That I am not ultimately responsible for the happiness of my parents. Even after Hugo and I were married, I felt guilty for not being able to make my parents, especially my mother, happy. I thought it was just one more failure of mine."

You may question, if we as children don't make our parents happy, then who will? God. God? But what if they are not even Christians? The fact that they are not believers does not alter the fact that God is the ultimate source of our happiness, or more accurately, our joy.

Joy is the character of God. The fruit of the Spirit includes joy. Every other source of joy is a counterfeit. As I asserted earlier, a codependent person makes another human act in the place of God. This is what I have called relational idolatry. It does not have to be another adult; children can be put in that position. It can easily develop into the perversion of emotional incest. But the apostle Paul proclaimed the ultimate source for meeting our needs: "My God shall supply all your needs according to His riches in glory in Christ Jesus" (Phil. 4:19).

You may contend that if our parents do not know God, we should do all we can to make them happy. No argument there! But the key is realizing we're not responsible for their *ultimate* happiness. The finest adult child or grandchild is a poor substitute for what God offers. Often people expend a lot of energy to make life work apart from God.

Parents are responsible for their own responses to life as long as their minds are clear. Often dementia, strokes, seizures, and other malaise such as Alzheimer's disease affect the brain. It breaks the hearts of adult children to have their parents look them straight in the eye and ask who they are. Yet there are parents who do not have these physical conditions but have been angry and bitter most of their lives. They may suffer physically now because of it. But as long as they have their rational minds, they are responsible for their behavior.

Assigning proper responsibility to in-laws may mean that the adult child stops assuming ultimate responsibility for his/her parents' happiness. The adult can pray that God would grant her parents grace to see their need to trust Him for their salvation, comfort, fulfillment, and happiness. Frankly, that is all the adult child can do. Parents can choose on their own whether or not to seek God.

When pressure mounts at the holiday season, how can we avoid hurting the parents we love? The sad reality is that we can't. *But no adult child is responsible to correct or make up for his/her parents' unmet childhood needs, unprocessed issues (bitterness, insecurity, fears), or responses to life.* We can encourage, suggest, appeal, urge, and hope. But our parents' response to God and life is within their own circle of responsibility. Our response to God and to life is in our own circle of responsibility.

Many of us grieve over our parents' lifestyle. It's sad to see people devoted to bitterness. But we have to let God be God. We have to let Mom and Dad assume responsibility for their lives and allow God to work in them as He wills. It is our responsibility to pray that any spiritual blindness in their minds and hearts will be lifted.

King Solomon's adult children may have had the same problem.

Sad Ending to a Great Beginning

There are few men in Scripture who started out so right but ended their lives so wrong. What Bible student hasn't gleaned practical insight from the wisdom Book of Proverbs. King Solomon, under the guidance of the Holy Spirit, articulated most of it.

A wealth of wisdom did not make King Solomon happy. He tried everything. If he lived today, I believe he would have even tried drugs to give his life meaning. He declared, "I explored with my mind how to stimulate my body with wine [then the drug of choice] while my mind was guiding me wisely" (Eccles. 2:3). Solomon built houses, made ponds, planted vineyards, bought male and female slaves and flocks and herds. He collected gold, silver, and a large harem of concubines. He provided himself with every pleasure. His conclusion? "Thus I considered all my activities which my hands had done and the labor which I had exerted, and behold all was vanity and striving after wind and there was no profit under the sun" (Eccles. 2:11). How sad.

That was bad, but it wasn't the worst. The writer of 1 Kings draws the strands of Solomon's life together. He recorded that the king loved many foreign women from the nations that God commanded Israel to avoid. The tragic result was that they turned his heart away from the one true God, and he went after the pagan gods, Ashtoreth, Milcom, Chemosh, and the detestable Molech (1 Kings 11:5–7).

74

Who was responsible for Solomon's happiness? He tried wisdom, works, wealth, and women. In his old age, he turned away from the only source that could give him ultimate meaning and joy—God Himself. Somewhere Solomon latched onto the idea that women could be his ultimate source of happiness. Did he learn that from his dad, King David, who morally violated Bathsheba, got her pregnant, had her husband murdered, then married her? The second child born from this new marriage was Solomon. It was illicit sex that brought his parents together. It was the desire for unrestrained sex that ultimately destroyed the character of Solomon.

What could the adult children of Solomon have done to save their dad? Were they responsible for his immoral behavior? God judges the one who is responsible. He judged King Solomon (1 Kings 11:9–13). The glory of Solomon ultimately turned into the grief of his family.

WE ARE RESPONSIBLE FOR THEIR CARE

No parents have had the wealth of Solomon to provide for them in their older years. As part of the way we honor our parents, God does make us responsible for our parents' general care in their declining years.

Jesus made this perfectly clear to the hypocritical Pharisees. They were clever fellows. The fifth commandment, to honor father and mother, included providing adequate financial support for them. But to skirt this responsibility, they would declare all their possessions to be *Corban,* a gift devoted to God (Mark 7:11). Such gifts could be utilized only for religious purposes. Why would the Pharisees do this? Because they loved to receive the praise of men for their lavish gifts to the Temple. It fed their pride, increased their power, and enhanced their position and prestige among men.

This scheme validated Isaiah's prophecy as Jesus quoted it: "This people honors Me with their lips, but their heart is far away from

Me" (Mark 7:6). The apostle Paul said it this way: "If anyone does not provide for his own, and especially for those of his household, he has denied the faith, and is worse than an unbeliever" (1 Tim. 5:8).

Jesus Himself was not excused from establishing responsible boundaries with his own mother. During a seven-day wedding feast, a problem surfaced that was to be the occasion for Jesus' first miracle. The wine supply was depleted. Mary turned to Jesus, thinking that He could solve the problem. How? It is not clear, because Jesus had not performed any miracles up to that point.

After Mary informed her Son that "they have no wine," He answered, "Woman, what do I have to do with you? My hour has not yet come" (John 2:3–4). (As strange as it may seem to hear Him address His mother as "Woman," in that day it was a polite and appropriate expression.)

Mary's response reflected a new aspect of her relationship with her Son. She told the servants, "Whatever He says to you, do it" (v. 5). Mary expressed her submission to Him. It is evident she did not fully understand, yet she trusted Him. This is significant because she participated in His ministry but had no control over it. He was totally in submission to His heavenly Father. He made it clear that He came to do the will of the One who sent Him, not the one who birthed him (John 6:38).

Excruciating pain did not relieve Jesus of personal responsibility. Mary, with a group of four women at the foot of her Son's cross, stood hopeless and hurting. His agonizing pain was piercing her heart just as Simeon had prophesied while holding the infant Jesus in his arms (Luke 2:35). When Jesus saw His mother's anguish and the apostle John standing by her, He said to her, "Woman, behold, your son!" And to John, "Behold, your mother!" (John 19:26, 27). From that point on, John assumed the responsibility for the over-sight and care of Mary. Apparently Jesus' own brothers and sisters were in Galilee and not in a position to meet her needs. Jesus was responsible.

For Nick's wife, Traci, though, the parental situation was harder to resolve. She was enmeshed.

ADULT-TO-ADULT RELATIONSHIP

Traci was teachable. She wanted God's best. I proposed again a practical project to begin this new adult-to-adult relationship, and to my pleasant surprise she accepted it. In preparation, I warned her of her mother's possible negative response. On the other hand, I told her, if she responded to God's grace and accepted the new biblical role that was to be established, the positive potential was enormous.

"Traci, when your mother calls tonight to inquire about your counseling session, may I suggest you thank her for her call? Express your appreciation for her thoughtfulness and concern, not just for now but for all your life. Share with her that you have come to realize that you need to make some adjustments in order to focus more on your own home and family responsibilities. Then gently share that you will not be calling her every single day. But ask if you could plan on a special time once or twice a week to touch base." (This was not to be a hard-and-fast rule, but an important goal to begin with.)

The look in Traci's eyes said it all: fear, panic, dread, terror. To her credit, she determined to do it. Nick's love and support encouraged her.

At their next appointment, I inquired how the call went. "Mom didn't call that night," Traci said. "I called my sister. We talked and I told her what I was going to do. She later called my mom. The next morning my mother called me. She asked me what this whole thing was about. I shared with her what we were doing. I was shocked at her response. Mom said frankly, 'I wondered when you were going to grow up.'" Traci's mother agreed it was a good idea to space their calls, and it was perfectly all right to focus more on her responsibilities. Nick said everything had been great since.

Traci did not have control over her mom. But when Traci exercised the tremendous power of personal responsibility, she began to work it out in a healthy way with her mom.

The "leave and cleave" principle may require some time away from a closely enmeshed parent in order for the adult child to regain some self-control and a new, healthy perspective. This is true especially if there has not been a healthy emotional separation and the relationship is characterized by overt dependence. It takes time to reestablish one's own circle of responsibility and then develop healthy ways to relate with one's parents. A word of caution: this will not be easy for the dependent parents. They may react out of their own immaturity and feel alienated or call you selfish. But for healthy adult children and bewildered parents, the time spent separately readjusting the relationship can be of tremendous value. This should be followed by a time of honestly sharing each other's expectations, then negotiating a healthy balance.

Over the course of a few weeks, we coached Traci and Nick in how to build an adult-to-adult relationship by assigning to each other and members of their extended family their own respective circles of responsibilities. Something else changed.

Traci had been responding like a young child to her mother. She also seemed to respond to Nick more like a daughter than a wife. But when she made the shift to relate more on an adult-to-adult level with her mom, she also began to relate that way to Nick. For a while this change made for a little marital awkwardness. Nick discovered that his strong, controlling manner needed mellowing; he was called into a mutual partnership that God calls coheirs of His grace (1 Pet. 3:7). This partnership did not alter the roles God defined in Ephesians 5, but it did initiate a mutual respect that took some time to develop. Nick shifted from a dominating leader to a loving servant-leader by personally becoming a living example of Christ to his wife.

We were elated over Traci's mom's positive response and for a very good reason: many times these situations blow up in your face. The sword that Jesus spoke of regarding in-laws pierces through the enmeshed family (Matt. 10:34–37). Making a healthy separation between the parent and adult child is often painful. Jane experienced this with her dad.

DADDY'S LITTLE GIRL

I had already met with Jane's older sister. She never felt wanted and loved by her dad. Broken marriages, live-in boyfriends, and abusive men filled her past. Then I met her younger married sister, Jane. In her father's eyes, she was still Daddy's little girl. Jane was his total focus and his favorite. This favoritism tore her sister apart. Favoritism is never expressed for the benefit of the child. It is all about how the child makes the parent feel.

Jane needed to make some changes in her relationship with her dad for the same reasons Traci did with her mother. She had her own home and children to raise. Jane chose to write a letter and meet with her dad in a park, as they often did just to chat.

She read the letter to her dad. It was full of gratefulness and appreciation. She shared that she had come to realize she needed to make some adjustments in her life. She wanted to relate to him more on an adult-to-adult level while still honoring him as her father. His immediate response in the park was warm and understanding. He went home. She learned later he ranted and raved and cursed me as her counselor. How could I rob him of his little girl? He has been cool but courteous to Jane ever since. Jane still loves her dad very much, but he will not allow her to grow up and have a Christ-centered, adult-to-adult relationship with him based on honor.

Jane and her sister rebuilt their relationship and worked through the anger and bitterness there. They are healthy. Dad is not. He is still stuck where he was thirty-five years ago.

Identifying, assigning, and establishing biblical responsibilities with in-laws may not bring peace. It may bring a sword. For Traci and Nick, it was not a matter of standing up for their faith with nonbelieving parents; instead it was assigning biblical roles and responsibilities for the new and extended families who were believers.

Marriage creates new roles and responsibilities. The relationship with parents changes. As you relate to them on an adult-to-adult basis, you will honor rather than obey them. As new boundaries are established, you can tell them "no" in an honoring way. Children are not ultimately responsible for their parents' happiness. That is a choice their parents make. But as adult children we are responsible for their general care in their declining years.

Traci and Nick faced pressure from without. But for Pastor Tim's couple, Mark and Kari, the sword was about to be raised within their family. Assigning responsibilities to the extended family is one thing, but to identify and assign responsibilities within the family may prove to be yet a bigger challenge.

FIVE

How to Mend
Fractures in the Family

Pastor Tim looked at the green chalkboard. Two big circles listed what Mark and Kari had done and what they wanted to do in their marriage. There was still one thing missing. Without it, our efforts were doomed from the start. I started the conversation. "Mark, do you know what a plumb line is?"

"Sure, it's a lead weight on the end of a cord that a builder suspends to get a true perpendicular line to the ground. It helps you build a straight brick wall, fence, or building."

"What is always consistent about a plumb line?" (Bible)

"It's always the same—true up and down. It is the same anywhere."

"What else can you do with it?"

"Well, you can use a plumb line to test existing walls to see whether they are tilted and need to be reinforced or just torn down."

"This is exactly what the Word of God is, a plumb line of truth. It is important to test our behavior and attitudes against the plumb line of God's Word."

THE PLUMB LINE OF TRUTH

God did this with His people, Israel, when He attempted to restore His relationship with them. The prophet Amos announced to the rebellious house of Israel that God was setting the plumb line of His Word among His people. It would indicate how out of line they were with His covenant law and why they were about to be torn down (Amos 7:7–9). God's people thought they were okay, normal. The truth of God's Word was about to show differently. It did the same with Mark and Kari.

I asked Mark to open the Bible to Proverbs 14:12 and read it. "There is a way which seems right to a man, but its end is the way of death." This truth is so important, its concept so sobering. Solomon was explaining in principle what Mark and Kari were experiencing in real life. Solomon was saying there is a path or a way of life, a lifestyle, that appears to be right, normal, or even straight, but the end result of that path is death.

Death means separation. In physical death, the spirit is separated from the body. In spiritual death, one's spirit is separated from God. But there is another kind of separation: relational separation. To a husband or wife certain behaviors may *seem* right or normal, but if continued they would actually result in dysfunction, separation, or divorce. The incidence of divorce among Christians now parallels that among non-Christians. Believers are not exempt from the reap-what-you-sow principle in relationships (Gal. 6:7).

The three most common causes of Christians' divorce are adultery, abuse (physical/emotional), and abandonment. It takes Christians longer to come to the point of divorce than non-Christians, but the results are the same. The basic lesson is simple. The Christian who does not adjust his actions and attitudes to the plumb line of God's ways will end up at the same place as anyone else doing the same thing. Sin produces separation and ultimately kills a relationship. Kari and Mark were well on their way to a relational separation and ensuing divorce.

"Mark and Kari, you can see on the chalkboard your destructive behavior patterns. Should they continue with no change, they will end in the death of your marriage. What should be in your circles of responsibilities that would lead you to mutual fulfillment and a vibrant relationship with Christ and each other? The power to make your marriage work is found in the power of fulfilling your own personal responsibilities."

I went up to the board and looked at their circles. Then I asked, "Which of your current ways do not line up with the plumb line of Scripture?" It is one thing to identify one's *wrong* behaviors, attitudes, and words, and quite another to correct them with healthy, biblical roles and responsibilities.

It is not within the scope of this book to give an exhaustive treatment on the theology of marriage. But it is important to point out some of the responsibilities that are common to both spouses and those that are unique to each.

WHAT ARE HEALTHY RESPONSIBILITIES?

Time was running out, so I asked Mark and Kari what personal responsibilities in marriage they could recall from any Bible teaching or preaching. The first one mentioned was "love." I wrote it in each of their circles.

Mark quickly chimed in, "Wives are to submit." I wrote that in Kari's circle while she sighed in disgust. I glanced at Mark, then Kari. I picked up a Bible and handed it to Mark. "Would you look up Ephesians 5:21?"

Mark read, "Be subject to one another in the fear of Christ."

"Based on that verse, Mark, what should I put in *your* circle?"

His wrinkled brow and glare reflected his reluctance to answer. He was confronted with a new reality, the responsibility of mutual submission. He believed that only wives were to submit; men were to control. Personally I believe God wanted to establish the concept of mutual submission first in verse 21 before the wife was singled out for emphasis in verse 22.

The apostle Paul illustrated mutual submission in the area of marital intimacy: "The wife does not have authority over her own body, but the husband does; and likewise also the husband does not have authority over his own body, but the wife does" (1 Cor. 7:4).

Since Mark had my Bible open to Ephesians 5, I asked if he would read the balance of the chapter, looking for his and Kari's biblical circles of responsibilities. He began to read verse 25. "Husbands, love your wives, just as Christ also loved the church and gave Himself up for her." I wrote in Mark's circle next to the word *love* "as Christ loved the church."

Mark piped up, "Yeah, but she has to love me too!" What a perfect setup! But nowhere in Scripture is a wife specifically commanded to love her husband. Though there are many "love one another" passages (John 13:34–35), no command to love is aimed specifically at wives as it is for husbands. True, the older women are to teach the younger women how to love their husbands and children, but it is not a direct command to love (Titus 2:3–4).

As Mark concluded reading Ephesians 5, another responsibility surfaced for Kari: "And let the wife see to it that she respect her husband" (v. 33). Kari rolled her eyes. I reminded her, "We are only assigning responsibilities now. Later we will look at what the hindrances are to fulfilling them."

I pointed out to Mark that he was responsible to take the spiritual initiative that would include family spiritual instruction, prayer, and church participation (Eph. 5:26–27). Several more responsibilities stood out as I had him read other passages. "You husbands likewise, live with your wives in an understanding way, as with a weaker vessel, since she is a woman; and grant her honor as a fellow heir of the grace of life, so that your prayers may not be hindered"(1 Pet. 3:7). Mark's look indicated some confusion. And with good reason.

Most teachers and preachers center their study of marriage on Ephesians 5. It is an important passage. Rarely, however, do they stress Peter's clear instruction for a man to understand his wife. Mark had never heard it was his responsibility to live with his wife with an intelligent understanding of the biblical nature of the marriage relationship. This is the reason I recommend that men read Ken Nair's excellent book, *Discovering the Mind of a Woman*. Mark, like many men, felt it was his wife's responsibility to understand and accommodate herself to him.

On the other hand, God does not command wives to understand their husbands. There are at least two possible reasons for this. First, women, on the whole, have more caring and relationship skills than men do. Second, women usually know more about men than vice versa. While women major on relationship building, men usually focus on their work. Few are the men who have come to me for marriage counseling because they wanted a deeper, more loving, intimate relationship with their wives. Intimacy to most men means more sex. To a woman, intimacy starts with understanding, tenderness, and emotional closeness.

Furthermore, I explained to Mark, men are to grant their wives honor. The word *grant* means "to bestow," the way an Olympic official bestows a medal to a winning athlete. This is the only time this word is used in the New Testament. A man may reason that if his wife were a real winner, he would grant her honor. Sorry, that is not God's example. He chose to grant us grace and favor when we were lacking any merit. "For by grace you have been saved through faith; and that not of yourselves, it is the gift of God; not as a result of works, that no one should boast" (Eph. 2:8–9). God bestows favor as a gift, not a reward. Men are responsible to reflect God's ways by giving their wives the gift of honor. Many women are still waiting to receive that gift.

Drs. Gary Smalley and John Trent's book *The Gift of Honor* is one of the most practical guides on how to grant the gift of honor in all your relationships. Dr. Smalley's video series *Homes of Honor* is a creative and invaluable resource on this subject for every home.

It was time to summarize what Mark and Kari were both responsible for. Some of the things listed in both of their circles of responsibilities were to forgive, encourage, rejoice, and "be harmonious, sympathetic, brotherly, kindhearted, and humble in spirit; not returning evil for evil, or insult for insult, but giving a blessing instead" (1 Pet. 3:8–9).

As Mark and Kari looked at their respective responsibilities on the chalkboard, they were overwhelmed. But one advantage they possessed was a willingness to work on their fractured marriage together. They also had a dedicated pastor who was committed to help them mend their relationship. This was not the case in Jerry and Susan's marriage.

Shattered Ideal

Jerry and Susan started dating when she was fifteen and he was seventeen. They were each other's first serious relationship. After dating for six years, they knew each other pretty well—right? Yes, Susan knew he had a temper, but she felt she could live with it. *Besides,* she thought, *nobody is perfect. I can change him.* And yes, she knew his mother strongly disliked her, but that was a small issue in light of their love. Or so she thought.

It did not take six months for Susan to find out how little she knew about Jerry. While making the bed one day, she found two pornographic magazines discreetly tucked under their mattress. Shock! Betrayal! Susan had reasoned that his lack of interest in sex with her was because he had a low sex drive. Then she began to find other clues that confirmed her worst fears. He was addicted to pornography. When confronted, he became violent to avoid his guilt. Susan kept apologizing for upsetting him and tried to keep peace and harmony by avoiding the subject.

When she became pregnant with their first child, Jerry made it clear that the only reason he agreed to have the baby was so she could have company while he went out with the guys. Months passed with no physical intimacy. Susan blamed her appearance and her performance in bed. A few years passed.

Then one day she inadvertently walked in on him in his private sexual activity. Her shock turned to rage. Instantly she lost trust in and respect for him. But Jerry affirmed his love for her and said he wanted to work it out. She recommitted herself to him and thought he did to her.

More years passed. When Susan was expecting their third child, Jerry announced, "I want out of this marriage." Daily he urged her to get an abortion. Finally she asked the dreaded question, and he admitted he was having an affair.

Susan told me, "I felt like my whole insides had just fallen out at my feet. I was totally empty inside." His affair was an extension of his sex addiction.

Jerry was outraged when Susan would not get an abortion. He really exploded when a lawyer said they could not get a divorce because she was pregnant. He threw everything he could get his hands on before storming out the door.

Susan's crushed heart became the fertile seedbed for the Word of God. While watching an evangelist on TV talk about a loving God who wanted to help and forgive her, Susan felt her heart soften. The evangelist emphasized that nothing is impossible with God. Susan said, "I knew I could no longer handle life by myself, so I asked Jesus Christ to forgive my sins and come into my life. I felt totally forgiven by God." Later a Christian counselor led her to forgive her husband, his mistress, and her mother-in-law.

When Susan delivered her third daughter, Jerry was not there. He did come to the hospital hours later with his mistress to see the baby and announce he still wanted a divorce. Six months later the divorce was final. God's ideal for Susan and Jerry's marriage was shattered.

DIVORCE AND RESPONSIBILITIES

Assigning circles of responsibilities for marriage when there has been a marriage failure is not easy. Susan realized it was her responsibility to learn how to deal with the painful aftermath. She wanted to be free of the control from Jerry's hurts, even though he stubbornly refused to acknowledge his sin against her. Her life changed, though, when she realized that Jesus felt her grief and loss. He Himself was a "man of sorrows, and acquainted with grief" (Isa. 53:3), who was able to sympathetically feel her loss (Heb. 4:15). Knowing Jesus understood her deep pain firsthand was greatly reassuring to her.

Susan had many practical questions, one being primary: "What are my responsibilities toward Jerry now that we are divorced?"

PURSUE PEACE AND TRUST GOD

Divorce is not new. The sword that separates, which Jesus spoke of in Matthew 10, results in the death of a marriage also. As the gospel was first preached, frequently a husband or a wife would hear the life-changing message, repent, and be saved, but the spouse would not. What were these new believers to do if their unbelieving spouses did not want to live with them because of their newfound faith? Paul clarified the believer's options. If the unbelieving spouse was willing to live with the new believer, the Christian mate was not to divorce him or her. If, however, the unbelieving one wanted to leave (like Jerry), the believing spouse was to let him go (1 Cor. 7:12–15). It was and is not in the believer's circle of responsibility to force the unbeliever to stay. It is the Christian's responsibility to pursue peace and trust God to do the convicting and changing.

Jerry wanted out. It was not Susan's choice. She did not fail. God gives us the power of choice for ourselves, but not for others. I told her, "Susan, God does not hold you solely responsible for the reconciliation. You are to fulfill all the responsibilities in your circle. It is a fact of life that you can do everything right to work it out and your husband still may not respond. Jesus did everything right, and He was still rejected. Was that His fault or theirs?"

That's not exactly what she wanted to hear. "I still feel I could have done something to prevent what happened. It's just hard to accept." There were a few things Susan could do, but they would not be easy either.

PROTECT YOUR SPIRIT

"I did forgive him," Susan asserted one afternoon, "but he keeps doing hurtful things to the girls and me. What am I supposed to do?"

I suggested a project to her. "Each time there is a new offense, mentally reopen Jerry's file of offenses before the Lord, and add the new conviction to it." I explained to Susan that frequently a police department in another jurisdiction will discover an additional crime the convicted criminal committed before he is sentenced for the most recent offense. Those charges are added to his criminal record.

"Susan, you have transferred Jerry over to the Lord Jesus, and you have put him, so to speak, in the Jesus Jail! Revenge is God's responsibility." We looked at Romans 12:19: "Never take your own revenge, beloved, but leave room for the wrath of God, for it is written, 'Vengeance is Mine, I will repay,' says the Lord."

I went on to explain that it is one thing to be hurt through a divorce that is not under your control. It is quite another thing to allow yourself to become bitter about it. Susan's response to the divorce was under her control. Honestly, one painful loss is bad enough.

Jerry shattered the marriage, but he couldn't steal Susan's peace. Jesus, not Jerry, was the source of her peace (John 14:27). Above all else, Susan could protect her spirit from bitterness. A bitter heart can be a painful tormentor.

LOVE THE EX-SPOUSE

"Love! Are you kidding? He has killed every emotion I ever had for him. He brought his mistress to the hospital to see our baby and to tell me he was divorcing me. Is there something about that picture I'm missing?"

Susan's outburst was understandable. But in reality, yes, she had missed something. I acknowledged her pain, deep hurt, and abandonment. True, Susan saw the historical situation accurately, but she was not aware of God's response to it. God felt Susan's pain just as He felt the pain Saul of Tarsus inflicted on Christians. Saul attempted to stomp out any traces of Christianity. He even stood by in approval as his friends brutally stoned Stephen (Acts 7:54–8:1). Then God stopped Saul cold in his tracks en route from Jerusalem to Damascus and plainly said, "Saul, Saul, why are you persecuting *Me?* . . . I am *Jesus* whom you are persecuting" (Acts 9:4–5, italics mine). When Saul abused Christians, Jesus felt and absorbed their pain. When Jerry hurt Susan, he hurt the Lord Jesus as well. But in spite of their abusive behavior, God still loves these people (John 3:16).

"Susan, you may not be able to love Jerry as your husband, but you will at least, according to Matthew 22:39, have to love him as your neighbor."

"Neighbor! I can't stand to be around him now," she said and quickly turned her head away from me.

"OK, then, you will have to love him at least as your enemy, according to Matthew 5:44."

She looked back in surprise.

"And if you are going to view him as an enemy, then another responsibility becomes yours, 'Pray for those who persecute you.'"

"Love? Pray? That's too much," Susan said, rolling her eyes in frustration.

"It may seem that way now, but you are the winner if you do," I told her. At that point, I shared a personal story. Almost twenty years ago I had been deeply disillusioned by a national religious figure and his father. I had worked for them. I left their organization because of the rampant immorality and cover-up, and I became a college professor and administrator.

For two years I prayed regularly for these two men. One day, while working at my desk, I thought back to the tumultuous events. Something happened. Normally when I thought of them, hurt and pain accompanied the memory. This time there was nothing. I waited a few more minutes. No hurt, pain, or anger came up. This was strange. Then God prompted me with this thought: *What have you been doing these past two years?* My prayer *for* them became, in time, my release *from* them, especially emotionally.

"I desire for you, Susan, to be free from the emotional control of Jerry's sin against you. God has empowered you with the key to attain it. Would you begin today to gain your freedom through your obedience to Him?"

She took a deep breath. Her face softened. God's work was being accomplished. Susan was letting herself out of her own prison. Months later she said she actually felt her former anger turn to sadness for Jerry. I commended her for that—that is how God feels. Finally she was able to do something else in prayer—thank God for her experience. How was she able to do it? It took some time, but she was willing to acknowledge God's sovereignty in allowing even painful events to touch her and the children's lives. Thanking Him for the trial was only possible when she honestly believed that nothing could touch her life that could not be turned to good (Rom. 8:28).

This worked for her. But what about the kids?

In regard to the children, assigning responsibilities after a divorce is no small challenge. Susan wrestled with how to respond when the children visited their father and he constantly bad-mouthed her in front of them.

The first test both Susan and the children faced was not to pay back evil for evil (Rom. 12:17). She had to learn how to interpret Jerry's behavior to the children and how to answer their questions appropriately and honestly. "Yes, your father is living with a woman who is not his wife. No, this does not please God. It hurts His heart just like it hurts ours.

"Yes, they say bad things about Mommy that are not true. Sure, it hurts! I have to ask Jesus to forgive them. I have to forgive them. Jesus is having to heal Mommy's heart.

"No, I don't hate Daddy. Jesus had to take my anger away. I am sad now for Daddy and his friend. I pray that God would bring them to Himself and they would invite Jesus into their hearts."

Susan did a masterful job translating adult pain into terms that her children could understand.

It is important to avoid, at all costs, using the children to carry the heavy burden of the divorce. I urged her to share her pain with another adult—a pastor, a trusted friend, a Christian counselor, or a support group. And she needed to distinguish between giving the children a heavy "steamer trunk" of answers to their questions when a light "overnight case" would be adequate. I reminded her that sin may need to be named, but not described.

I also encouraged her to avoid triangular communication. One day one of Susan's daughters reported, "Mommy, Daddy said he wanted you to let him see us twice a week instead of once a week." Jerry's intent was to get a message to Susan through the children because he was afraid to talk to her except when he was angry. He also hoped that the kids could influence her to let him have his way.

Susan's response took the burden off her child: "Honey, thank you for giving me that message. That is Mommy's and Daddy's responsibility. I will talk to him personally."

It is not the child's fault she is being used as a go-between. A divorced parent should never put a young child in the role of explaining to the other parent why he or she can't be a message carrier. Older children and teens may be able to respectfully request that the questioning parent call the other parent directly. Divorce or separation is *not* about children. It is about the parents. But in divorce or separation, children need something that is very difficult to give—especially for the abandoned parent.

ENCOURAGE LOVE AND LOYALTY

Susan faced the challenge and did everything within her power to encourage her children's love, respect, and even loyalty to Jerry. I received the opposite of this as a child myself. My father was an alcoholic and adulterer who abandoned our family. My mother has struggled with bitterness toward my father for more than forty years. She has attempted to make me as angry and bitter at my father as she is. I had to fight bitterness on two fronts: first, my own at what my dad had done to our family, and second, my mom's that tried to poison me toward my dad. Today I love both my parents. I dedicated my first book, *I Should Forgive, But . . .* , to a loving mother and a forgiven father.

No parent ever wins by poisoning her child toward the other parent. Honestly, at that time it was easier to love my forgiven dad than my bitter mother. Mom was deeply hurt, but she wouldn't release her bitterness and receive full healing from her devastating pain. But I knew my future happiness depended on honoring both my mother and father.

At first Susan wanted to strangle her ex-husband. But her bitterness was an issue she had to deal with for her benefit and the sooner the better. She had the responsibility to build as much love, respect, and loyalty in her children toward Jerry as was in her power to do. Just as Peter declared, we are not to return "evil for evil, or insult for insult, but giving a blessing instead; for you were called for the very purpose that you might inherit a blessing" (1 Pet. 3:9). Susan would pass a blessing on to her children, affecting their present and future well-being, by choosing not to dishonor her former mate or retaliate with bitter revenge.

Be Real

Another step in Susan's circle of responsibilities was to help her children see reality at their age levels of understanding. Dismissing Jerry's bad behavior with "Daddy's just not feeling well" was not the truth. It was more realistic to tell them, "Daddy has been drinking and is not feeling good. We need to pray that Daddy will get help for his drinking. We want Daddy to feel better and be happy."

God gives grace only for the truth. A physician-friend who was an alcoholic told me he went into treatment after he overheard his young son say to a friend on the phone, "My dad is a drunk."

Before you scold the seven-year-old for calling his dad a drunk, remember he was having to work through a harsh reality. Furthermore, when he reads the story of Noah, he will be faced with the fact that Noah "drank of the wine and became drunk" (Gen. 9:21). And someday he will read Paul's description in 1 Corinthians 11 of the Lord's Supper, the Communion service, and realize that some of the believers in Corinth were getting drunk at the love feast. Paul had to name and correct the reality of this evil practice. So, you see, the seven-year-old was dealing with reality as he saw it.

In the dysfunctional home, truth and reality are rarely acknowledged. Three unwritten rules govern the fractured home: Don't talk (tell), don't feel, and don't trust. Each of these is totally contrary to Scripture. Some of the saddest times I have had counseling with adult children are when they find out in adulthood something that should have been shared in childhood. Why? Because life did not make sense to them then because of family secrets. They wrongly concluded that something must be wrong with them. Why else could Mom or Dad not share the truth with them?

Rarely are there family issues that cannot be told. In almost forty years of ministry, I have noticed that dark secrets are more damaging than openly expressed truths. Through Nathan the prophet, God revealed King David's cover-up of his affair with Bathsheba and subsequent murder of her husband. The prophet made it clear to David that by his sin he had given the enemies of the Lord great opportunity to despise and blaspheme Him (2 Sam. 12:14). God was the greatest loser. God's enemies mocked and ridiculed Him. But God's very nature is truth, and He will not cover up the sins of believers to protect His reputation or theirs.

LET THEM LOVE IN TIME

Children may need time—lots of it—before they can love a stepparent. Every child has one birth mother and one birth father. The child did not get a divorce, the parents did. Parents need to let them grow in love in their own time and at their own speed.

Another of Susan's responsibilities was to encourage her children to be respectful now to Jerry's girlfriend, even if love came later. Children should respect stepparents or "significant others" because they are adults. That is appropriate.

The reverse is also true. A wise stepparent will build appropriate love and loyalty toward the natural parents when possible. The reason is simple: if the child is forced to love the stepparent and dislike, dishonor, or hate the birth parent, that bitterness could in time poison not only the child but the lives of many others (Heb. 12:15).

At all costs, Susan needed to avoid using the children as pawns for revenge. This was the very thing Jerry did. Here I will let Susan tell her story.

White Roses Made Me See Red

How could he? He just wanted to hurt me, I thought as I took the six white roses and gave them to my daughters, ages five, four, and one.

"These beautiful roses are from your daddy for you. Isn't that special?" I could hardly get the words out as I fought back the tears.

We were divorced. He knew white roses were my favorite. The more I looked at the whiteness of the petals, the more I saw red.

When I came for Christian counseling, I worked through the issues of forgiveness and what to do with my memories. I was able to be emotionally free from the control of Jerry's hurt even if he would not acknowledge his sin against me. I now knew that Jesus understood my feelings.

Then came the six white roses. Jerry rarely gave roses. Here I was, trying to forget the pain, and the roses arrived. The proverbial salt in the wound. My anger returned.

As I shared this latest setback, Chuck began to ask some probing questions. "Who made the rose? Who designed its color, shape, and fragrance?"

I began to see that I had put a negative meaning on something God created for my enjoyment. Even if Jerry meant to hurt me with the roses, God meant them to be a delight to enjoy as part of His creation (Gen. 1:26–30).

Something was pointed out that I never had realized before. Jesus is also called the Rose of Sharon (Song of Sol. 2:1). Even the thorns on the rose are a reminder of the crown of thorns He wore as He suffered for my sins (Mark 15:17). Then it dawned on me. Regardless of Jerry's purpose for the roses, God wanted to send me a message of His love and care, life and death, and the purity He gives me through Christ (Isa. 1:18).

I came into that session crying. I left rejoicing. What Satan may have intended for my evil, God intended for my good (Gen.

50:20). Though the roses from Jerry were a gift to our girls, now I see that they were a reminder of God's love for me.

Susan saw God's grace in the midst of her pain. The road to mending a fractured heart after divorce is never easy. Those who have experienced both divorce and death of a mate affirm that divorce is much harder to endure. With death there is closure; with divorce there may not be. One may still have to interact with the former mate, if for no other reason than the shared responsibility of the children.

BE AN ANCHOR

When a single parent focuses on being a consistent, godly person, the children will have at least one stable anchor in their lives. My mother was not perfect. She failed in areas. She often told me that she had to be both mother and father. She was great as a mother but made a poor father. But Mom remained our family anchor.

Often single parents fear that they have no impact on their children. It is hard—very hard! Yet I can personally attest I would not be in ministry today, walking with the Lord, or have a Christian home, if not for the one anchor in my life, my mother. It is in all parents' circles of responsibility to walk holy and humbly before God and their children.

What happens if the godly anchor gets consumed with his/her own unmet needs and slides into moral failure, hoping that the children will just understand? They will! They will wrongly conclude that God and His ways do *not* work in adulthood. Then when they are older, they, too, will seek to get their needs met any way they can. The tragic cycle will repeat itself (Exod. 20:5).

CLEAR YOUR CONSCIENCE

Finally, it is part of the divorced parent's circle of responsibility to correct, make restitution, or clear her conscience for anything she did to bring the marriage to an end. The only thing worse than a mistake is an uncorrected one. I urged Susan to correct anything she could.

In my first church, I had a carpenter-friend, Max, who was divorced. His wife was unsaved and abandoned the family, and Max was given custody of the kids. He remarried. Years later, his ex-wife received Christ as her Savior. She contacted him. They both asked for and were granted forgiveness. Max's new wife was a Christian too and was grateful for the former wife's salvation. They all became and remained congenial friends. There was a sense of sadness that they had to go through so much before reconciliation took place. But through it all, the five children were able to move freely between their birth mother's home and their dad's home with their blessings. This took a great deal of grace. Yet this is the kind of reconciliation God majors in.

Assigning responsibility in the family has at least one other facet: what to do if one's adult children return home. Pam and Glenn had to work this one out.

DEALING WITH ADULT CHILDREN

The fall leaves had all dropped off the large oak, ash, and walnut trees that dotted Glenn and Pam's ten acres. Their grown daughters, spouses, and grandchildren trekked home for Thanksgiving dinner.

No one made flaky-crust apple pies like Pam. No one roasted the large, golden-brown turkey or made the mouth-watering chestnut dressing like Pam. No one cleaned the house, served the Thanksgiving feast, and washed all the pots, pans, and dishes like Pam. No one!

"My children don't pitch in and help," she complained. "Rarely do they volunteer for anything. They are on vacation and want to visit with each other. They expect to be served. One of our daughters and her family may even show up two or three hours after dinner.

I know I probably trained them like this, but I'm tired and I can't keep up with it."

Pam and Glenn were like most parents of adult children. If we had it to do over again with the insight we have now, we would do some things differently. But we can't. How could Pam and Glenn assign responsibilities now to their grown kids? They couldn't, except as it impacted them.

STOP ENABLING IRRESPONSIBILITY

There is a little principle tucked away in the letter to the church of Thessalonica that speaks to this: "If anyone will not work, neither let him eat" (2 Thess. 3:10). The apostle Paul had modeled to the Thessalonians the need to be industrious. He targeted this pithy statement not to those who were unable to work, but to those who for their own reasons would not work. They expected others to support them out of a sense of charity. The cure was severe; allow them to experience the pangs of hunger so they would be motivated to be responsible and go to work. The deeper principle here is that each person is responsible to help or to contribute as he is able.

Pam would be the first to admit it was easier to take on big tasks herself than to face the hassle of getting others to help. But doing for others what they could or should do for themselves is called *enabling*. Enabling encourages another, either actively or passively, to be powerless and irresponsible. A wife who keeps her husband's severe drinking problem a secret from the family or from those who could help him, or her, is enabling. A husband who excuses his wife's belittling comments to the children as "Mommy is just having a bad day" is enabling wrong behavior. If inappropriate actions are not addressed but are ignored or denied, the offender feels permission to continue business as usual. Our children get the message too that it is normal to ignore.

This injunction to stop enabling irresponsibility may seem as ill-timed as the farmer's comment after his horse had been stolen:

"Lock the barn." Good idea, just too late. What could Pam and Glenn do now about irresponsible grown children? The place to start was not with a lecture on how irresponsible they were, but how as parents Pam and Glenn were irresponsible in not training them to be team players with family chores. This would not be easy. It would mean stepping on parental pride and humbling themselves before their children. (Yet even that could be an effective example to their adult children. Parents make mistakes and need to acknowledge and correct them when possible.)

That was what Pam had to decide. Was it worth it? She loved her girls. She knew she needed to do it for their sake and hers. Hers? Often a mother realizes these parental oversights later in life and chooses not to do anything about them. She continues to let the grown children use her. What is the result? Irresponsible adult children and a bitter mom.

Adults find it hard to change, but remember, the ways of God were not given exclusively to children. The three thousand people saved at Pentecost were adults. The gospel impacted lives at every age. The Bible is about change. If the ways of God are learned young, that's great. If they are learned later in life, that's grace!

Pam learned much about herself and the ways of God later in life. God's ways are always appropriate. They are timeless, and now was the time.

ESTABLISH RESPONSIBLE BOUNDARIES

Glenn and Pam's son-in-law, Bob, needed a typewriter. (This was B.C., before computers.) Because of his poor track record of returning what he borrowed, they were reluctant to lend it but eventually did so. "I will get it right back to you," he assured them. After much urging on their part, he returned it three years later. Would you believe he then asked to borrow it again? They reminded him how long he took to return it the last time. He promised to bring it back by the next Wednesday; Pam and Glenn didn't see it for two more years.

Adults who do not have boundaries or understand assigned responsibilities by the time they reach adulthood rarely change. Bob will do what Bob will do. But Glenn and Pam are equally responsible to do what they need to do. If Bob requested the typewriter again, they were free to loan it again, give it as a gift, or decline. If pressed for a reason, Pam and Glenn could gently remind Bob of his borrowing track record or decline. If Bob then tried to intimidate them for a further response, he would be violating their boundaries and respect. There is nothing wrong in refusing to get into a discussion that will not produce the fruits of righteousness (James 1:19–20). One of those fruits is peace.

This couple had another problem. Because Pam did not set responsible limits regarding the grandchildren, Glenn and Pam had become the expected babysitters at the whim of their daughters. Often at the root of a failure to set healthy limits is fear, primarily the fear of rejection. "But I just can't say no!" Pam told me. "They get upset, then I get upset, and everyone is mad at everyone."

All parents and grandparents have to ask themselves, "Is the problem that I can't say no or that I can't act like a mature adult?" Mature adults know they are not going to be liked all the time when they act in a responsible manner (2 Tim. 3:12). "Instead of saying, 'I can't say no,'" I told Pam, "ask yourself, 'Can I be a responsible adult and assign the proper responsibilities that belong to another?'"

Pam may have thought, *But I am a responsible adult.* True—but she may be overresponsible. Overresponsibility is not maturity either and is usually motivated by fear, not faith. It is a fear of rejection and abandonment. This fear has parents saying yes when they mean no. Jesus addressed this issue head-on.

The Pharisees were notorious for their oaths, yet they devised an ingenious scheme to avoid keeping them. If they swore an oath by heaven, earth, Jerusalem, or their own heads, they reasoned the oath did not need to be kept because God Himself had not been involved; therefore, it wasn't binding (Matt. 5:33–37). Jesus cut right through this system of irresponsibility: "Make no oath at all. . . . . But let your statement be, 'Yes, yes' or 'No, no'; and anything beyond these is of evil." He was declaring that one's own integrity should be enough to validate his words.   _recognize +_

It is always appropriate to take responsibility for the stewardship of your own time, energy, and assets. If a parent allows others to control her in these areas, it reinforces in her not servanthood but a bitter heart. When she says yes but means no, anger swarms internally. And anger will turn to bitterness.

ALLOW SUCCESS THROUGH FAILURE

Adult children are responsible for their own wise or unwise decisions. Phyllis and Gerald learned this with their college daughter, Carissa. Somewhere in her early years, Carissa got the idea that college was a four-year party, then life began. At the end of her first year, she failed all but two classes, and she earned a D in each of those. Gerald and Phyllis paid all of her college expenses. They paid; she played. At the end of the fall semester, Carissa was on probation and had to take her classes over again.

Gerald was hopping mad. I made a suggestion. Though she had failed on many fronts, Carissa now seemed sincere about changing. It was Gerald and Phyllis's responsibility to forgive her, and hers to earn their trust. My suggestion to make Carissa successful was simple: have her borrow the money for the next year's expenses. If she finished the second year satisfactorily, they should pay off her debt and have her borrow for the next year. If she was assigned the financial responsibility for herself and proved to be responsible, they should reward her success.

Gerald and Phyllis did this. Carissa graduated and went on for her master's degree. How did they work it out? What made the difference? They empowered her by assigning the responsibility where it belonged. This was relatively easy for Phyllis and Gerald, but it was not for Helen, who was divorced, and for Ron, her drug-addicted adult son.

BE RESPONSIBLE, NOT MEAN

Ron moved back home after his two-year marriage failed. Initially his behavior was okay. But then he was off to the bars and wrecked the family's second car. When he enrolled in an airline school, Helen financed his retraining. Ron passed at the top of his class. She bought another car; he wrecked it when he was drunk. Ron was arrested and incurred lawyer fees; Helen paid them.

Helen started to go to Al-Anon for herself. That did not change Ron. Things began to disappear from her home. She found herself asking Ron, as when he was young, "Where are you going? Where have you been and who were you with?" Ron's drug use only increased. He was always remorseful and tearful after a binge. Helen continued to excuse his behavior.

While Helen was on a trip to Israel, Ron stole her checkbook and forged thousands of dollars in checks. After further thefts Helen found herself filing formal charges against her own son.

The case was plea-bargained away, and Ron was released from jail. He called his mom at 12:30 A.M., cold, broke, and hungry, requesting to come home. And she let him. He did well for a while. Then Helen felt that queasiness return to her stomach when he didn't come home at night. Her sleep was fitful. She prayed every waking hour. The worry pattern returned.

It was then that Helen realized how "sick" she was. She began to understand that she was codependent. She had factored God into many of her waking moments, but she still felt she needed her son's validation and approval too. She learned that no relationship means anything to an addict. For Ron, the need for money was the only relational link he had with anyone, including his mother. It was not until Helen became a responsible adult that she could act in a responsible way toward her immature adult son. It was difficult to change a lifelong pattern.

If her son had been instead just an acquaintance, an employee, or even a distant relative, Helen would have found it easier to lay down the law. But when a parent has to deal with her own child, that's hard. The emotions are complex. I asked her, "Helen, is there a particular reason your son is living in your house?"

"He hasn't any other place to go. I just can't turn him out with no place to go."

"Is it your responsibility to provide a home for your grown son?"

"Well, where can he go?"

"Where did he live when he was not living with you?"

"Wherever he could."

"Would you allow him to be responsible for his own housing?"

"I can't do that. He will not eat well or have a safe and clean place to live."

"May I ask you a personal question? Are you as much concerned for how he feels or how you feel about what he is going through?"

"I'm his mother! I can't just turn him out."

"Why turn him out? Why not establish some biblical ground rules for him to live by in the house? If he accepts and fulfills them, let him stay. If he doesn't, you have not rejected him; he has rejected you. You are free to do what you want. But after he steals you blind and there is nothing left to pawn, where is he going to go then? And where will you go?"

I could see the wheels turning. Helen felt for years it was her responsibility before God to provide her son a clean, safe home, regardless of his addiction. Two words got confused in her thinking: *mean* and *responsible*. Helen felt that if she put reasonable limits or boundaries on her son, she was being mean to him. Often people who are not used to being held responsible for their behaviors, habits, choices, or feelings call the one holding them responsible "mean." That is blame shifting. Such a person is not mean; he or she is responsible. (If the responsible one holds someone accountable in a mean spirit, however, that is wrong.) Helen had to tell herself her feelings were not responding to truth or reality. Feelings often need to be brought in line with truth.

When Helen was able to assign biblical responsibilities to her son and was willing to be hurt if he chose to leave, she restored the personal power in her life to be a responsible parent. When she combined both love and limits, something remarkable happened.

Months later at an antique shop of a mutual friend, Helen told me how much better things were. She had defined the household limits in love, coupled with firmness, and Ron had responded. When she exercised the power of personal responsibility, she was able to work it out, and a new, healthy relationship began with her son.

Assigning responsibilities in marriage, in divorce, or in a blended family is not as easy as it first appears. In each case, it begins with holding up the plumb line of God's Word to behavior. Pastor Tim's couple, Mark and Kari, had to begin at square one to identify and assign their individual responsibilities in their seriously fractured marriage. Susan had to learn what her new continued responsibilities were after her painful divorce. Glenn and Pam needed the wisdom of King Solomon to understand how to be responsible parents with their adult children. Gerald and Phyllis realized before it was too late that they needed to allow their college-age daughter to grow up, become successful, and develop into a responsible adult. Helen was able to discover the power of personal responsibility and stop enabling her adult son to think and act without regard for her or anyone else. Each of these difficult situations needed the wisdom of God. They also needed to understand something else.

Thus far I have omitted one major truth: God has His own circle of responsibilities. Without this understanding, we can become angry at God. Susan learned this the hard way with Jerry.

SIX

WHAT DOES GOD HAVE TO DO WITH IT?

Jerry had a temper. If things did not go his way, if unforeseen changes affected his plans, he blew. Susan saw this. She discounted his behavior because, after all, "nobody is perfect." Character flaws should be overlooked, ignored, or tolerated. Susan also believed she could change Jerry. If she could just love and care enough, create a happy little nest for him, he would be fine. He just needed to get away from all those "bad" people who made him unhappy. She would make him happy.

Tragically, I have heard this rationalization often, from believers and nonbelievers alike. The truth of the matter is that our hearts are deceitful and can trick us into believing anything that is not true. Jeremiah stated it plainly: "The heart is more deceitful than all else and is desperately sick; who can understand it?" (Jer. 17:9). The apostle John also puts believers on notice that they can be self-deceived: "If we say that we have no sin, we are deceiving ourselves, and the truth is not in us" (1 John 1:8). But a naive, deceived heart was not Susan's only problem. She felt she could change her husband, something only God can do.

When I met with Nick and Traci and Pastor Tim's couple, Mark and Kari, I pointed out that some things are God's responsibility. The couples confronted me with strong questions: "God's responsibility? What does God have to do with it?" It was a foreign thought. But every biblical conflict resolution must not only factor God's presence into the conflict but also acknowledge His circle of responsibilities.

It is not our purpose here to exhaust the character, attributes, and responsibilities of God. But when we can identify many of God's responsibilities in working out human conflicts, we get a better picture of what is or is not in our circle of responsibilities. One of God's responsibilities that may be hardest for us to accept is that only He can change people.

GOD IS ULTIMATELY RESPONSIBLE FOR CHANGE

Peggy had been married almost twenty years. She had been the epitome of hope. Repeated setbacks in her marriage only strengthened her resolve to work harder, please better, and excel as the Proverbs 31 superwoman. "I can and will do it, and he will change," was her motto. But her strategy and tireless efforts were not working. Peggy was tired of trying. She had almost made herself sick attempting to change her husband, Martin.

In relationship conflicts the words *change* and *influence* are easily confused. Peggy believed her godly performance in life would effect a real change in Martin. She began to admonish me, "But God said in His Word that if I will just be submissive to my husband, even if he is disobedient to God, he will be won without my saying a word." Peggy was paraphrasing 1 Peter 3:1, "In the same way, you wives, be submissive to your own husbands so that even if any of them are disobedient to the word, they may be won without a word by the behavior of their wives." This is the hope of every godly wife who is married to an unsaved husband or disobedient believer. But what Peggy did not understand is that this is a principle, not an absolute promise. It does not say husbands *will* be won by their wives' behavior but that they *may* be.

The opening phrase in 1 Peter 3:1, "In the same way," refers back to 1 Peter 2 and the ways servants should serve their masters. Servants are to be submissive to their masters with all respect whether those masters are good or unreasonable. Obedient servants find special favor with God if they do the right thing and suffer for it. There is no guarantee that a servant's right behavior will change his master or make life better for himself. Neither does a wife's godly behavior guarantee that her husband will change.

Furthermore, saving faith comes from hearing the Word of God (Rom. 10:17), not just a righteous example. What Peter addressed is the wife who tries to preach, teach, plead, or manipulate her husband toward obedience with no real Christlike character in her life to back her up. He is addressing a modern cliché, "Your life speaks so loudly, I can't hear a word you say." Peter urged wives to confirm the truth of the gospel by the godly way they live their lives. Being an example is in the wife's circle of responsibility. Changing the husband is in God's circle of responsibility.

The Scripture states that a thing is confirmed in the mouths of two or three witnesses (Deut. 17:6; Matt. 18:16). The Word of God is one witness. The wife's godly life is to be another.

I asked Peggy a seemingly unrelated question based on 2 Peter 3:9. "Is it God's will that none should perish?"

"Yes."

"Just from your own experience, are there people who are perishing?"

"Well, yes."

"What more could our Lord Jesus do to convince the world of His love and their need for a Savior?"

"I guess nothing."

"Peggy, you can do all the right things to influence your husband.

Unless he responds to God, he will not change. May I ask you a personal question?"

She nodded.

"Were you performing to convert or change your husband, or were you doing this because it pleases God?"

Her eyes dropped.

"If you are bitter because your husband did not change as a result of your diligent behavior, what is the real motivation of your heart? Have you accepted the reality that it is ultimately God's responsibility to change a heart?"

To godly women who desire their husbands to become Christians or their believing husbands to be obedient to Christ, Peter recommended a different tack: "But let it be the hidden person of the heart, with the imperishable quality of a gentle and quiet spirit, which is precious in the sight of God" (1 Pet. 3:4). I told Peggy, *"Even if there is no change in your husband, you have succeeded in pleasing your heavenly Father, which is your highest priority in your circle of responsibility.* Influence your husband as you can, but remember, God is responsible to effect a lasting change in him. You must trust Him. Yes, this is hard."

The apostle Paul also felt a deep anguish over those of his own Jewish people who were not responding to his best efforts to reach them for Christ: "I have great sorrow and unceasing grief in my heart. For I could wish that I myself were accursed, separated from Christ for the sake of my brethren, my kinsmen according to the flesh, who are Israelites" (Rom. 9:2–4). Note, he even wished the worst on himself if it meant they could be won to Christ. He carried the sad truth to his death that he couldn't change them in and of himself. Peggy had to accept the same reality as Paul and understand who is ultimately responsible for change. It is God.

A hardened look came across Peggy's face. Her angry glance said it all: "Then why doesn't God do it?" The apostle Paul anticipated the same question: "Why does [God] still find fault? For who resists His will?" (Rom. 9:19). If God makes the choice or even opens or blinds the heart of man, how can He hold man responsible for his behavior? God does not answer that question for the apostle Paul or Peggy. He merely responds by saying, "Who are you, O man, who answers back to God?" (Rom. 9:20). Why so strong an answer from God? Simple. It is in God's circle of responsibility to save, change, open, or close. It is our circle of responsibility to be obedient to live and to share, regardless of the change or lack of change on another's part.

Years ago, while a student at Biola University, I spent many leisure hours debating with fellow theological students about God's sovereignty and personal evangelism. My Calvinist friends said that God knew who would be saved and that He would get them saved with or without us. My Armenian friends said if we did not evangelize, no one would get saved.

It was not until I understood the circles of responsibilities principle that I brought the two realities of God's sovereignty and man's responsibility to rest for myself. I came to understand that it was in God's circle of responsibility to draw whomever He wanted to Himself (John 6:44). Who is saved is not my responsibility. I am to witness to whomever I can (Matt. 28:19). The apostle Paul defined who is responsible for what: "I planted, Apollos watered, but God was causing the growth" (1 Cor. 3:6). We are to plant and water, a word picture describing our responsibility to share the gospel with unbelievers. God is responsible to bring about their salvation and to cause spiritual growth in the new believer.

There is a major distinction between the *means* of salvation and the *cause* whereby a person believes. A farmer can plant the seed, but he cannot make it grow. Peggy felt it was her responsibility to both plant by means of her life and cause what she planted to grow. She had, in effect, blurred her circle with God's. God never gives a person grace to do His job. If we try, we will break and ultimately become bitter. That was Peggy's state of mind.

I have met scores of bitter wives who have given up on their spouses and God. Why?

"It didn't work," they tell me.

"What didn't work?"

"What God said in 1 Peter 3. I gave and gave for years and he never changed."

Here we are again. Change is confused with influence. Influence is our responsibility. Change is God's.

Consider the situation of a Christian brother living in overt sin. Matthew stated what is to be done and by whom: "And if your brother sins, go and reprove him in private; if he listens to you, you have won your brother" (Matt. 18:15). This is Plan A. "But if he does not listen to you, take one or two more with you, so that by the mouth of two or three witnesses every fact may be confirmed." We will call this Plan B. "And if he refuses to listen to them, tell it to the church." This would be Plan C. Finally, "if he refuses to listen even to the church, let him be to you as a Gentile and a tax-gatherer" (vv. 16–17). Plan D is the last resort. We are to do what God has instructed us to do to work it out, and then we are to trust God by faith for the change.

The apostle Paul instructed Timothy in God's and our spheres of responsibility: "Be kind to all, . . . with gentleness correcting those who are in opposition, if perhaps God may grant them repentance leading to the knowledge of the truth" (2 Tim. 2:24–25). We confront. We correct. We influence, but God does the changing. What if you feel the person deserves to be punished for the painful hurt he has inflicted?

God Is Responsible for Revenge

I introduced Fred in my first book, *I Should Forgive, But . . . .* His father was a verbally abusive alcoholic. Fred concluded that if he did not forgive his deceased father, he could somehow exact revenge on him. Fred was not about to let his father off scot-free. I explained to him that when we let a person off our hook, they are still on God's hook. Fred had the same choice Susan had with Jerry. Fred could stand guard over his father twenty-four hours a day in the jail of his own bitter heart or transfer his dad over to the "Jesus Jail."

This word picture captures an important principle of Scripture we looked at in chapter 5: "Never take your own revenge, beloved, but leave room for the wrath of God, for it is written, 'Vengeance is Mine, I will repay,' says the Lord" (Rom. 12:19). This New Testament passage is a quote from the song of Moses, which he taught to the tribes of Israel poised to enter the Promised Land. Near the end of this song, Moses gives a key insight on when God will act (or vindicate) on our behalf: "For the LORD will vindicate His people [from their enemies], and will have compassion on His servants; when He sees that *their* strength is gone" (Deut. 32:36, italics mine). God will activate His judgment on Israel's enemies when His people relinquish all their trust in their own efforts. For Israel, this did not happen until they stopped trusting in foreign gods and restored their trust in the one true God.

Fred became free when he let God act out of His own character and justice. God will unleash His wrath in His time. He will repay with vengeance. Read what God has in store for the unbeliever in the Book of Revelation. Revenge is His responsibility, never ours.

Susan struggled with wanting revenge against her ex-husband, Jerry. She could not change him. She felt he fully intended to hurt her by sending those white roses to her daughters. Before the divorce, he never gave white roses to his daughters, only to Susan.

GOD KNOWS THEIR END

After the divorce, Susan wound up with custody of the three girls and a limited income. She had to go to work; so much for being a full-time mom. Her dream was smashed to pieces. Jerry appeared to get the best of both worlds: he could have the kids when he wanted as well as all the sex and fun with his mistress that he desired. But that's not the whole picture. God's judgment on all who mock Him and His children is described by Asaph in Psalm 73.

Asaph felt as cheated as Susan. He was one of King David's top choir directors. He was in charge of thousands of musicians. But he struggled with God's fairness. It seemed to him that though he stayed pure, he had little materially to show for it. The wicked opposed God and prospered. God had to do for Asaph what He wants to do for Susan and all those mistreated by others.

God brought Asaph into His sanctuary and shared what is really taking place in the lives of those who are enemies of God and are abusive to His children. Let Asaph tell you what he came to understand:

> When I pondered to understand this,
> It was troublesome in my sight
> Until I came into the sanctuary of God;
> Then I perceived their end.
> Surely Thou dost set them in slippery places;
> Thou dost cast them down to destruction.
> How they are destroyed in a moment!
> They are utterly swept away by sudden terrors!
> Like a dream when one awakes,
> O Lord, when aroused, Thou wilt despise their form.
>
> *(Ps. 73:16–20)*

We could summarize what Asaph learned in three words: *revenge is God's*. The wicked and disobedient seem to get away with a lot. But God writes the last chapter of their lives, and it reads like the Apocalypse.

On the negative side, we're told not to take revenge on those who hurt us. On the positive side, "Do not be overcome by evil, but overcome evil with good" (Rom. 12:21). Why let the evil actions of others control you? Instead, use your personal power to master evil by doing good.

Susan did just that. Jerry purposed to hurt her by sending the white roses to the girls. His subtle message was, "I don't love you, and here's a reminder." But Susan was ultimately able to see God's goodness in what Jerry meant for evil. He tells the children lies about her. She tells them the truth, then prays with them that Daddy will come to know Jesus. He does everything he can to make the children's weekend visits as difficult or inconvenient as possible. Susan goes the extra mile to be more than fair, which only inflames him more. Susan is able to work it out within herself and to go on with her life. Jerry is still obsessed in getting even with her for the rest of his life. The children see these opposite responses and desire the companionship of their mother.

GOD IS RESPONSIBLE TO CONVICT

"I shout at the top of my voice, and he still doesn't listen!" Kari exclaimed as she looked from Pastor Tim to me. "He will not listen to me. I have been trying to tell him these things for years. Even the kids don't listen. I have to do something drastic just to get their attention. They just don't get it!"

If there is one common complaint that weaves itself through family conflicts, it is ineffective communication. Kari said it for all, "They just don't get it."

There are a number of hindrances to communication that are in our circle of responsibility. According to *Taming the Family Zoo* by Jim and Suzette Brawner, less than 10 percent of our communication is words, what is said. At least one-third is tone of voice, and more than half is body language. The meaning of our words can be changed just by our tone of voice. We can say, "I love you" in a soft, gentle voice, in a harsh, angry tone, or in an expressionless monotone: each conveys a totally different meaning. Even animals read our tones more than our words. Try saying all kinds of mean things to a dog in a loving, accepting voice, and the dog will just wag his tail. Why? He believes your tone, not your words.

We do the same thing with body language. A warm smile conveys acceptance and love while a disgusted look communicates rejection. Hands on the hips, teeth clenched, and eyes squinted are signs of anger. Their language is heard in every heart.

It is our responsibility to communicate His Word as clearly, sincerely, and graciously as possible. But it is ultimately God's responsibility to take it where we cannot go, to the heart. As the apostle Paul joined a group of women gathered by the riverside for prayer, he began to speak to them regarding the Scriptures. These women were already worshipers of God and were listening intently. Unseen by anyone present, God was at work. Dr. Luke was made aware of it by the Holy Spirit of God when he wrote of a woman named Lydia, "The Lord opened her heart to respond to the things spoken by Paul" (Acts 16:14). Paul spoke. Lydia and her friends listened. God opened the door of their hearts through faith.

When the heart is hard, understanding is darkened (Eph. 4:18). How then can we make a person listen to us from the heart so that he or she can understand what God may be communicating through us? Simple: we can't. That is God's circle of responsibility. Only God can convict.

"Well, then, are we just to sit back and let God do it?" Now we are back to the sovereignty and evangelism issue. We do what we have the power to do, but God is responsible to take His Word where we cannot go. "For the word of God is living and active and sharper than any two-edged sword, and piercing as far as the division of soul and spirit, of both joints and marrow, and able to judge the thoughts and intentions of the heart" (Heb. 4:12).

God's Spirit is responsible to convict the world of sin, righteousness, and judgment (John 16:8). Note that conviction is not the same as conversion. Many are convicted and feel guilty as they are presented with the truth of the gospel. Instead of accepting it, though, they react or reject.

The evangelist Stephen clearly explained the gospel to the Sanhedrin council. They did not respond with acceptance; they attacked. "When they heard this, they were cut to the quick [conviction], and they began gnashing their teeth at him. . . . They cried out with a loud voice, and covered their ears [rejection], and they rushed upon him with one impulse. And when they had driven him out of the city, they began stoning him" (Acts 7:54, 57–58). Stephen preached. God convicted. The Jewish leaders rejected.

Peggy believed she would bring Martin to conviction by her life. She was doing her part, but Martin was not changing. He did not appear to be convicted of anything. She was facing the hardest part for her—trust. She had to trust the heavenly Father. Anger, anxiety, agitation, and frustration do not express trust. It's true, trust is hard when you are feeling the pain of hurt, neglect, loneliness, and rejection.

We may or may not live out what we really believe from day to day, but we will always live out what we truly believe in a crisis. Peggy was in a crisis. Would she ultimately trust God with the outcome, whether Martin changed or not? I was told as a young preacher, "Holiness is not how high you climb, but how straight you walk when you hit the bottom." When you are at the bottom with your family, marriage, or a close relationship, that's when your mind cries out for something else that only God can give—wisdom.

GOD IS RESPONSIBLE FOR WISDOM

Total disruption. Turmoil. Displaced. Scattered. Unsettled. Unfamiliar environment. Problems galore. These words describe the condition of the hearts and lives of those James sought to encourage in his letter.

James knew turmoil, confusion, and misunderstanding. He

was the half brother of Jesus. He witnessed the life and death of Jesus. Though raised in the same home as Jesus, he didn't believe He was who He claimed to be (John 7:5) until after the Resurrection. Then the past and present began to make sense for James.

Less than fifteen years later, James attempted to help his Jewish brethren in Christ to make sense out of their lives after they had been scattered to the east in Babylon and Mesopotamia. They had big-time problems in these strange lands. They needed megawisdom just to survive. Trials literally surrounded these dispersed believers. Notice that James referred to these difficult situations as *trials,* not problems. The word *problem* does not appear in the King James Bible. It appears only twice in the New American Standard Bible (Dan. 5:12, 16) and three times in the New International Version (Deut. 1:12; Dan. 5:12, 16). God calls the difficult situations, conflicts, and tragedies we experience *trials,* not problems. Trials occur for a purpose, for our benefit. They test and expand our faith, which results in the character quality of endurance.

These stressed-out believers had the same need Susan had in dealing with her unfaithful husband, Jerry. It was the same need Peggy had in dealing with her unsaved husband, Martin. Phyllis and Gerald had it with their irresponsible college daughter, Carissa. Helen had it in coping with her drug-addicted son, Ron. Nick and Traci had it in dealing with her mother. What was it? Wisdom. God's wisdom.

James explained in simple terms how to access this godly wisdom. "If any of you lacks wisdom, let him ask of God, who gives to all men generously and without reproach, and it will be given to him" (James 1:5).

This is the edge we have over all the king's horses and all the king's men, who could not put Humpty Dumpty together again. We, too, face the shattered pieces of our lives. Only God has the wisdom to work with those pieces. He is abundantly generous with His wisdom, but you must ask. That is why I start every counseling session in prayer. Hundreds of times I have paraphrased Proverbs

3:5–6 in prayer: "Lord, each of us wants to affirm to You that we are going to trust in You with all of our heart. We are not going to lean or rely on our own understanding or insight. But we now acknowledge You in all our ways, words, and attitudes; and we thank You for making our paths straight, holy, and pleasing to You. For Your wisdom we thank You in advance. Amen."

What keeps this from being a trite ritual for me? Simple. God never brings people into my life with trivial problems. Rarely a counseling session passes that I do not silently ask the Father for His direction and wisdom. It is His circle of responsibility to grant true wisdom.

How do you know when you have His wisdom? James spells out how to distinguish between wisdom that is from above (from God) and that which is from below (from the world). Understanding this distinction is vital. You may see some of the ways you are dealing with a difficult situation and realize you are not reflecting godly wisdom. Understanding the difference between godly and worldly wisdom could give you the life-changing key to your current trial.

WISDOM FROM BELOW

James introduces the need for God's wisdom in chapter 3, verse 13: "Who among you is wise and understanding?" Then he distinguishes between God's infinite wisdom and Satan's infamous wisdom. Their characters are radically different and their fruits are as opposite as day and night. James gives clear criteria to evaluate if you are using God's wisdom or selfishly motivated wisdom in working out a conflict. James begins this important comparison with the characteristics of the counterfeit wisdom from the evil one, which is guaranteed to further destroy your relationships. How can you detect that you have behaved unwisely? Consider the four major characteristics of counterfeit wisdom.

Bitter Jealousy

First, counterfeit wisdom spills forth "bitter jealousy" (James 3:14). Bitterness is like a raging river with many sources. These tributaries usually reflect unfinished business—past pain in the heart. Grief is just one tributary that feeds bitter jealousy. Because grief is so prevalent, it deserves a brief consideration.

Grief is the normal emotional response to loss. The believers of Ephesus were "grieving" the pending loss of their beloved friend, the apostle Paul, especially since he had told them that they should see his face no more (Acts 20:38). The word *grieving* literally means "tormented by intense pain of loss." If grief is not identified and expressed in a healthy way, it will convert into bitterness of heart. Every word, action, attitude, and decision will reflect shades of bitterness. That is the reason a very high percentage of parents who lose a child to death eventually divorce. We turn the anger of loss loose on those closest to us. Healthy grief, by contrast, has a sense of release and acceptance. Bitterness reflects a determination to hang onto the lost person or circumstance because one did not deserve the loss. A wife whose husband abandons her may say bitterly, "I deserve a happy marriage." She may stubbornly hang on to what may not be restored.

Decisions issuing from bitterness will result in even more conflict within and without (Heb. 12:15). The "root of bitterness" will show itself in more animosity, deeper resentment, and subtle or blatant harshness. It will not produce a godly closure because the bitter heart is not working through the loss in a godly manner.

Bitterness can also reflect unprocessed disappointment. Something or someone may have deeply disappointed us, crushing our hope. A deeply desired expectation plummeted to the ground, creating more loss, more need to grieve. Peggy's repeated efforts to effect change in her husband's life resulted in repeated disappointment. Refusal to accept disappointments or to modify her unrealistic expectations sprouted into bitterness. She was back to square one.

My farmer-friend Doug was very angry over his wife's over-spending. His anger over that hurt mushroomed into bitterness. His wife's spending first hurt Doug; then as it continued, it fanned his anger. Doug's anger turned to bitterness over her lack of concern for their worsening family finances. Bitterness is the house that anger built. It is not a condominium; it is a prison. The good news is that the lock and key are not on the outside, nor are they in the hands of another. Always they remained in Doug's hands, whether he used them or not.

The counterfeit wisdom from below germinates not only in the fertile soil of bitterness but also in the well-watered field of jealousy. The Greek word for *zeal,* when used negatively, is translated "jealousy." Jealousy is a strong envy built upon the foundation of fear—the fear of being replaced. When we experience jealous love, we fear the loss of our place in the heart of another.

If we feel someone is threatening our position, prestige, power, or possessions, jealousy raises its ugly head. Rooted deeply in the Jews' hostile persecution of the apostle Paul was not a love for God but a deep-seated jealousy. They used wicked men to attempt to frame Paul and get him executed (Acts 17:5). Why? He was a threat to their comfortable and secure religious system.

A bedfellow of jealousy is envy. Jealousy is the fear of losing what one has. Envy is discontent or resentment over another's advantage; it is wanting what another has. Envy was at the heart of those who plotted the death of our Lord Jesus (Matt. 27:18).

From a heart rooted in jealousy come distorted insights, thoughts, and attitudes. The wisdom that comes from a fear of loss will be skewed and dark and will produce conflict. Jesus made a comparison with the human eye: "The lamp of the body is the eye; if therefore your eye is clear, your whole body will be full of light. But if your eye is bad, your whole body will be full of darkness. If therefore the light that is in you is darkness, how great is the darkness!" (Matt. 6:22–23). Until one deals with bitter jealousy by forgiveness and restored trust in God, his continued conflict is virtually guaranteed, along with something else—selfish ambition.

SELFISH AMBITION

The second major characteristic of counterfeit wisdom is "selfish ambition" (James 3:14). The Greek denotes "self-seeking" and "rivalry." *Rivalry* is translated in the King James Bible as "strife" or "factions." The underlying meaning is self-will. Self is boss of life's control system, the heart. Place a group of adults motivated by self-will and personal agendas together and you will have the essence of a kindergarten free-for-all; the following words will dominate discussion: *I, me, mine, and no* (see 1 Cor. 3:1–3).

Pseudowisdom results in only further conflict in relationships and avoids biblical resolution. It is a totally juvenile, selfish program, not an adult system based on negotiated give-and-take. This was the very reason the Corinthian believers were going to court and suing each other (1 Cor. 6:1–7). The thought of experiencing personal loss and not winning was totally foreign to them. Why? Because they were not responding with the wisdom from above.

Satan first attacked perfect humanity through Eve. He appealed to her selfishness: "'For God knows that in the day you eat from [the tree of the knowledge of good and evil] your eyes will be opened, and you will be like God, knowing good and evil'" (Gen. 3:5). Counterfeit wisdom is selfish, plain and simple, first and last.

PRIDE

Third, worldly "wisdom" exudes arrogance or pride (James 3:14). Surprised? Like a facet on a diamond, pride merely reflects a different angle of carnal wisdom.

James flatly states, "Do not be arrogant." In Greek this is an intense word meaning "to vaunt oneself against another with contempt." No one feels good when demeaned. When looking into the eyes of contempt, one experiences a feeling of wrath, not personal worth. Pride cannot say, "I was wrong" or be responsible. It reverts to the demonic strategy of blame shifting. You will never be able to work out a difficult situation if pride remains the controlling attitude.

LYING

The fourth characteristic of pseudowisdom is lying, not only in word but in action. Look at what Satan did to Eve. God warned, "You eat, you die." Satan said, "You surely shall not die!" (Gen. 3:4). That was one person's word against another. Why did Eve choose to believe the creature rather than the Creator? Simple. She was deceived.

THE SOURCE OF COUNTERFEIT WISDOM

A person who claims to be Christian but whose behavior is characterized by bitter jealousy, selfish ambition, pride, and lying is what James called a hypocrite. Hypocrisy is from the dark side of evil, not from the kingdom of light and righteousness. Hypocrites are pretenders. The word *lie* comes from the Greek verb that means "to play false." We would paraphrase it by saying, "Don't live a lie." Don't claim godly wisdom and live like a self-deceived fool. A hypocrite aims to deceive others with lies in both word and action. One's life should not contradict the truth he professes to believe.

James clarified counterfeit wisdom's source. "This wisdom is not that which comes down from above, but is earthly, natural, demonic" (James 3:15). It all has the familiar fingerprints of Satan. The word *earthly* indicates things of this world, where Satan is the "prince of the power of the air" (Eph. 2:2). *Natural* refers to the sensual or unspiritual. Those who are unsaved are under the control of the prince of the power of the air and are "dead in [their] trespasses"—they are "by nature children of wrath" (Eph. 2:1, 3). *Demonic* describes anything that Satan energizes. Jesus nailed the hypocritical Pharisees by exposing their true motivator: "You are of your father the devil, and you want to do the desires of your father. He was a murderer from the beginning, and does not stand in the truth, because there is no truth in him. Whenever he speaks a lie, he speaks from his own nature; for he is a liar, and the father of lies" (John 8:44).

The results of counterfeit wisdom are "disorder and every evil thing," including complicated, unresolved conflicts (James 3:16). Think through how you have been working through a conflict. Ask yourself if you've reflected any of these characteristics of counterfeit wisdom.

- Does my action or attitude come from a bitter, jealous heart?
- Am I motivated by selfish ambition?
- Does my action or attitude reek of pride?
- Does my life match my words?
- Do my choices reflect secular (earthly) values?
- Do my choices lack Christian values (natural)?
- Do my choices have an evil twist to them (demonic)?

Using ungodly wisdom will not resolve conflicts; it is futile and unproductive. Allow God to enrich your life with His wisdom. He will do it.

If God is ultimately responsible for granting us wisdom to handle difficult situations, how will we know if we have His wisdom or the world's? What does godly wisdom look like? We know what it is not. But what exactly is it?

WISDOM FROM ABOVE

Godly wisdom reflects the character of God. Jesus is the wisdom of God (1 Cor. 1:24), so His life reflected the qualities of godly wisdom. James describes its eight characteristics.

PURE

Purity is the foundation upon which wisdom rests. "The wisdom from above is first pure" (James 3:17). It is the absolute starting point. The word *pure* is from the same root as the word *holy;* it means totally clear and unadulterated, flawless, and faultless. It is not 90 percent good and 10 percent bad. It is guiltless, blameless, and completely above reproach. There is no hint of selfish contamination, no polluting defilement.

Pure motives, character, and intent will not reflect politics, selfishness, hidden agendas, or veiled manipulation. *My wise decision should be able to be spoken from the mouth of God.* I believe that is one of the reasons Jesus sternly warned the Pharisees, "And I say to you, that every careless word that men shall speak, they shall render account for it in the day of judgment. For by your words you shall be justified, and by your words you shall be condemned" (Matt. 12:36–37). Because we have deceived hearts, we alone could never initiate a pure train of thought. It has to originate from God. Just look again at the lawsuits that took place among the Corinthian believers; no doubt they believed their decisions to go to court against fellow Christians were wise. The apostle Paul cut to the selfish heart of the matter with two penetrating questions: "Why not rather be wronged? Why not rather be defrauded?" (1 Cor. 6:7).

Every fiber in the Corinthians screamed out for fairness, justice, and equality. Take a loss? Accept being defrauded? Not on your life! The Corinthians' response underscored the truth that God's ways are not our ways, neither is God's wisdom our wisdom (Isa. 55:8). *Loss* is a time-oriented word. Every single thing we view as a loss here and now is, in God's eyes, merely a transfer of assets from here to heaven for eternity (Matt. 6:19–20).

Anything that smacks of selfishness—with the words *me, my, mine*—does not reflect the wisdom from above. If we really understood that, frankly, I am not sure many of us would pray for God's wisdom. The potential for temporal loss for us would be too great. So we go with the counterfeit wisdom from below, from the evil one, and deceive ourselves into thinking it is okay to look out and act solely for ourselves.

PEACEABLE

Godly wisdom does not promote peace at any cost. We don't gain the true peace of godly wisdom by trading off our inner peace to buy that of another. Compliant pleasers are usually guilty of this. They lie about their true emotions. They say they are fine when they are livid with anger. They have bought peace for the moment only to have their rage erupt later in violence or mental breakdown. That is the reason James states, "But the wisdom from above is first pure, *then* peaceable" (James 3:17, italics mine). The word *then* means that purity that includes honesty must precede the next quality of being peace loving or harmonious.

The application of godly wisdom usually brings about a peaceful result, but not always. Consider Susan, who displays pure motives in treating her ex-husband better than he treats her. No doubt she experiences some peace from her efforts, but the situation isn't resolved. She still has to contend with her husband's difficult behavior and lifestyle choices.

GENTLE

The next characteristic of godly wisdom is gentleness. The Greek word for "gentle" does not have an English equivalent. Shades of meaning include *reasonable, fair, seemly, equitable, moderate, forebearing, not insisting on the letter of the law, not legalistic.* A person exercising this type of Godlike wisdom can respond in a given situation without harshness. Any approach you take to working out a difficult situation must be gentle. It is one of the fruits of the Spirit. If God is at work in you, you will be gentle.

126

REASONABLE

Reasonable may be rendered "easy to be entreated." When we are reasonable, others feel safe to come into our presence and earnestly ask for consideration or reconsideration. God encourages us to come into His presence with confidence and boldness (Eph. 3:12).

One of the biggest hang-ups young people have is feeling parents are not approachable or reasonable. It is "their way or the highway." This does not reflect the heart of God, who is utterly approachable yet has more absolutes than any parent could possess.

God opened Himself up to a lot of strong urging when Jesus told the parable about the annoyed judge. Because the widow kept coming to the judge and asking for legal protection, he relented and listened. He did so, "lest by continually coming she wear me out" (Luke 18:5). This is how Jesus said we ought to exercise diligence, to pray and not become discouraged. He even invites us to come (Matt. 11:28–29).

You can reason with God the way Abraham did at the time of the imminent destruction of Sodom (Gen. 18:22–33). He requested that God spare the area from His judgment should ten godly men be found there; God agreed. Moses reasoned with God, who was about to completely destroy Israel for worshiping the golden calf. After Moses appealed to God's faithfulness, "the LORD changed His mind about the harm which He said He would do to His people" (Exod. 32:14). The Hebrew word for "changed" carries the idea of relief or comfort from a planned course of direction. God chose another course of action in accomplishing His will. This reveals that the response of God is not inflexible; He does respond to our needs, attitudes, and actions. God's Son can respond to and sympathize with our feelings (Heb. 4:15). Why? He is full of mercy.

FULL OF MERCY

Open the heart of godly wisdom and mercy pours out. Grace is God granting us favor we do not deserve. Mercy is God withholding judgment that we *do* deserve. But mercy has a broader meaning. It includes a deep well of compassion, even pity. Mercy responds to a weak, hurting person suffering affliction, deserved or not. It is a tender, emotional response to a deep need in another.

Why is wisdom from above full of mercy? Because this wisdom has to reflect the character of God. God Himself is rich in mercy (Eph. 2:4) and more than willing to save anyone (Titus 3:5). We are invited to boldly approach a loving God for mercy: "Let us therefore draw near with confidence to the throne of grace, that we may receive mercy and may find grace to help in time of need" (Heb. 4:16). Therefore, in attempting to work out a difficult conflict, a wise response will be full of mercy. You may have to go the second mile for the person you're struggling with when he or she does not deserve an inch of consideration.

FULL OF GOOD FRUITS

If the seed of godly wisdom is planted in our hearts, what does it look like? God's wisdom produces a bumper crop of good fruit. "By this all men will know that you are My disciples, if you have love for one another" (John 13:35). Love is the first of many fruitful evidences of God's wisdom at work in your life. "But the fruit of the Spirit is love, joy, peace, patience, kindness, goodness, faithfulness, gentleness, self-control" (Gal. 5:22–23).

Jesus repeatedly challenged His listeners to evaluate the results of people's actions. He firmly warned of false prophets who would come into the congregation in sheep's clothing yet inwardly be ravenous wolves (Matt. 7:15). How can you identify them? "You will know them by their fruits. . . . Every good tree bears good fruit. . . . A good tree cannot produce bad fruit, nor can a bad tree produce good fruit" (Matt. 7:16–18). Godly wisdom yields ever-increasing good fruit.

The wisdom from God reflects the fruit of God's Holy Spirit in its conception and expression. This type of wisdom will produce a bumper crop of good results. And in abundance in these good results will also be rock-solid stability.

UNWAVERING

The simplest rendering of the word *unwavering* is "firm." Wisdom from the heart of God is straightforward, wholehearted, and impartial. It is unhesitating. God does not waver in His character, "For I, the LORD, do not change" (Mal. 3:6). God is not political. He does not sense the wind of public opinion, then act. He always acts true to His character, so He never wavers in purity, love, gentleness, reasonableness, and mercy. The fruit of His character is always the same because He never wavers.

We saw in the story of Israel and the golden calf that God sometimes changes His course of action, but His character *never* changes.

We make some of our saddest decisions when we try to bend God's precepts and principles in deference to someone or something (James 2:1–9). All too often I have seen that when there is a conflict between Christian convictions and, for example, cash flow, the latter wins. It is a pathetic commentary on political reality to hear the axiom "People vote their pocketbooks." It is not so with God. Pray it will not be so with us.

Unwavering wisdom will lead into the final characteristic of Godlike wisdom from above.

WITHOUT HYPOCRISY

Hypocrisy and godly wisdom are as compatible as oil and water. The Greek word translated "without hypocrisy" is actually one word with a limited use in the New Testament. The word *hypocrite* was developed from the Greek and Roman theater where actors wore large, exaggerated masks and projected their voices with a mechanical device. These people portrayed characters different from who they actually were; therefore, they were "hypocrites" (later rendered "actors"). *Actor* came to mean someone who presented himself one way but in reality was a different person. He professed qualities, beliefs, and feelings that he did not possess.

Of the six times the word translated "without hypocrisy" is used in the New Testament, it deals with that issue of giving a false impression. In three of the six instances it is used to qualify love, as in Romans 12:9: "Let love be without hypocrisy." Paul makes the same recommendation regarding faith (1 Tim. 1:5). Faith is not to be affected by expediency. Finally, it is used in reference to wisdom (James 3:17). The wisdom from above is foundationally based on the character of God and reflects a transparent life. It is not a front. It is a fact, based on reality and truth.

When you are seeking God for wisdom in working through a difficult situation, ask these simple questions:

- Are my words, actions, attitudes, and motives pure?
- Will this action produce a peaceable end?
- Does this action reflect genuine gentleness?
- Have I listened to the reasons of those this will affect?
- Does this action reflect compassion and mercy?
- Does this action reflect the nine fruit of the Holy Spirit?
- Is it consistent?
- Is it void of hypocrisy?

The Pain of the Unwise

The nation of Israel was ripped apart into two separate kingdoms as the result of an unwise decision. This same decision devastates families and other important relationships today. The details vary, but the essentials remain the same.

Solomon failed his son Rehoboam in many ways. He failed to be a moral example. In fact, Solomon was a spiritual and moral disaster. And despite his own wealth in wisdom, which he asked for and received from God, in the end, he failed to teach his own son to make wise decisions. How did it happen?

Solomon had burdened the Israelites with excessive taxes and heavy labor constrictions. When his son, Rehoboam, was about to be made king, a delegation from the ten northern tribes pleaded for the new king to lower their taxes. Rehoboam consulted the elders who had served his father, Solomon. They responded by saying, "If you will be a servant to this people today, will serve them, grant them their petition, and speak good words to them, then they will be your servants forever" (1 Kings 12:7). In other words, by reducing this burden, Rehoboam could win his people's hearts and loyalty and solidify the kingdom.

Then Rehoboam asked the young men who grew up with him what they thought he should do. They responded, "Thus you shall say to this people . . . , 'My little finger is thicker than my father's loins! . . . I will add to your yoke; my father disciplined you with whips, but I will discipline you with scorpions'" (1 Kings 12:10–11). Rehoboam chose this advice and conveyed his decision. At that, the ten northern tribes rebelled, just as the prophet Ahijah foretold (1 Kings 11:31).

Rehoboam lost ten of the twelve tribes of Israel in the same manner many parents have lost their sons and daughters to teenage rebellion. Submit Rehoboam's "wisdom" to God's eightfold test: Was it pure? No, it was very self-serving on his part. Was it peaceable? The people reacted in anger and said, "What portion do we have in David? . . . To your tents, O Israel! Now look after your own house, David!" (1 Kings 12:16). The nation went from peace to pieces. Did Rehoboam reflect gentleness? We are told that he "answered the people harshly" (12:13). Was he approachable? Yes, but only once. The tribes learned quickly not to do that again. Did he offer an abundance of mercy? Rehoboam's cruelty can be seen in his impudence, "I will discipline you with scorpions." (He referred to an unusually cruel kind of whip with sharp pieces of jagged metal tied on the ends.)

Did this "wisdom" reflect any of the fruit of the Holy Spirit: love, peace, patience, kindness, gentleness? Rehoboam's response was totally void of any hint of the presence of God's Spirit. Was he consistent or unwavering? He was consistent only in his cruelty. Finally, was his decision void of hypocrisy? He initially appeared to be a righteous man when he chose the city of Shechem for his coronation. Shechem was a special place in the eyes of Israel. That was where God first appeared to Abraham in the land of Canaan (Gen. 12:6–7). Jacob later lived there (Gen. 33:18–20). Joseph was buried there (Josh. 24:32). The people of Israel dedicated themselves to be faithful to keep the Mosaic law at Shechem (Josh. 24:1–27). This was a sacred place. In asking to be crowned there, Rehoboam associated himself with the divine destiny of a nation under God. What a religious front! He appeared to be a man of godly character, but in reality he was selfish and insecure. He hoped to intimidate his people with fear rather than lead them by faith and godly wisdom.

More homes are ripped apart by selfish decision making based on the wisdom from below, than by anything else. Daily I challenge individuals and families to evaluate how they are to relate to each other based on these eight evidences of God's wisdom. I have yet to see God's wisdom fail. But sadly, I have watched many fail to use godly wisdom.

Up to this point, what have you done to work out the conflicts you are facing? If you were to evaluate your approach with the plumb line of God's wisdom, how would it look? What do you need to start doing? If whatever you are doing is not working, it's time to reevaluate your strategy and make appropriate adjustments. There is tremendous personal power to be gained through utilizing the wisdom which is from above.

Using and abiding by truth and wisdom can be painful as we

seek to resolve conflicts. Yet God is responsible for something else in conflict resolution that is readily available: His comfort.

God's Responsibility to Comfort

Comfort is what Peggy needed when Martin did not respond to her efforts to change him. Susan desired God's comfort when Jerry sabotaged her at every juncture. Helen needed comfort when her drug-addicted son persisted in damaging behavior. It is ultimately God's responsibility to comfort us as only He can.

The apostle Paul felt this same need when burdened excessively and pushed beyond his strength. He even despaired of his life. But Paul met God in a new way in Asia. After feeling crushed beyond belief yet consoled by God, Paul wrote, "Blessed be the God and Father of our Lord Jesus Christ, the Father of mercies and God of all comfort" (2 Cor. 1:3). Friends, fame, and family all paled into insignificance compared to how God met him at his deepest point of need.

Another truth hit Paul. God comforts us in all, not just some, of our crushing emotional and physical pain. His comfort gives us hope and strength and, as we discussed earlier, the ability to convey the same to others out of the overflow of our own comfort (2 Cor. 1:4).

What happens when we give it our best shot and our family, mate, or friends don't respond as we hoped? God Himself gives us hope when all looks hopeless. He grants strength when we feel we can't take it another day. That's His responsibility. "But," you may ask, "what if someone really needs to pay for what he or she has done to me?" Revenge is God's responsibility. "What if I can't convince my spouse, my kids, or my family that they need to change?" Ultimate change is also God's responsibility.

How will I know if the steps I am about to undertake reflect the wisdom from God? Again, measure them by the eight characteristics of the wisdom from above. Compare them with the description of the wisdom from below. Ask, seek, and knock, and God's wisdom will be opened unto you (Luke 11:9–13).

Identify and assign what is biblically in each person's circle of responsibilities whether it is in marriage, divorce, or in-law conflicts. Acknowledge that God, too, has His circle of responsibilities. I know from experience that identifying and assigning responsibilities may be difficult, but it's not as hard as the next step. Our friends, Kari and Mark, were soon to find that out.

SEVEN

HOW TO REGAIN
PERSONAL POWER

Mark and Kari had it all lined out on the chalkboard in Pastor Tim's classroom. Almost three hours had passed. They had worked hard. They knew where they were *At* in their marriage and agreed where they ought to *Be*. They had the content of their circles of responsibilities clearly identified.

In years past, at this point I would have looked at Pastor Tim with a weary but satisfied look and thanked God for what He had directed us in His wisdom to accomplish. We would have closed the marathon in prayer and departed—mission accomplished. Another family had seen their needs and understood who was responsible for what.

But a few weeks later, I would see the couple, and they would be just as troubled, if not more so, than when we last met. A major oversight on my part would have failed to accomplish the desired end. Something was still missing.

When I began the pastoral ministry as a young man, I made many mistakes. To this day I thank God for the patience possessed by the members of my first church. More than forty years ago, I naively believed that if I could just get people to see their spiritual condition, they would automatically accept it and change. Wrong!

Even after spending thousands of hours counseling, I still ignorantly believed that *seeing* responsibility was the same as *assuming* it. I now realize that a person coming to understand what's in his circle of responsibilities does not automatically mean he will embrace them. And there's a double loss at work: when one fails to assume his personal responsibilities, he also rejects the personal power he needs to work out his conflict.

Because my time was coming to a close with Pastor Tim, Mark, and Kari, I knew we had to bridge this last hurdle. If they would not take this next step, there was no need to continue.

Continental Divide Decision

The Colorado Rockies are one of my favorite mountain ranges. I have spent many delightful days among them with my family. Running north and south throughout this range of breathtaking peaks is the Continental Divide. All the water on the west side of the Rockies drains into the Pacific Ocean. All the water on the east side flows to the east and drains into the Gulf of Mexico. The Divide is a separation, a line of demarcation. That was where we were with Kari and Mark. We had to decide to move forward or to come to a standstill. It was a Continental Divide decision.

When helping people with biblical wisdom, we never give up in spirit, but those we're trying to help can end our efforts. If they do not want to go forward, we can't make them. That is in God's circle of responsibility. We can pray, urge, plead, exhort, and reinforce, but only they can respond to God's pressure.

In the past I guided people to see their circles and just hoped they would assume them. Then I would go on attempting to bring reconciliation, rebuilding, and finally restoration, only to have the relationship fail. Usually it could be traced back to one point: the failure to fully assume personal responsibilities.

The saying is true: "A man convinced against his will is of the same opinion still." Unless a person "owns" his own circle of responsibilities, the end of a relationship may be near. Some Christian counselors start with the easy responsibilities. I don't. I asked, "Mark, are you willing to assume total responsibility for your alcoholism and your recovery? Will you assume responsibility to end this affair?

"Kari, will you accept responsibility to correct your un-Christlike temper? Will you purpose to correct or greatly reduce your overt criticism?

"Mark, will you assume your responsibility to rebuild the trust you have so flagrantly betrayed? Will you accept the responsibility to end your use of bitter sarcasm?

"Kari, will you accept responsibility to stop your revengeful behavior and to learn how to forgive?"

You may be thinking, *Why wouldn't they? They've acknowledged their wrong behavior.* But that wasn't enough. They had to assume full and complete responsibility for their words, actions, and attitudes before growth, change, reconciliation, and closure could take place. As we saw in chapter 2, Jesus illustrated this with the rich young ruler.

This successful politician plainly asked Jesus, "Teacher, what good thing shall I do that I may obtain eternal life?" (Matt. 19:16). Jesus instructed him to "go and sell your possessions and give to the poor, and you shall have treasure in heaven; and come, follow Me" (v. 21). Go, sell, give, come, and follow: these were clear instructions. It was as if Jesus said, "These are your responsibilities. Will you assume them?" As the words penetrated the young man's understanding, he instantly visualized only personal loss and pain. He turned and walked away. He heard and identified but would not assume.

Identifying one's circle of responsibilities is a function of the mind. Assuming responsibilities is a function of the will. Sadly, that is what failed to happen with Kari and Mark. The Cinderella ending, with everyone living happily ever after, didn't happen. Both spouses came to a clear understanding and agreement that the issues listed in their circles were right. There was very little debate. But why did they, and why do others, fail to assume their circles of responsibilities? Because of the age-old behavior of blame shifting.

BLAME SHIFTING

You met Pastor Martin, who served in a small rural church, in chapter 3. When his teenage daughter described how her father abused her physically and emotionally, he piously responded, "I take no responsibility for her wrong decisions. It is not my fault. She is a young adult." This is a classic example of pride-filled blame shifting—wisdom from the dark side.

Pastor Martin did not start shifting responsibility off of himself and onto others that day. In further sessions, it became evident that he had developed a lifelong pattern of blame shifting. He reduced his responsibility in his own thinking. Then, as a clever mind would have it, he began to focus on his daughter's behavior and her responsibility to correct it. Remember that this is what John did to Alice. He cunningly reduced his circle to the size of a pea and inflated Alice's circle to the size of a basketball. The reason remained the same: John could then blame Alice and Pastor Martin could then blame his daughter to avoid identifying and assuming any fault of their own. It's another strategy from hell.

The young farmer, Doug, was totally locked into his wife's overspending habit. If she did not spend, he reasoned, they would not have financial—or marital—problems. He could not see his own absentee parenting, his lack of care for or relationship with his wife, his violent anger, or his obsession for the approval of others. These never even registered in his conscience. Doug's motto was clear—"It can't be me; it must be thee." Jesus identified this time-worn pattern in the lives of the first-century Pharisees.

Jesus often rebuked the Pharisees by calling them "hypocrites." They were familiar with classical Greek and Roman theater and the masks actors wore to play their roles. The Pharisees' lives were just such an illusion. They placed a heavy burden of performance on others but did not practice it themselves (Matt. 23:3–4). Their focus was on how right they were (like John and Doug) and how wrong others were (like Alice and Doug's wife). A Pharisee stood and prayed, "God, I thank Thee that I am not like other people" (Luke 18:11). Blame shifters do the same thing.

They also do something else. Blame shifters serve the idol of public approval and acceptance. Jesus clearly revealed the Pharisees' motives: "They do all their deeds to be noticed by men" (Matt. 23:5). They are addicted to the approval of others. They need frequent human validation.

Furthermore, blame shifters experience guilt over their hypo-critical acts, so they major on the minor issues to give the public appearance that they've covered all the major issues in their lives. Jesus pointed this out in the Pharisees: "For you tithe mint and dill and cummin, and have neglected the weightier provisions of the law: justice and mercy and faithfulness" (Matt. 23:23). They meticulously tithed the smallest spices but shifted into selective amnesia and avoided the more important issues of the law—fairness and compassion. These religious leaders knew deep in their hearts they were hollow, empty, and seriously failing, so they focused on the outward show to hide their hidden depravity and shame.

This is the heart of legalism, when the length of men's hair or women's skirts becomes more important than the depth of inner holiness, compassion, love, and other fruit of the Holy Spirit. There is a simple reason for this. It is easier to perform outward actions than it is to develop inner character. It is easier to trim the hair than to purify the heart. Outer acts of righteousness are a camouflage for shallow inner character.

Jesus did not mince words. "Woe to you, scribes and Pharisees, hypocrites! For you clean the outside of the cup and of the dish, but inside they are full of robbery and self-indulgence." Then He drew a devastating word picture: "For you are like whitewashed tombs which on the outside appear beautiful, but inside they are full of dead men's bones and all uncleanness. Even so you too outwardly appear righteous to men, but inwardly you are full of hypocrisy and lawlessness" (Matt. 23:25, 27–28).

The result of their blame-shifting hypocrisy was personally devastating. Jesus warned, "Behold, your house is being left to you desolate!" (Matt. 23:38) Whether "house" refers to their city (Jerusalem), the temple, or even the Davidic dynasty, Jesus clearly stated it would be devastated. And it was—the city, the temple, and all genealogical records were destroyed by the Romans in 70 A.D., forty years later.

Again, what is the purpose of this lifelong habit of blame shifting? Simple. Blaming someone or something else for your responsibility is a self-defense mechanism designed to avoid any personal responsibility and loss of pride. We see this enacted at the trial of our Lord. At least four times Pilate declared Jesus innocent. In Matthew 27 we see that Pilate knew the Jews wanted Jesus killed not because of evil in His life but because of envy in their hearts. If he executed an innocent man, he could be held liable by his superiors. If he did not stop the riot that was about to start, that, too, would have been bad for him. So in one of the greatest travesties of justice in human history, he performed a physical act to illustrate his devious act of blame shifting. Pilate took water and washed his hands in front of the crowd, symbolizing his refusal of responsibility for putting an innocent man to death. Then he turned Jesus over to the Jews and allowed them to assume an unbelievable responsibility, which they embraced zealously: "His blood be on us and our children!" (Matt. 27:25).

Blame shifting does not prevent loss. It only postpones it. Protecting one's pride by shifting the blame is the beginning of the end. Pride comes before the fall (Prov. 16:18). We saw earlier that blame shifting began with Adam. When God confronted him for eating the forbidden fruit, Adam could not admit he ate until he shifted the blame, first to God and then to Eve.

Aaron, Moses' older brother, is another classic example of a blame shifter. As Moses descended from the mountain, having received from God the Law, he discovered the people of Israel dancing before an idol in the shape of a golden calf. Throwing down the stone tablets, which shattered to pieces, he smashed the golden calf, burned it, and ground it to powder. After scattering the powder over the stream, he made the people drink it. Then he turned his attention to Aaron and asked, "What did this people do to you, that you have brought such great sin upon them?" (Exod. 32:21).

Aaron mixed truth with the most ludicrous lie when he said, "They gave [the gold] to me, and I threw it into the fire, and out came this calf" (Exod. 32:24). He had actually molded the idol himself. Aaron could not face the truth or the potential loss through consequences.

Blame shifters use two reasons for self-justification: "I had no choice but to do it" and "They made me do it." The heart of the issue is a refusal to own or assume responsibility for their own choices. It is always someone else's fault. They are self-deceived into thinking they are passive—that others have control and, therefore, responsibility. Self-control, the ninth fruit of the Holy Spirit, is replaced with an attempt to control others. When self-control is replaced by blame shifting, personal responsibility and personal power vanish. This deceptive thinking only muddies the issue of any reconciliation and closure.

Some favorite blame-shifting statements are

"Well, you always . . ."

"If only you would . . ."

"Well, when are you going to . . ."

"Look who's talking . . ." (My favorite.)

"When is the last time you . . ."

"I will when you . . ."

BLAME SHIFTERS REWRITE HISTORY

Blame shifters also tend to recast events in their favor. This happened repeatedly while I was working with Rex and Marylee. He worked in real estate and she was a high school administrator. One of her complaints was his virtual disappearance during deer hunting season. He insisted that he actually went hunting only once a season. Later, under extreme pressure from mutual friends, he admitted going twice. To her, any time he was out in the woods with his gun was hunting. To him, he was hunting only if he was gone for three or more days.

For the next three months, he reminded us that we were the confused ones and that he went hunting only once. You may be thinking, *He is a pathological liar.* That could be, but he is definitely a blame shifter who rewrites history to avoid fault. He sees himself as innocent, maybe even a victim of a nagging wife. The sad part is that a wife who lives with such a deceived person may begin to believe her deceptive husband and think she is going crazy. These kinds of manipulations are called "mind games."

According to Doug, his wife allegedly spent him into a $45,000 debt. He was an innocent, hardworking farmer victimized by his unsubmissive wife. Through decades of counseling folks I've learned that when something does not make sense, the whole story has usually not been told. In Rex's and Doug's cases, they had rewritten the story in their own minds, then used misinformation to convince their wives and others of their innocence.

When Lois, the wife of a chronic blame shifter, came to me she was an emotional basket case. I had not seen such results of emotional spouse abuse in years. She and her husband were in a fine evangelical church. While at church, he was the picture of love and devotion. At home, it was hell. Before Lois came for her first appointment, she had found herself curled up, shaking, in a fetal position in the corner of the garage. Her husband stood over her, heaping abuses and profanities of the most vulgar sort.

Lois separated from her husband. He went to the church leaders and told them he could not understand his wife's behavior. She must be sick. She was acting strange. She would not submit to him as her husband. The leadership called her in for a conference. She attempted to tell her story. They didn't believe her. They scolded her for her lack of unilateral submission. How could she hurt her children and husband by breaking up the family? She was reabused emotionally by the church elders and ultimately disciplined by the church. She left. He stayed.

For years afterward, Lois's husband called her and quoted Bible verses that said she was wicked and rebellious. At the same time, her teenage sons reported that their dad encouraged them to watch pornographic movies during their visits with him. This man quit his job and quickly disposed of the retirement money so Lois would not have any of the family assets. As God-appointed authorities (Rom. 13:1–7), the civil judges righted the wrong in court that the true ministers of God failed to even investigate.

Lois's husband exhibited the pattern of one who shifts the blame and rewrites history. He first attacked her verbally and when she reacted, he turned into the victim in his own mind. Then he shifted into wanting to rescue the marriage, only to repeat the pattern down the road. What he reported to the church leadership was her reaction to him, making himself out to be the abused person. He would cry and lament that he wanted his wife and marriage back, then turn right around and use the foulest gutter talk imaginable to her on the phone. He was not too smart. He also left this language on her answering machine. Those tapes did not play well for him in court.

This is a very sick pattern, which unfortunately is happening all too often even in our church families. A situation like Lois's touched another church family. But this pastor knew abuse when he saw it, and he had the leadership protect the wife while the husband was urged to get professional help. He refused. In his mind, he did not have a problem. If his wife would only submit to his authoritarian position, there would be no problems. It was all her fault! Notice the familiar pattern: history is rewritten, he believes he is the good guy and she is bad.

The basic motivation behind blame shifting and rewriting of history is to avoid, at all cost, any shame, pain, or conviction that God may bring. It is also deeply rooted in the fear of discovery, the fear of rejection, and ultimately the fear of being alone. Legitimate conviction, shame, and guilt are designed by God to draw us to confession and repentance, resulting in forgiveness and restoration of fellowship (2 Cor. 7:10).

The blame shifter believes the guilt, shame, and chastening are too great for him to endure and he refuses to go to God in confession to gain forgiveness, freedom, and consolation. Instead, he rewrites the events in his mind so that he no longer feels responsible to others or God. But he is still left with the guilt, shame, and fear of perceived or real rejection.

I grieve for Rex. I grieve for Doug. It is my opinion that Satan has deceived them into thinking that confession and repentance are too difficult. Satan offers temporary relief. He has convinced them to avoid the biblical response so they can save face and keep their pride intact. Now their relationships are based on a lie (energized by Satan) and not the truth (energized by God). Satan is the progenitor of deception and lies. Jesus, by contrast, is the way, the source of ultimate truth, and the life (John 14:6). God gives grace only for the truth. Jesus' way fosters humility. Satan's way bolsters pride, followed by a horrific fall.

Blame shifting to avoid assuming responsibility is also seen in arguments. One of Mark's pet peeves with Kari was that she frequently misplaced the car keys. To remedy that, they mounted a pegboard at the entrance to the back door. Upon arriving home, Kari and Mark were to hang all keys there. Whether it was due to Kari's passive-aggressive behavior, revenge, selective amnesia, or plain forgetfulness, she often forgot to do this.

Consequently Mark frequently got ready to leave for work but couldn't find the car keys. He launched into rages over this. The missing car keys are the perceived issue. Kari felt the emotional pain of his attacking anger and reminded him of the time he forgot to pick up the kids at school. Not to be outdone, he reminded her he would not have to pick up the kids if she had not taken that stupid computer class. The opening issue is soon lost.

Why is blame shifting so devastating? The shifter's underlying motive to win and to gain control brings death to a relationship and drives the nails in its coffin. Blame shifting does not reflect the wisdom that is from above. It flunks all eight tests of godly wisdom. It is certainly not pure and is far from peaceable. Gentleness is replaced with harshness and anger. It is devoid of mercy. It is capricious at best. It is the epitome of hypocrisy.

Blame shifting remains the first reason many fail to assume legitimate responsibilities. Diffusion of responsibility is the second reason.

Diffusion of Responsibility

Scarcely a year goes by that we don't hear in the news of someone being physically assaulted while a group of onlookers stands idly by. It is a strange phenomenon, yet there is a logical reason for this lack of involvement. If one person witnesses a victim in distress, he feels totally responsible to help and will bear all the guilt or blame for nonintervention. On the other hand, if several people are present, each assumes someone else is going to help. The net result? No one does anything.

This happens Sunday after Sunday in churches across the land. Sincere pastors plead for more church workers from among the congregation. Most people think he is looking for someone else and are willing to let that someone else do it.

When I turned to Mark and Kari in our session, I did not ask them collectively if they would assume their circles of responsibilities. I would have run the risk of diffused accountability. Instead, I turned to each one individually in the presence of all and asked, "Will you assume each item in your own circle of responsibility?" Years of people helping has taught me that diffusion of responsibilities can happen in the smallest groups as well as the largest. This explains Nathan's approach with King David.

The prophet Nathan directly confronted David with his adultery and murder. David finally confessed, "I have sinned against the LORD" (2 Sam. 12:13). He admitted he was guilty and assumed full responsibility for his actions. Psalm 51 reveals David's heart of repentance and the resulting release of guilt and shame.

To assume responsibility now that for years has been ignored or blame shifted away can be initially painful. For some, it may be a new experience. But they will feel a new surge of energy from God. They will experience firsthand the reality of Jesus' own words, "Come to Me, all who are weary and heavy-laden, and I will give you rest. Take My yoke upon you, and learn from Me, for I am gentle and humble in heart; and you shall find rest for your souls. For My yoke is easy, and My load is light" (Matt. 11:28–30).

Weariness comes from struggling under heavy burdens, whether it is sin and its consequences or not identifying and assuming our own legitimate responsibilities. Jesus promises an inner rest for our souls because *His* yoke is easy and *His* load is light. By yoking ourselves to the Savior, we assume only the responsibilities He designs for us (Gal. 6:5; Matt. 11:30).

The responsibilities and instructions Jesus delegates to us will reflect the wisdom from above. Assuming our responsibilities from the Lord may seem initially unmanageable or totally exhausting. That, however, describes Satan's load, not our Lord's.

Kari looked overwhelmed as she realized the legitimate load she was responsible for. I strongly suggested that she take one responsibility at a time and work on the rest as God gave her the strength. Mark also appeared to be overwhelmed. Then it became quite evident that they both expected the other to continue assuming their responsibilities. Why is this practice so dangerous?

RESIST ASSUMING OTHERS' RESPONSIBILITIES

There are at least seven reasons why people take on others' responsibilities to their detriment. Through each, let me explain why this practice is so destructive.

TO MAKE PEACE   #1

Peace at any cost is not peace. It is only delayed warfare, inevitably coupled with further emotional pain. There are times we need to do a little extra to maintain the peace. But assuming another's circle of responsibilities in order to keep peace over the long term is irresponsible. This is called enabling: one person picks up the responsibility of another, empowering him to continue being irresponsible.

fear lies beneath standing up

When a Christian wife allows her believing husband to verbally and physically abuse her, she is not securing peace; she is only delaying the inevitable—more abuse. There is a higher law than that of the husband. It is civil law. Civil authority is established by God, and it prohibits spouse abuse. The wife may need to put a space between herself and her husband until he admits he has a major problem, assumes responsibility for his behavior, and seeks appropriate help. This can be equally said of a verbally abusive wife. Distance may need to take place first before reconciliation can be affected.

If a wife continues to endure abuse in an effort to keep the peace, she is removing her husband's most powerful motivator for change: suffering the consequences or loss. If he displayed that behavior at work, he would lose his job, a costly consequence. Part of his circle of responsibility is to bear the loss incurred by his inappropriate behavior: in this case, no peace.

In less extreme cases, when parents make a reasonable request of their children and do not follow through to see that it is done, the parents' irresponsibility is at fault. Making a habit of picking up after children just to avoid hassling them to do it only prolongs the irresponsible pattern in both the adult and the child.

To assume others' responsibilities to avoid their getting mad at us is faulty thinking: we assume that if we please them we can control their anger. The reality is that their anger is going to erupt somewhere else. It is not a matter of if, but when. Nick's wife, Traci, felt she was responsible to make her controlling mother happy and secure at any cost. Traci sincerely believed that if she did this, she could avoid her mother's anger and subtly imposed guilt trips. It didn't happen. But ignoring reality, she asserted, "It's worked for years, hasn't it?"

"Is that why you and Nick are in my office tonight?" I gently probed.

"Well . . ."

"Until you acknowledge that taking responsibility for your mother is not working and assume appropriate steps to correct it, the triangular conflict between you, your husband, and your mother is only going to get worse."

There is another downside to keeping peace by assuming others' responsibilities. In time, you get tired and realize that trying harder does not work. You begin to reflect how you have been used. Then the stuffed anger and hidden resentment surface. There is no peace. There is only delayed bitterness. Then you are faced with both bitterness and burnout, a physical evidence of overresponsibility.

Jesus said, "Blessed are the peacemakers, for they shall be called sons of God" (Matt. 5:9). These peacemakers help others identify their responsibilities, urge them to assume them, and encourage them to follow through with action. They do not make a habit of doing for others what they are fully able and responsible to do for themselves.

To Avoid Guilt Feelings   #2

True guilt says, "I am worthy of blame." False guilt makes you *feel* worthy of blame when in reality you are not. The confusing part is that true guilt and false guilt feel the same. Guilt must be tested to see if it is based on reality.

Traci's obedience to her mother was creating havoc in her marriage. Her husband was at his wit's end because of his mother-in-law's constant intervention and Traci's emotional entanglement with her. Tracy is Exhibit A of one's assuming another person's responsibilities out of false guilt. We used these questions to test her guilt:

"Are you to honor your mother?"

"Yes."

"Are you responsible to obey your mother?"

"No."

"Is honor an attitude of the heart or obedience to her commands?"

"Attitude of the heart."

"Are you responsible for your mother's ultimate happiness?"

"No."

"Who is?"

"God."

"Is your mother responsible for her own response?"

"Yes."

"Are you responsible to correct or make up for your mother's unmet or unprocessed needs?"

You won't get God's help on taking on someone else's responsibilities.

149

"No."

"Are you willing to take back the control or ownership of your own life as a responsible, mature young woman?"

Did you notice what I attempted to do for Traci? I simply asked questions that brought out the truth and her responsibility. The only way to identify genuine or false guilt is to test it with truth. God gives grace only for responsibilities assumed in truth, those given under His yoke, not ours.

To Protect from Pain   # 3

Our friend has a neighbor who is a registered nurse. She worked her way up to the position of a nursing supervisor. She brought in more than seventy thousand dollars a year in salary. She also signed up for extra overtime.

Her husband, however, rarely kept a position. He used up more than twenty years looking for just the right job. He spent money on extravagant clothes, cars, and hobbies. The more he spent, the harder she worked. Their credit card debt was astronomical.

She was a brilliant, talented woman. But she struggled with just one small fear: the fear of being alone. She assumed total financial responsibility for the family in order to keep her husband from being unhappy with her. She was fully convinced that if she did not do this she could find herself alone. That fear drove her.

To Maintain a Childish Perspective   # 4

Adults who seek approval based on their performance maintain an immature, childish perspective. When they were children, they pleased Mom and Dad and received approval. As adult children they look for the same approval by assuming responsibilities that are not theirs. To them, pleasing equals acceptance. This is how they continue to relate to their parents and to others in adulthood.

Adults who cling to the childlike perspective of assuming others' responsibilities perpetuate a false sense of security to maintain a feeling of acceptance. Immature adults need encouragement and help in putting away childish things (1 Cor. 13:11). They need to transfer their childlike security base of collecting others' responsibilities to accepting only those that God wants them to shoulder. All other performance-based security is sinking sand.

TO GAIN ACCEPTANCE ≠ 5

One devastating effect of the Fall in the Garden of Eden that continues to this day, even in the lives of believers, is the feeling of separation and rejection. Though we are completely accepted by God through our relationship with Jesus Christ (Rom. 8:15–16), the scar of separation remains. We all still struggle, more or less, with a desire for acceptance and a fear of rejection.

Even a believer, though positionally secure in Christ, can emotionally feel the need for human acceptance and approval. Notice I used the word *need,* not *want.* It is healthy to want to be accepted and generally pleasing to others. It is not healthy to need this from others. Codependent persons need it. Healthy, interdependent persons want it.

need is bad

One of the unhealthy human strategies to gain acceptance and approval is to assume others' responsibilities with an air of pride. "I can do anything asked of me through sheer determination and sacrifice." People who are locked into a performance-based acceptance cannot say no. They therefore assume responsibilities that are not theirs. If you wonder whether or not you are addicted to others' approval, ask yourself, "Am I neglecting any God-given responsibilities to do people-pleasing responsibilities?" This was a source of conflict in Deidra and Keenan's marriage.

Deidra was deeply hurt every time she saw her husband, Keenan, dart out the door to help someone on a moment's notice. While her "Honey Do" list was gathering dust on the refrigerator door, her neighbors' needs received Keenan's prompt attention. It was the same way at church. If anyone wanted a responsible person to do something, Keenan was the one to ask. His winsome smile always said yes. Dread controlled Deidra. Every phone call was like a fire alarm to Keenan. He was in his boots with hat in hand before the receiver was replaced on the phone.

The hurt deepened in Deidra's heart, resulting in bouts of depression. Their five kids longed to be with their ever-popular but increasingly absent dad. Everyone loved Keenan. But while he served others, his own family suffered neglect. Though Keenan was saved and a faithful church member, deep inside of him was a gnawing need for people's approval. It was not the work that attracted him. It was the praise, acceptance, and euphoric high of being a hero.

More than once I have heard pastors' children wish they could be parishioners' children instead. They longed for their parents' undivided attention and a sense of value and honor. Neglect communicates rejection. When a dad claws his way through life, seeking approval in adulthood for what he did not get in childhood, he is setting up his children for the people-approval trap of Satan that says, "Serve others at all costs. Ignore God-given responsibility at any cost."

An emotionally and spiritually immature person takes on responsibilities that are not his to gain acceptance and approval and avoid rejection. This pattern of behavior may indicate the need to grow into a more secure relationship with Christ. This will result in an adult who can balance his priorities.

When Keenan saw how out of balance his priorities were and how it was hurting his family, his eyes filled with tears. His heart sank. He saw that what he was doing to his five children was the same thing his dad unintentionally did to him. His grief was almost too much. Yet this was beneficial. Often a personal breaking precedes a permanent healing (John 12:24–25). Keenan now readily allows his wife to be a reality check for him. When asked to help someone, he does not tell others he has to check with his wife—that shifts his responsibility from himself to Deidra. He just says, "I need to check my schedule. I'll get back with you. Thank you for asking."

Deidra did not resent the use of his spiritual gift of serving. She did resent Keenan's overt neglect of her and the children, which they translated as rejection. A secure relationship with the Lord Jesus Christ and an open relationship with his wife and children is now Keenan's basis for serving others.

Those who feel the need to rescue or fix everyone are approval addicts, not mature, secure believers in Christ. Rescuers and fixers often assume responsibilities that are not theirs and neglect those that are. The need for human validation is a trap set by the evil one. He leads you to believe you need people's validation, which becomes the doorway to approval dependency. This pattern is like a two-edged sword. It cuts one way to gain acceptance, then it cuts the other way to avoid rejection.

TO AVOID REJECTION   # 6

Because we are motivated by a desire for personal gain and a fear of personal loss, we purposely seek the approval of others. The downside of this is our fear of loss by rejection if we do not assume others' responsibilities. This fear of rejection prevents us, like Keenan, from saying no to people's requests. Instead our radar is always on as we try to *avoid* rejection. Rather than doing something for praise, approval, or self-fulfillment, we do it out of a fear of rejection or abandonment.

This avoidance of rejection is the motivation that a perfectionist often feels. He pursues not excellence, which would be fulfilling and peace giving, but perfect performance, which is both impossible and defeating. He lives in constant fear of others seeing his flaws and rejecting him. A perfectionist rarely experiences satisfaction in what he accomplishes. If he has a list of ten things to do and gets only seven of them done, he is depressed. He can scarcely enjoy the accomplishment of seven things because he failed to complete the other three. Blame, shame, and fear of failure resulting in rejection consume his private thoughts. So he reverts to serving the god of public approval.

A perfectionist has most all the earmarks of what the New Testament calls a "Pharisee." Both hide behind a mask of false pretense, fearing rejection. But mature growth in Christ can handle rejection, even though it still hurts.

Along with the desire to avoid rejection is the strong motivation to please.

To Please #7

Pleasers are notorious for assuming responsibilities that are not theirs. Pleasers' one goal is to have no one upset with them. It is a rule they live by. Compliant pleasers often marry angry controllers. The number one emotion that controllers use to manipulate pleasers is anger. So pleasers learn to "walk on eggs." They pursue peace and assume others' responsibilities at any cost, and they feel guilty if they fail to please. They, too, crave acceptance and fear rejection. In the course of trying to please and be who others think they should be, pleasers lose their identity. In time, they even lose touch with who they are in Christ. This happened to Marylee.

Rex's wife, Marylee, was a classic pleaser. Although in her professional career as an educator she received outstanding evaluations, she experienced an identity crisis. She did not know who she was. As ludicrous as this may sound, it is very logical. While Marylee spent her whole life pleasing others, she had to deaden her own feelings, interests, desires, goals, gifts, and dreams. But these important things are never buried; they are put in "cold storage." In time, they thaw and begin to activate, but by then the pleaser is aware she is getting older. This is a setup for a midlife crisis. She feels, *There is so much to do and so little time left to do it.*

Like perfectionists, pleasers assume responsibilities that are not theirs out of a need for approval and a fear of rejection. As

Christians, we are to please others for their good (Rom. 15:2). A husband is to find ways to please his wife and a wife her husband. The apostle Paul sought to "please all men in all things, not seeking my own profit, but the profit of the many, that they may be saved" (1 Cor. 10:33).

Paul's goal was to reach both Jews and Greeks for Christ. He avoided certain activities to keep from being a stumbling block. He did not want to do anything that would prevent someone from entering God's kingdom or would impede the growth of anyone already in the kingdom. He did not seek to please for personal benefit, acceptance, approval, or praise. His efforts to please were on a higher plane. It was for others' gain and God's glory.

It is important to underscore something here. Although the apostle Paul did his best to please, he still met with rejection, if not outright persecution (2 Cor. 11:23–27). Yet because he assumed only the responsibilities that were from God, he was able to say at the end of his life that he had fought a good fight, finished his course, and kept the faith. He eagerly looked forward to a crown of righteousness that awaited him on that day (2 Tim. 4:7–8). Paul's motivation to please was rooted in his understanding of being totally accepted by the Father, not in an unhealthy desire to gain the acceptance and approval of others.

Your spouse, family, or friends may get angry with you for not assuming their responsibilities. That should be a signal to confirm in prayer what is and is not your responsibility. Failure to do this could drive you to the breaking point of overcommitment and the temptation to blame God for it. Yet, taking no responsibility can be even worse.

No Decision Is a Decision

Not to decide to assume legitimate responsibilities is a decision—a decision by default. This is how Keenan handled conflict in his life.

He ignored, avoided, and denied it. He reasoned, *If I do not deal with conflict, it will just go away.*

Keenan came across as spiritual, saying he was always going to take the "high road" and avoid conflict. That sounds good, but it is not biblical. What Keenan called taking the high road was really copping out of his responsibility as a husband and father. It hurt Keenan to realize this about himself. Denial was his lifelong method of survival. But he learned that he needed to forgive and release his past. Now he sees current requests for his time as an opportunity to serve based on already being accepted by God and not to gain others' acceptance. And he realizes that his family's needs come first. Deidra has been a terrific soul mate to help Keenan maintain this balance.

How do you regain personal power in your life? It starts by identifying and assigning legitimate responsibilities where they belong. But then the key is to assume your own responsibilities. Stop all forms of blame shifting. Tenaciously resist taking on others' yokes. That will not strengthen you. It will only weaken you. But God will dynamically empower you personally to do all that *He* requires of you.

※

Possessing the incredible power to work out difficult situations through assuming God-given responsibilities is a good start. There is one more ingredient that actually makes it all work. Phyllis and Gerald learned this the hard way with their college-freshman daughter, Carissa.

EIGHT

HARNESS THE POWER OF RESPONSIBILITY

follow-through, fulfill

College years are fun times. I have good memories of those days. I pursued my life's work and forged lifetime friendships. These were the expectations that Gerald and Phyllis, the couple we met in chapter 5, had for their college-bound daughter. Carissa had the grades for college. She shopped around and selected the one that just suited her.

Phyllis and Gerald believed that Carissa would work hard and they would pay the bills. This was their plan, not Carissa's. Instead she partied hard—they still paid the bills. Consequences ensued: first came academic probation, then dismissal. Phyllis and Gerald were understandably devastated. Gerald was on disability and Phyllis worked part-time. Money was available, but tight.

Carissa had fulfilled two of the three ingredients of an unspoken contract for success in college. First, she identified the school and major she wanted to pursue. Second, she took the initiative to apply to the college and sign up for classes. The third ingredient, which Carissa discounted, was acting responsibly—attending classes, completing her assignments, studying for exams, and passing courses. Carissa felt it would somehow just work out and she would graduate.

Her parents' expectations were as obvious to them as if they were written in contract form. But Carissa didn't or wouldn't fulfill her responsibilities. The result? Mom and Dad fulfilled theirs and were very angry. Carissa was very irresponsible and having a ball.

While teaching on the collegiate level, I never ceased to be amazed at students' reactions when informed they were on academic probation or worse yet, dismissed. The look on their faces asked, "How could you?" Rarely was it, "How could I?" The attitude of many seemed to be that a college education was a birthright, not a privilege. They often wanted to continue an academic career with little effort on their part. Some failed to understand that a student does not merely receive a degree. He *earns* a degree.

As we saw previously, Phyllis and Gerald decided to transfer the ultimate financial responsibility over to Carissa. They would love her, encourage her, and let her become a responsible young adult. If she wanted to continue in school she would have the privilege of paying her own school bills. If she fulfilled her academic responsibilities well, they agreed to pay for the successfully completed semesters. This principle of fulfilled responsibilities worked well for Carissa through college and graduate school. It works well in industry too. Many employers will reimburse employees for the successful completion of classes. The power of personal responsibility provides a strong motivation for employees to persevere with excellence and fulfill their assumed responsibilities.

Failure to fulfill responsibilities is second in seriousness only to not assuming responsibilities at all. Just as identifying responsibilities is not the same as assuming them, neither is assuming responsibilities the same as fulfilling them. The power of personal responsibility to restore relationships works only if you do your part.

If there is one running battle God has had with mankind, it is the issue of obedient follow-through. From the very beginning,

God assigned responsibilities to man to fulfill. In the Garden of Eden He established one prohibition with Adam and Eve: no eating from the tree of the knowledge of good and evil. Did they not follow through because the command was unclear? No way! Eve was able to clearly repeat God's command when Satan questioned what God had said. But she disobeyed anyway. The rest is history. From that point on, God's thrust in human history has been to clearly identify man's responsibilities, then to convince him to assume and to *fulfill* them.

The first murder in history sprang from a failure to fulfill responsibilities. Adam's first son, Cain, refused to offer the prescribed sacrifice. God pleaded with him to reconsider, saying, "If you do well, will not your countenance be lifted up?" (Gen. 4:7). He would feel better after obedience. Abel, in contrast, acted out of faith and fulfilled what God required (Heb. 11:4). Cain's anger at God for rejecting his sacrifice turned on Abel, resulting in cold-blooded murder. Failure to follow through with personal responsibility may not result in murder, but it can kill relationships.

ROOT OF CONFLICT

When Deidra and Keenan first shared the issues that were creating marital disharmony, I was particularly interested in one complaint of hers regarding Keenan. He was extremely talented and very successful in his profession. He was also a people pleaser who hated conflict. In his desire for peace, he often agreed to do something at home but did not follow through. It rarely dawned on him that "Yes" meant "Yes, I will do it."

Keenan was not lazy, as his work ethic evidenced. But because he said yes to everyone in order to gain approval and avoid rejection, he was not able to fulfill all his commitments. There were not enough hours in the day to do it all. The needs at home suffered the most neglect.

My older brother, Carl, used to say to me, "The road of life is strewn with the bones of good intention." Keenan would promise to do something for his wife, fully intending to do it. His good intentions usually fell short. Deidra translated his failure to follow through on her requests as personal rejection and a lack of love for her. What do love and following through on promises have to do with each other? Jesus makes it clear: "If you love Me, you will keep My commandments" (John 14:15). He reinforced it again six verses later: "He who has My commandments and keeps them, he it is who loves Me" (John 14:21).

When we met and talked about this issue, Keenan sheepishly flashed his million-dollar smile and admitted, "I need to work on that." To his credit he not only acknowledged it, but he purposed to do something about it. We cannot correct what we do not acknowledge. Conflict can often be traced to a failure to acknowledge, assume, and then fulfill responsibilities.

Fulfilling Responsibilities in Marriage

Although not currently pastoring a local church, as an ordained minister I perform weddings from time to time. They are happy, joyful, and sobering occasions. Taking vows before God and witnesses is a serious matter (Eccles. 5:4–5).

In marriage counseling, I often refer a couple back to what they vowed on their wedding day. This is what one couple vowed to each other in an outdoor chapel, framed by the Colorado Rockies: I asked the groom, "Do you take Elizabeth to be your wedded wife, to have and to hold from this day forward, to lead, to love her as Christ loved the church, to nourish and cherish her, to live with her in an understanding way, and to grant her honor as a fellow heir of the grace of life, to cleave to her, so that together you may become one in Christ and serve Him throughout your lives? Do you promise these things with complete dependence upon our Lord to enable you to fulfill them? If this is the intent of your heart, will you say, 'I do'?"

Then I turned to his lovely bride and asked, "Elizabeth, do you take George to be your wedded husband, to have and to hold from this day forward, to submit to him as unto the Lord? Do you promise to allow his leadership in your home, to respect and honor him as your head, to adorn yourself with a gentle and quiet spirit, and to be a helpmate to him? Will you now cleave to George so that together you may be one in Christ and together you may serve Him throughout your lives? Do you promise these things with complete dependence upon our Lord to enable you to fulfill them? If this is the intent of your heart, will you say, 'I do'?"

Notice what George vowed: to lead, love, nourish, understand, honor, and cleave. Note what Elizabeth vowed before God and those witnesses: to submit, respect, honor, cleave, be gentle and quiet in spirit, be a helpmate, and allow George to lead. Those are serious vows.

very serious

I agree with M. Scott Peck, who observed in his book *The Road Less Traveled,* "If it were not for the blindness of love, we would all run in terror from the reality of our wedding vows." When the responsibility of those vows is not fulfilled, conflict is inevitable.

Although every couple may have unique features in their particular marital conflict, most of it can be traced to a husband's failure to love and cherish his wife and a wife's failure to respect and admire her husband. Both of these failures stem from not fulfilling the identified responsibilities laid out by the apostle Paul in Ephesians 5:21–33.

Pastor Tim and I had helped Mark and Kari list the conflicts in their marriage. Kari listed Mark's hurtful behavior—his lying, infidelity, lack of love, cursing, vengefulness, and dishonoring spirit. Mark's list of Kari's destructive behavior included fighting, yelling, criticism, and sarcasm. I asked Mark and Kari individually which of these words, attitudes, or behaviors showed love and respect and which didn't.

The words *love* and *respect* are easily spoken but have different meanings to different people. Love according to whom? Respect by whose standard? God gave us the plumb line of true love and respect in His Word. First Corinthians 13 synthesizes what love looks like and how it is to be expressed.

Is patient under stress (v. 4)

Is kind under hostility (v. 4)

Is secure under threat of loss (jealousy) (v. 4)

Avoids marketing self (boasting) (v. 4)

Is humble under pressure to exert pride (v. 4)

Acts appropriately when under pressure to come unglued (v. 5)

Is calm when provoked (v. 5)

Forgives when tempted to keep track of wrongs (v. 5)

Is joyful when truth wins out (v. 6)

Endures under pressure to quit (v. 7)

Hopes regardless of the circumstances (v. 7)

Perseveres when tempted to give up (v. 7)

Continues to love when tempted to quit (v. 8)

Not just one spouse, but both husband and wife are to love, respect, and honor each other. Often in counseling a couple, I will lead them to agree at the outset to fulfill their identified responsibilities to love, honor, cherish, and respect each other. Then later, if they engage in hurtful behavior, I am able to appeal to them to follow through with this earlier commitment. I remind them there is no power to restore relationships apart from fulfilling personal responsibilities.

What if spouses do not love, honor, or respect each other before coming to counseling? No problem. I ask them to read the appropriate passages (Eph. 5:21–33; 1 Pet. 3:1–12; Col. 3:18–19). Then I ask if they are fulfilling their respective responsibilities as defined in the Word of God. If not, are they willing to learn how?

You may ask, *What if they say no?* Then I ask if what they are doing is working for them in a healthy, mutually fulfilling way. The fact that they are in counseling is an outward indication that whatever they are doing is not working. The result of sin is still death (Rom. 6:23). The temporal effects are relational, even physical, and ultimately spiritual separation from God. A couple may have come to counseling to learn how to make their "sin-functional" system work better. That I cannot help them do. I have to adhere to the plumb line of truth as revealed in God's Word. All other systems are destined to fail and for good reason. They do not reflect the character and ways of God. His ways reflect His character.

Humpty Dumpty shattered into many pieces, as do people's relationships. There are fewer pieces, however, than one would expect in a conflict. How do we know? "No temptation [testing] has overtaken you but such as is common to man" (1 Cor. 10:13). The variety of testings is unlimited, but the basic ingredients are relatively few.

There are few basic ingredients in a cake recipe. One can vary their amounts, but they usually include flour, sugar, eggs, shortening, baking powder, and salt. All cakes include some of these basic ingredients. At a supermarket bakery you can find a wide variety of exotic shapes and sizes of cakes made from a few basic ingredients. So are the variations in relational conflict—though they come in many shapes and sizes, they can be reduced to a few basic ingredients.

Divorce can result from the failure to fulfill vows and God-assigned responsibilities. Those who reduce the marriage vows and commands of God to nothing more than avoiding adultery somehow think they can violate other godly behavioral principles with no consequences to the relationship. This was the case with Rex and his wife, Marylee. He emotionally abused her by cussing, yelling, belittling, demeaning, lying to, and embarrassing her—then rewriting history. His response to her accusations of abuse was to say

Marylee had no biblical grounds to separate temporarily from him because he had not had an affair.

Many believe that adultery is the only basis for permitting divorce. But separation may be necessary in order for each mate to get appropriate personal help and then reestablish a biblical foundation to reunite.

In extreme abuse situations, rarely will the husband change until the wife takes drastic steps to force the issue. It may be necessary for her to separate with the firm ultimatum that he must undergo serious counseling before she will return. As hard as it is to accept, this is usually the only effective means a wife has of ending the abusive cycle.

Rex felt he had the right to mentally, emotionally, and sometimes physically abuse Marylee to control her, but since he hadn't been unfaithful, he told her she couldn't even consider a separation. I have a hard time with that reasoning. The apostle Paul gives a spouse at least three options in a difficult marital situation: to remain in the situation with no change, to leave and remain unmarried, or to leave temporarily but be reconciled (1 Cor. 7:10–11). There may be other options, but Paul gave these three clear ones. Reconciliation may be the most difficult.

Successful Couples Work Hard

God has brought some unique people into my life. Such were Amanda and Steve. She had won the title of Mrs. Missouri. Steve and Amanda shared on our television series, *Fresh Start,* their devastating behavior in the early years of their marriage. Each confessed to having affairs. There was a lot of rebuilding to do in both of their lives.

I recall their first visit with me. They worked hard to honestly admit where they were *At* personally in their marriage and where they thought the marriage was as a whole. Before the session was over, they were able to agree where they wanted to *Be*. I could affirm them in those goals because they were God's goals as well.

Then it fully hit Amanda. She had been sitting on the edge of the couch all evening. Her eyes instantly shot open as if she had been suddenly shocked. She fell back on the couch and exclaimed, "Marriage is work!" We all looked at each other and laughed. She got it! And so did he! I was elated they both got it!

Got what? Marriage partners have to work hard to fulfill their own circles of responsibilities. How do you use the power of responsibility to benefit your relationships? Simple. Fulfill all that you are responsible for before God. For where your investment of time and energy is, there will your heart and commitment be also.

Amanda realized that in order to make her marriage work in a meaningful way, she had to identify, assume, and fulfill her own circles of responsibilities. Up to this point she expected Steve to work harder to please her. She thought he was the one who needed to make changes. After looking at their own circles of responsibilities, they agreed, "We both have to change, and it will take work."

This young couple rolled up their sleeves and went to work. What was not right was made right. They learned to talk "honor," the language that God designed to build mutually fulfilling relationships. Instead of looking at each other through squinted eyes of anger and disgust, they viewed one another with value and respect. They learned to speak to each other as the most valued person they knew. As Dr. Gary Smalley says in his *Love Is a Decision* seminars, "Stand and speak in 'awe' of them." That is the essence of honor.

Words of honor are full of grace. They meet the need of the moment. The apostle Paul described it this way: "Let no unwholesome word proceed from your mouth, but only such a word as is good for edification according to the need of the moment, that it may give grace to those who hear" (Eph. 4:29).

The word *unwholesome* means "rotten and putrid," as in decaying fruit (Matt. 7:17) or fish (Matt. 13:48). "Good" is in contrast to "rotten." Steve and Amanda had to change their words from those that rotted their marriage to wholesome words, based on the needs of the other. In fact, at the heart of most of their arguments was an attempt to get their legitimate needs met illegitimately.

Changing their thinking was not easy. It was hard work. Both Steve and Amanda were raised in "rotten word" homes. They were only reproducing what they saw growing up. Although they found it difficult and sometimes overwhelming to change, in the end they were richly blessed (Matt. 5:9). They were able to work it out. Now they are leading marriage enrichment seminars in their own church.

Doers Are Blessed

The Letter of James was written to believers evicted from their homeland and scattered in foreign countries. Imagine the question that loomed in each exiled family's mind: *How can we be blessed by God in these awful circumstances?* James takes this opportunity to explain the source of God's blessing, regardless of the situation: read the Word, don't ignore it, but put it into practice. James wrote, "Prove yourselves doers of the word, and not merely hearers who delude themselves" (1:22).

The key that distinguishes a blessed doer from a frustrated listener is that the listener rewrites what is in his circle of responsibility. He believes listening is doing. The word *delude* is used only in James 1:22 and in Colossians 2:4. It means "to cheat or deceive by false reasoning." How were the listeners deceiving themselves? Easy. They believed that if they just heard or read the Word of God, they had done all that was necessary. This happens every Sunday morning. Ask most people if they are religious, and they will say, "Yes." If you query further, you may hear, "I go to church." Unfortunately, they translate going to church and merely listening to a sermon as acceptable piety. These are hearers who delude or lie to themselves

166

"by false reasoning." They are deceived into believing that listening *is* fulfilling one's circle of responsibility. Listening is a good start, but a poor finish.

James draws a very realistic word picture at this point: "For if anyone is a hearer of the word and not a doer [fulfiller], he is like a man who looks at his natural face in a mirror; for once he has looked at himself and gone away, he has immediately forgotten what kind of person he was" (James 1:23–24).

The word *looks* literally means "to consider attentively." It means he takes serious note of what he sees. It is not just a glance. When he looks at his "natural face" or "the face of his birth," he registers in his mind his origin, roots, and lineage. He sees who he really is. But then through mental gymnastics, he forgets his identity and lives like someone else, just like the ancient actor (hypocrite) complete with exaggerated face mask and mechanically projected voice. The sad part is that only he believes his false persona.

The self-deceived listener is a loser. Life will not work for him. James does not dwell on the failure but highlights the winner, the blessed one: "But one who looks intently at the perfect law, the law of liberty, and abides by it, not having become a forgetful hearer but an effectual doer [fulfiller], this man shall be blessed in what he does" (James 1:25). Doers are powerfully blessed—even in their relationships.

What is the continental divide that defines relationship success? First, a person must be honest enough to look at himself intently. The words *looks intently* in James 1:25 literally mean "to gaze, to peer into." It's a thorough, honest evaluation to identify responsibility. So far, so good.

Second, a blessed person in God's eyes assumes responsibility for what he sees in the Word about himself. But just looking intently into the Scriptures does not in itself guarantee success. Something vital is still missing.

Third, a blessed person has become "an effectual doer." He is a doer who fulfills his responsibility. It is hard work. The insight that floored Amanda was precisely what James is saying: "A doer is a worker." He is not an observer who merely agrees, then forgets. The only one who will be blessed, regardless of circumstances, is the doer of God's Word.

Sadly, I see in my office the same thing every pastor sees. Men like Rex will finally admit their wrong behavior and acknowledge the righteousness God desires in their lives and marriages. They will leave my office refreshed, loved, accepted, and ready to work into their lives what God has revealed. Then something happens. Honestly, I have cried over this next reality.

Those who remain hearers only and not doers are doomed, not for eternity, but in their relationships. More pain, loss, confusion, loneliness, conflict, hurt, and sorrow are ahead for them. Relationship challenges do not work themselves out by wishful thinking but by fulfilling personal responsibility. When the people I meet with tell me about conflicts they had during the week, I ask a simple question, "Did you use your biblical tools this week in the conflict?" Silence usually means no. Harmony is in direct proportion to being a doer, not just a hearer of the truth.

Time after time Rex left my office ready to make changes in his life. Then he sent me faxes totally rewriting all that he had agreed to do. His pride, guilt, and shame surfaced. Rex believed Satan's lie that the truth was too painful to face, that changing was too hard, if not impossible. He rewrote his circle of responsibility to make Marylee wrong.

What was Rex's problem? Look how Jesus described such behavior in the parable of the sower. In this parable (Luke 8:4–15) Jesus identified the seed as the Word of God. Then He explained, "Those [people] beside the road are those who have heard; then the devil comes and takes away the word from their heart, so that they may not believe and be saved." I sowed the Word, Rex received the Word, Satan stole the Word from his heart, and he refused to fulfill his responsibilities. What a contrast to the faithful doers who are greatly benefited.

BENEFITS OF FULFILLED RESPONSIBILITIES

Pastor Tim asked me a question after Mark and Kari left his office one afternoon. "How do you get people to do what they need to do?" I suggest that each of us has two imaginary scales in the back of our mind. One side of the scale is gain and the other is loss. Each of us was born with a desire for gain and a fear of loss. In weighing the two options with Mark and Kari, I attempted to point out to both of them their gain from fulfilling personal responsibility and their loss if they failed to follow through. I appealed to them to make wise decisions based on the benefits (gains) of obedience. There are at least three.

PERSONAL SECURITY ①

Dr. Luke gives a *Reader's Digest* version of the Sermon on the Mount. Although this sermon was primarily directed to Jesus' disciples, a crowd also listened intently. Jesus concluded with this probing question, designed to clarify the very thing we have to address: "And why do you call Me, 'Lord, Lord,' and do not do what I say?" (Luke 6:46). Those words—"Lord, Lord"—so devotedly spoken, may be only superficial. Only actions validate the beliefs and sincerity of the heart. When the talk is in conflict with the walk, the walk becomes hypocrisy. Knowing down deep they are not who they profess to be deepens people's feelings of personal insecurity. They live in terror of being discovered.

Jesus emphasized the importance of calling Him "Lord" and fulfilling His commands by using a word picture from the building trade. "Everyone who comes to Me, and hears My words, and acts upon them, I will show you whom he is like: he is like a man building a house, who dug deep and laid a foundation upon the rock" (Luke 6:47–48). By digging deep he struck bedrock before he laid the foundation. Likewise, those who call Jesus "Lord" *and* act on His Word are grounded on the bedrock of God Himself, thus establishing the basis for personal security.

Jesus then pictured a major weather front moving in: "A flood rose, the torrent burst against that house." Responsible doers experience the same trials, distresses, and afflictions as anyone else. Obedience does not excuse us from difficulty. We may be tax-exempt but we are not trial-exempt. The torrential downpour did not destroy the house. The reason? "It had been well built." It was secure. Those lives built through obedience on the bedrock of God's Word cannot be shaken. Yes, they feel the storms. They cry. They ask, "Why?" They hurt.

Like Job they may stand up, tear their clothes, shave their head, and fall to the ground. But rage out of control? No. Cuss like a reprobate? No. Suffer loss? Yes. Worship? Yes! Like Job who cried out from his core belief based on his rock-solid faith, "The LORD gave and the LORD has taken away. Blessed be the name of the LORD" (Job 1:21).

There is a difference between being shaken and being emotionally disabled. Everyone is shaken in life. But not everyone falls apart in a crisis. As stated before, we may not act out what we believe from day to day, but we will always act out what we believe (foundational truth) in a crisis. A crisis reveals the basis and stability of our personal foundation.

Self-deceived people think that just hearing God's Word is all it takes to make life work for them. Not so. Jesus goes on to describe the second type of house builder. "But the one who has heard, and has not acted accordingly, is like a man who built a house upon the ground" but note, "without any foundation" (Luke 6:49). Hearers' lives appear as lovely houses. They may be in the Parade of Homes for all to see. They look good. They are clean, painted, landscaped, beautiful at every point. But the same tragic storms of life strike hearers as well as doers. A child is killed. A company fails. A job is lost. A teenager rebels. A mate is unfaithful. A daughter gets pregnant. Jesus' description of a house with no foundation parallels a life without obedience to Him: "The torrent burst against it and immediately it collapsed, and the ruin of that house was great" (Luke 6:49). "Immediately . . . collapsed . . . ruin." This devastating end awaits those who build their lives on anything but God Himself. The real basis of security is found by those who fulfill their responsibilities to His commands and not those who only call Him "Lord."

INCREASED POWER

My friend Keenan struggled. A life of blame shifting, denial, and avoiding did not prepare him well for adulthood's responsibilities and challenges. He had a core belief that said: "I can't do anything God expects of me because I don't have the strength to do it." He sincerely believed this. He is not the only one.

I would be a wealthy man today if I had a dollar for every time I heard, "I can't do that." "That's just not me." "I'm too human." Or the classic, "That's just the way I am. I can't help it."

Those who are hearers only and not doers feel powerless. Their motto is, "I can resist anything but temptation." How can you help folks who feel this powerless? First, ask them to clearly identify what they are doing that is not working for them. This is important. If they do not see that a particular pattern of behavior isn't working for them, they will not abandon it for something more beneficial. Even then it is difficult to change. Habits run deep and often defy logic or reason.

Second, help them understand *why* what they are doing does not work for them. By understanding the cause and effect, they learn from their mistakes and avoid developing faulty future behavioral patterns. On one hand, Keenan dearly loved his wife, Deidra; but he also had a deep need for the approval of others. His seeming neglect at home contrasted with his enthusiastic help everywhere else and caused Deidra to withdraw in hurt.

I probed Keenan with a pointed question: Was his on-call rescue service working for him? Reluctantly, he admitted it was not. But he was not yet in the mood to change until he openly admitted to himself and his wife that misplaced priorities do not work. But properly balanced priorities do work, not just for him but for the whole family. Remember, the human heart has a built-in program that attempts to make life work apart from God (Rom. 1:21–23).

Third, have them tell you what *they* think God wants them to do, followed by why they think He wants them to do it. It is a variation of starting where they are *At* and seeing where God wants them to *Be*. Once we clarify this and address obstacles, we can discuss how God will help them to accomplish it. This will include His Word, prayer, and especially a support team of Christian friends, a pastor, a support group, or a biblically based Christian counselor.

Even after this procedure, some will claim, "But I already tried that." Further inquiry often reveals they attempted a *modified* form of obedience, just like King Saul. God had told Samuel to instruct King Saul to exact revenge on the Amalekites. They had savagely attacked the Israelites from the rear while sojourning in the desert. God promised to avenge Israel (Exod. 17:8–16) and gave the assignment to King Saul. He was not to spare man, woman, child, infant, ox, sheep, camel, or donkey.

God identified what was to be done. King Saul assumed the responsibility. He carried it out, but he did it his way. He saved some of the best of the flocks and killed the rest. He captured Agag, the king of Amalek, as a personal war trophy.

That night God told Samuel about Saul's incomplete obedience. Saul could no longer be king. He must now be removed. It was Samuel's job to tell him the next day. Perhaps weakened by grief and disappointment, Samuel confronted Saul. He reviewed Saul's mission, to search and to destroy. The very question Samuel may have asked the Lord all night he now asked the king, "Why then did you not obey the voice of the LORD, but rushed upon the spoil and did what was evil in the sight of the LORD?" (1 Sam. 15:19). Saul defensively responded, "I did obey. I went on the mission. I brought back King Agag and destroyed the Amalekites. The people saved the choicest of the things devoted to destruction to sacrifice to the Lord. What's the problem?"

King Saul chose to believe that sacrifice to God was more important than obedience to God. Yet the reverse is true. "To obey," says God, "is better than sacrifice" (1 Sam. 15:22).

God equates service without obedience with rebellion. Rebellion is as serious as divination or witchcraft. What was Saul's root sin? He rejected the command of God. He modified it to suit himself, rationalizing that he did it for God. Modified obedience is rebellion and demonically inspired (1 Sam. 15:23).

When I question those who say they tried obedience and were unable to accomplish it, in most cases I learn they modified their obedience, rendering themselves powerless. Consistent obedience taps into God's unlimited power. Obedience is the secret of harnessing the power of personal responsibility. This is precisely the key to power that the apostle Paul described to the believers in Philippi. God gives us the ability to respond to anything. We call it "response-ability." He describes the procedure: "Work out your salvation with fear and trembling; for it is God who is at work in you, both to will and to work for His good pleasure" (Phil. 2:12–13).

It is like two wings on an airplane. The left wing is our responsibility—"Work out your salvation." We are to work into everyday life the salvation God has worked into us through the Holy Spirit. That is our circle of responsibility. We are to factor the practical presence of God into whatever we do in word or deed, including conflict.

The right wing of the airplane is God's responsibility—"God is at work in you." He is working (energizing, operating) in us and giving us the will or desire to do what pleases Him. He is actually the One who is empowering us to obey Him. God does both the "willing" and the "working" (or energizing) in our lives. It is God's circle of responsibility to give us the energy and desire to do what pleases Him.

People who fulfill their God-designed circle of responsibilities experience power from Him. It is a work-work issue. We work, He works. It is a win-win situation. We win in every way through the power He gives. God wins in the glory He receives through our obedience. Doers harness power. That is the reason the apostle Paul can confidently declare, "I can do anything God expects of me through Christ who gives me the strength to do it" (Phil. 4:13, AMPLIFIED BIBLE).

It is for this reason I look for the hindrances to obedience that short-circuit the power in a person's life. If they can be identified and removed, obedience becomes a terrific source of power for the believer's life.

Not only does fulfillment of responsibility give us power, it helps us stay focused.

CLEAR FOCUS

I had the privilege to serve Dr. Gerald and his wife and family as he went through an alcohol recovery program for the fourth time. After his last three-month rehabilitation program, we began to discuss what he learned there. He was coached to use a profound but simple motto—five short words that could have been lifted from Scripture. Simply stated, the motto was: "Do the next right thing." It wasn't "Just do the next thing," which could be self-destructive. Or "Do what you see in front of you next." That is impulsiveness. But "Do the next *right* thing." That reflects focus.

Those who identify, assume, and fulfill legitimate circles of responsibility do the same thing. They do the next right thing in their circle. They have focus—the third benefit of fulfilling responsibilities. They zero in on what they are responsible for.

Focus is probably the hardest discipline to maintain in reducing conflict and bringing closure to a difficult situation. It is one issue that can completely derail the process of restoration. One of the primary reasons Rex could not follow through with his circle of responsibilities was that he was so obsessed with Marylee's failures, shortcomings, and character flaws. This blame shifting or blame refocusing became his excuse to neglect or even default on his own responsibilities.

Both Kari and Mark refused Pastor Tim's and my plea to make the significant changes necessary to restore their marriage. Why? Neither would budge until the other one changed. Both were out of focus. Each was attempting to remove the speck in the other's eye while attempting to navigate around the mammoth beam in his or her own.

Pastor Martin was totally locked in on his rebellious daughter's poor behavior as a means of avoiding his own un-Christlike attitudes and actions. He focused on the next right thing she should do. She did need to make some major changes in her life, but that had to be her decision. Pastor Martin's daughter illustrated a family dynamic concept called the "black sheep."

Often a drug-addicted, alcoholic, divorced, or rebellious child will be labeled the "black sheep" of the family. This becomes her family role. She accepts this demeaning role primarily because her family expects it of her. She serves a vital function for the rest of the family. The focus shifts off the rest of the family's dysfunction and concentrates on her. Often the weakest child becomes the scapegoat for the family.

The black sheep accepts this dysfunctional role because this is at least one way she can get the attention she lacks. Any attention, as bad as it may be, is better than no attention. Dr. Selwyn Hughes contends in *Helping People through Their Problems:*

If a child is not sure of his parent's love, then he will settle for the next best thing—attention. The child will begin to manifest extremely unacceptable behavior on the proverbial basis that attack is the best form of defense. This results in the child feeling the lesser pain of rejection for what he is. He finds it much easier to live with the knowledge that he is being rejected for his unacceptable behavior than with the knowledge that the rejection is due to his own worthlessness.

The other family members believe they would be just fine if it were not for the black sheep. This dysfunctional family must refocus back on individual circles of responsibility and fulfill them before the family can be healed. Each member must do his/her own next right thing.

Those in God's Faith Hall of Fame, summarized in Hebrews 11, have one thing in common. By faith they all fulfilled the next right thing God asked of them. Abel offered a better sacrifice than Cain. Enoch pleased God by faith. Noah did the next right thing and built an ark by faith. Sarah considered God faithful, even though she was well beyond childbearing years. She did the next right thing, believed God in spite of impossibilities, and conceived a son. The whole eleventh chapter of Hebrews is a catalog of men and women who were full of focus.

One of the people whom you meet in God's Faith Hall of Fame is Abraham. He, too, did the next right thing God required of him. He did this by faith.

God sovereignly selected and summoned Abraham to become the father of the nation Israel. God called him out of a totally pagan society. Abraham was middle-aged, very wealthy, and from a family of idolaters. God told Abraham to leave the security of Ur, the commercial and political capital of Sumer located on the Euphrates River, and enter the land of Canaan, more than five hundred miles to the west.

The writer of Hebrews summarized his life: "By faith Abraham, when he was called, obeyed [he did the next right thing] by going out to a place which he was to receive for an inheritance; and he went out, not knowing where he was going" (Heb. 11:8).

Here Abraham modeled a significant key to conflict resolution. He focused on the next right step of obedience, but not the actual destination. He knew only that he was looking for a city that had foundations, whose architect and builder was God (v. 10). Often we do not know in advance the twists and turns on the road to conflict resolution. There is not an identical route for all situations. God is responsible for the direction, and we are responsible only to focus on the next right thing we know to do.

The fantastic benefit of fulfilling your circle of responsibilities is that it gives you a clarified focus. Countless people leave my office having clearly in mind their next right step toward wholeness, healing, and restoration. Although many curves, side roads, detours, and traffic jams may lay ahead, God is faithful to lead the obedient ones who focus on fulfilling their circle of responsibilities and do the next right thing. But it may involve a struggle.

THE STRUGGLE FOR OBEDIENCE

Jesus told a brief parable that highlights a common experience we face in fulfilling responsibilities, namely that we may struggle before we obey. "A man had two sons, and he came to the first and said, 'Son, go work today in the vineyard.' And he answered and said, 'I will, sir,' and he did not go. And he came to the second and said the same thing. But he answered and said, 'I will not'; yet he afterward regretted it and went. Which of the two did the will of his father?" (Matt. 21:28–31).

Notice that Jesus did not attack the attitude of the son who said he would not obey but later did. Jesus affirmed his ultimate obedience.

I see this struggle to obey every day. There are those who profess instant obedience to God's conviction. That is ideal. Yet for the rest of us, it is a battle. God knows that our spirit wages war against the flesh and the flesh against the spirit (Gal. 5:17).

Many times I've been encouraged as I have read the apostle Paul's admission of his own inner turmoil described in Romans 7:15–25. Haven't we all felt this way? Traci did not want to take the next right step to call her mom. It took several sessions before she was ready. Her husband, Nick, could not speed up the process. It was God's responsibility to lead and to energize Traci to follow through.

Helen struggled to change from the enabling mother of her drug-addicted son, Ron, to a responsible mother who let him fail before he would seek professional help.

Peggy wrestled within herself to let go of her false belief that she could change her husband, Martin. It was God's responsibility to effect the change.

This struggle is actually productive. Change that requires little or no effort is rarely permanent. Often, the greater the struggle, the more lasting the result.

Jesus struggled in His humanity. It was not automatic for Him to identify, assume, and fulfill responsibilities. He knew before the foundation of the world what He was going to do. He was obedient to His Father even unto death (Phil. 2:8). But in the process of fulfilling what He came to do, Jesus experienced intense inner turmoil. In the Garden of Gethsemane He cried out, "My soul is deeply grieved to the point of death" (Mark 14:34). Jesus walked a little distance from His disciples and fell to the ground. In agony He prayed to His Father that if possible, could He be released from the torture and death that lay ahead? "Abba! Father! All things are possible for Thee; remove this cup from Me; yet not what I will, but what Thou wilt" (Mark 14:36).

Jesus' struggle was not in whether His Father was able to stop His impending death but in whether it was the Father's will to do so. Jesus knew that the moment He became the sacrifice for man's sin (2 Cor. 5:21) He would experience the full force of God's wrath physically, spiritually, mentally, and emotionally. The next right thing for Jesus to do was to offer Himself to die on a cruel Roman cross. Even the Son of God struggled with fulfilling His circle of responsibility on our behalf. But He did it!

How do you harness the power of personal responsibility? You choose to do the next right thing God tells you to do.

But what can you do when others don't fulfill their responsibilities and their failure impacts you? Susan and I have had similar painful events in our lives. Susan's husband abandoned her in the hospital as she delivered their third daughter. My father abandoned my mom and us three sons in our formative years. Both Susan and I faced dealing with others' failures.

NINE

How to Handle Others' Failures

The commencement exercise had been exciting. My older brother, Carl, had just graduated from high school. The temporary bleachers for the graduating seniors were erected on the fifty-yard line of the football field facing the hometown side of the permanent bleachers.

As I descended the family viewing bleachers, I happened to glance up and see a prematurely grayed gentleman leaning against the chain-link fence surrounding the athletic field. As I walked by at a distance, I noticed his arms outstretched, hands still clutching the steel links, as his gaze remained fixed on the empty stage and bleachers. I began to make out his features.

"It can't be," I muttered. But it was. Dad! My feet continued to take me to the car, but my mind stayed at that chain-link fence. The picture is indelibly fixed in my mind. It was just the way it had always been, Dad standing on the outside of our lives, pausing for only a moment to look in. Then he was gone. We were hurt again. Alcoholism devastated another family.

FAILURE TO FULFILL RESPONSIBILITY

My parents moved from the small rural community of Winchester, Indiana, to the sprawling suburbs of Los Angeles, California, when I was four years old. Then I did not know what an alcoholic was. As the years went by I received a firsthand education.

Dad stayed out late from time to time. Then he was gone every other weekend. Soon it was every weekend, then every night. The nights turned into days, months, and finally, years. Through those years the money stopped coming. Mom was left with three young boys and no job.

In the early forties, family roles were traditional. Mom worked at a small dry-goods store before she married. She worked a while afterward. Then the children came. She became a stay-at-home mom. It was the way they wanted it. Dad worked outside the home; Mom worked in the home.

Another factor came into play. Early in their marriage Mom and Dad had his parents live with them, and they cared for them until they died. Family responsibility was clear in those days, and my parents fulfilled it. But once alcohol became a permanent resident in our home, all of that changed. Alcoholism doesn't just visit; it takes over. The guest becomes the master.

It is brutally cruel. No human relationship is of value to the addicted. Dad ignored our feelings. He hid alcohol all over the house and garage. When we stumbled across it we poured it out, naively thinking this would halt Dad's addiction. We unintentionally were taking responsibility for Dad's longed-for recovery.

Dad eventually abandoned the family. But some things did not change. The mortgage bill still came due faithfully the first of each month. The gas and electric bills found their way to our mailbox like homing pigeons. Something else did not change: the appetites of three growing boys.

Carl reminded me recently of the day Mom brought the three of us boys together in his bedroom. Mom was now the CEO of the household. She laid the facts out as clearly as she could. We could either do nothing and starve, or each of us could get a job to help keep the home "ship" afloat.

Solutions were the first order of business. There was more to deal with. My father had racked up enormous credit card debt, and he had disappeared. Mom's name was also on those credit cards. Guess who had to pay them off?

Mom cleaned houses before she landed a minimum-wage job as a salesclerk. Carl stopped delivering papers and went to work part-time in the produce section of our neighborhood market. I mowed lawns. Every single day of my adolescent years, I faced the consequences of my father's failure in his responsibilities.

Broken promises. Lies. Betrayal. Abandonment. You find it; you can eat it. You earn it; you wear it. Little did I know that these experiences were forming an attitude in my subconscious mind. When the truth finally sank in—I was not wanted, loved, cared for, valued, or special to my dad—something inside me broke. I began to feel I was not lovable or worthy of love. My anger turned to bitterness.

For years I did not see the worm of bitterness eating away on the inside of me. I looked good on the outside. I felt good. The ache inside eventually seemed normal. But I had a task ahead I never envisioned. It was the same task Susan faced with Jerry.

Hard to Forgive

The hospital sounds were all too familiar. Susan was there for the birth of her third baby. Her heart was crying out for a thread of hope for the recovery of her marriage. How desperately she wanted to work it out. Her thoughts ran in circles: *He didn't mean it. It's not over. How could he just walk out? What went wrong with what I felt so right about ten years ago?*

Jerry, her husband, stood beside her hospital bed. The "other woman" stood framed by the threshold of the hospital room door. "I want a divorce," Jerry announced. "I'm going to get it!" Susan felt that a razor-sharp knife plunged into her chest could not have been more painful. It's true—emotional pain is always more excruciating than physical pain. The wounds of the heart go deeper than the wounds of the flesh.

Though he abandoned his family, Jerry still remained financially responsible for their basic needs. The courts are a little more effective today than they were forty-five years ago, when my father abandoned us. But the courts could not make Jerry love, care for, and cherish Susan. They could not force loyalty or fidelity. They can enforce payment of child support but not permanence of relationship.

Susan did not marry to be unloved, abandoned, verbally abused, dishonored, disrespected, ignored, criticized, betrayed, or to spend endless nights alone. Those deep wounds of the heart were not clean cuts but raw, ripped emotions. The anger from the pulsating wounds soon sprang into bitterness. The worm in Susan's apple devoured her from the inside. Wounded hearts find forgiveness hard, if not impossible. TRUE

BUT I'M NOT ANGRY

Susan had a tool she used to cope with pain. She had learned early in life to smile when hurt—to deny the anguish. Smiling when hurting is not biblical. God does not smile when we hurt Him by our actions. The apostle Paul exhorted the Ephesian church, "Do not grieve the Holy Spirit of God" (Eph. 4:30). It is a strong command that means "cease continuing to grieve" or "do not have the habit of grieving." In other words, Paul said, "Stop causing significant pain to the heart of God." The sins of believers cause deep emotional pain in the heart of God. Just ask Jesus. He did not smile in the face of crushing rejection by His people Israel.

Jesus rode a colt near the west side of the Mount of Olives. The people's thunderous cries of hosanna, as they threw their cloaks and palm branches before him, incited the jealousy of the Pharisees. "Teacher, rebuke Your disciples," they demanded. He quickly replied, "I tell you, if these become silent, the stones will cry out!" As Jesus approached Jerusalem, "He saw the city and wept over it" (Luke 19:39–41). He felt the rejection of the religious establishment and virtually the whole nation of Israel (John 1:11). Why did Susan hurt? She felt rejected by her husband. Why do I still feel the pain of a little boy who experienced loss and abandonment? Dad's rejection.

When Susan came to me for counseling, I gave her the same permission that someone had given me years earlier: permission to say, "Ouch." *Ouch* means "I hurt" and opens the door to legitimate anger. Anger does you a favor. It notifies you when you are hurt. "Do something about this pain" is its cry.

Anger is one of the most lied-about and covered-up emotions we have. How often do we hear the words "I'm not angry" from an unconvincing voice spoken through clenched teeth framed by a scowling face? The sense of shame and guilt we have been taught to associate with the normal emotion of anger usually prevents anger from doing its work: notifying us that we are hurt and need to do something biblical about it. When you put your hand on a hot stove, pain notifies you to move it so something worse doesn't happen. Pain motivates us to action; so does anger.

Why is it important? If anger does not notify you of the need, you will not acknowledge the offense. If you do not acknowledge the offense, you will not identify the offender. If you do not clearly identify the offender, you will not take the next hard but necessary step, to forgive.

Every month for years my mother received bills from credit card companies. The unpaid balances were painful reminders of my father's failure. Mom faithfully paid them all off over the course of years. But these monthly bills did something sinister; each one picked off the newly formed scab on an emotional wound that refused to heal.

I witnessed her pain and felt it myself. Sincere but naive friends through the years advised me, "You just need to forget it. If you have genuinely forgiven your father, you will forget it." Jeremiah 31:34 clearly states that God will forgive our sin and will remember it no more. What people fail to understand is that an omniscient God cannot forget. Instead when He forgives He purposes not to remember it against us again (2 Cor. 5:19).

When family, friends, employers, or others fail to fulfill their legitimate responsibilities, it will hurt. No, you will never forget. Instead, you have to allow God to do what you cannot do.

"But," you may say, "someone has to pay." If my dad had straightened out early on and dedicated the rest of his life to making up for his alcoholic failures, he still wouldn't live long enough to do so. My dad deserved to be punished for his incalculable sin against our family. But to insist that my dad "pay" for his sin is double payment, because Jesus paid for his sin. Double payment is not justice! Justice was totally satisfied on the cross (2 Cor. 5:21). Christ paid my dad's sin bill of irresponsibility. I now must grant to Dad what God has granted to me, full forgiveness from the heart (Matt. 18:21–35).

IRRESPONSIBILITY IS SERIOUS

The family conference in my brother's bedroom highlighted one thing. If we did not work, we would not eat. Dad was narcissistically self-absorbed with his own cravings. We could have lost our modest home, starved, gone threadbare, become sick, or even died. He did not care. How do I know? For a period of ten years, none of us boys received as much as a birthday card. Dad must have realized early in his marriage that Mom was a responsible person. If she was responsible, why did he need to be?

Dad did not show up for my graduations from high school, college, or two of three graduate degrees. Years later, after I located him, I took him to my doctoral commencement. He was not at my wedding nor present for the birth of my children.

When I counsel others who have experienced similar or worse losses, they raise a question: "Where was God when all this was happening?" The answer is simple but not easy to accept. God was with us. His name, *Immanuel,* means "God with us." "But if God was with us," they reason, "why didn't He stop the painful experiences?" God does not normally stop the cause and effect of sin, whether we do it to ourselves or it is done to us. Just ask the apostle Paul.

Paul experienced afflictions, hardships, distresses, beatings, imprisonments, hunger, shipwrecks, robberies, and stonings (2 Cor. 6:4–5; 11:23–28). If anyone should have questioned the protective power of God, Paul was the man. But he understood the same insight the apostle Peter offered: "If when you do what is right and suffer for it you patiently endure it, this finds favor with God. For you have been called for this purpose, since Christ also suffered for you, leaving you an example for you to follow in His steps" (1 Pet. 2:20–21). God has called us to suffer. Failure to acknowledge and accept this reality will lock a believer in a prison of anger and bitterness, resulting in depression and a host of physical problems.

I often hear another question as well: "Is God bothered when He sees people acting flagrantly irresponsibly? It almost seems like He does not care." Good question! God is clear about the seriousness of neglected responsibilities: "But if anyone does not provide for his own, and especially for those of his household, he has denied the faith, and is worse than an unbeliever" (1 Tim. 5:8). The meaning is, the person who has "denied the faith" has practiced the apostasy of neglect. The one who defaults on his family responsibilities undermines any personal claim to know God. It becomes a de facto denial of the faith.

Even the apostle John questioned the love a believer has for God if he is irresponsible toward the needy in his spiritual family. "But whoever has the world's goods, and beholds his brother in need and closes his heart against him, how does the love of God abide in him? Little children, let us not love with word or with tongue, but in deed and truth" (1 John 3:17–18).

How can a person who professes to know God be worse than an unbeliever? By avoiding, shirking, ignoring, or refusing the responsibility to meet the needs of his family. Even non-Christians generally understand and fulfill their familial responsibilities.

The words *provide for* literally mean "to think ahead, to provide for by anticipating needs in advance." That is exactly what alcohol and other mind-altering substances blunt. The addict allows the euphoria of the drug to replace the glaring needs of the family. Sadly enough, most long-term alcoholics or substance abusers eventually have to use their drug of choice just to feel normal again. The hook of pleasure entraps them into fighting to survive. As much as God disdains the selfish, irresponsible adult, to us who suffer because of them He holds up the only holy response: forgiveness.

WHAT FORGIVENESS IS NOT   vs denial / vs tolerance

We confuse many things with forgiveness. One might say, "I just don't let the hurt bother me any more." Good. But not letting it bother you is not forgiveness. That is denial. Any painful memory that surfaces just gets plunged back down into the cellar of denial. You try to deny the pain by suppressing the past, yet it rattles around, looking for creative ways to surface. You have to devote much energy to keeping the proverbial "lid" on it.

"I can be civil now around the person who hurt me." Civility is a form of tolerance. Tolerance is an admirable quality if it is used in a healthy way. But practicing tolerance is not forgiving.

"I try to have a good attitude." One major problem with this strategy is that it takes a great deal of emotional energy to maintain this facade. While one tries to hide or deny a bitter spirit, it may seep through as sarcasm or other cutting, critical remarks. Passive-aggressive personalities have mastered this hypocrisy, acting like people they are not—outwardly happy but inwardly hurt and bitter.

"I just overlook it." There are times when we should do this (Prov. 19:11), but usually overlooking is not the same as forgiving. God does not overlook sin. If anyone could, He could. He knows our frame, that we are "but dust" (Ps. 103:14). He knows we will sin again. Yet His holy character will not allow Him to "just overlook" it. Sin must be handled in a biblical fashion that is consistent with God's character and His ways.

"Overlooking" hurts is a means of avoiding potential consequences and the emotional energy of loss. If we don't deal with offenses biblically, we rob God of His glory and ourselves of the potential for closure and release. The irresponsible one may translate your "overlooking" as permission to continue unabated his narcissistic course of behavior. This is another form of enabling.

"I guess I have done some things wrong too." No doubt you have failed and need to acknowledge and confess your sin, and receive forgiveness (1 John 1:9). That is in your circle of responsibility. Often the power of reconciliation will be released only when we start with our own admission of wrongs in the relationship. But it is equally important to acknowledge other persons' sins against you and in turn grant them the gift of forgiveness for each of their failures. If you do not admit to yourself their failure to be responsible, you will not bring the forgiving grace of God to them. You will remain stuck in your tracks rather than be free to move on with your life. Those who have failed you by their irresponsibility need to be forgiven, just as we do for our failure (Matt. 6:12). Balancing offenses is not forgiveness. It is avoiding the hard work of true forgiveness.

WHAT DOES FORGIVENESS MEAN?

The basic meaning of the word *forgiveness* is "to send away." A very practical question may be, "Where do I send the irresponsible person and his sin?" The apostle Paul uses Jesus' execution scene to explain to the Colossian believers how they were once dead in their sins but are now living through Christ. How is this accomplished? "He made you alive together with Him, having forgiven us all our transgressions, having canceled out the certificate of death consisting of decrees against us and which was hostile to us; and He has taken it out of the way, having nailed it to the cross" (Col. 2:13–14). Jesus paid the debt that we could not pay. The sin must be sent away to Jesus to be nailed on the cross where it belongs.

But sending it away is not stuffing it. Stuffing is what Susan did with her ex-husband's offenses. I explained to Susan that forgiveness does not mean to deny or forget the sins, to be cordial to the offender, or to work hard so sin didn't get the best of her. You'll remember that I encouraged Susan to put Jerry in the Jesus Jail. I said, "Let's name all of Jerry's sins and send him to the Lord Jesus, who nailed his sins to the cross where He so brutally died. Since revenge is God's circle of responsibility, let's send Jerry to Jesus. Transfer him out of the prison of your own heart and put him into the Lord's hands. He will do what He feels is best. Either way, Jerry and his sin of failed responsibilities are transferred over to the Savior. Jerry is now off your hook. He's now on God's hook."

Forgiveness will never remove the memories. I will never forget my father's abandonment. He is conspicuously absent in all the family pictures. Thankfully, forgiveness greatly reduces the emotional pain and subsequent control of those memories. Memory is a chemical and electronic function of my brain, not my spirit. It functions in the physical, not the spiritual, realm.

That brings up another question. What do I do with the memories of those who failed me by their irresponsibility?

Forgiveness and Memories

Forgiveness handles the judicial aspect of others' failed responsibilities. But the lingering memories and consequences must involve another function of our will—acceptance.

Acceptance does not come easily. It did not for Susan. Most every young girl dreams of someday getting married and having a family of her own. A woman can substitute other callings, goals, or fantasies that do not include marriage. But she has a monthly physical reminder of one of the functions of her body that other endeavors cannot fulfill.

Susan wanted to be a wife and mother, to be loved and cherished. She pictured being with a friend, companion, lover, soul mate, one who would live within the covenant of marriage until "death do us part." Now she retires to her bedroom alone. She goes to family functions alone with her children. She lives single in a couples' world. She raises her three beautiful daughters alone. She makes the discipline decisions alone. Yes, she walks with God. He meets her at her points of need. Yet the painful loss is ever present. Death of a marriage must be grieved every bit as much as physical death.

In grieving a marital or any other relational loss, one will experience the same stages of grief that come after the death of a loved one. As Susan was lying in the hospital bed, recovering from the delivery of her third child, she finally passed through the first stage of grieving—denial. Wives have shed buckets of tears telling me they feel like they are watching a movie of themselves being divorced and they can't stop it. "I will not let this happen!" comes the screaming of a stunned heart. "I will not accept this. I am going to awaken and find out it is all a bad dream." They are right about one thing. It's like a dream; only it is a nightmare. The physical presence of the "other woman" standing in the doorway of Susan's hospital room opened her eyes to reality.

When the pain of reality finally sets in, then the second stage of grief kicks in—anger. It is normal. Anger makes you feel the reality of loss. It helps you identify those who have hurt you by failing to fulfill their responsibilities. Anger can then trigger another response—magical thinking. "If I had just worked harder to please him, I know he wouldn't have left me. If only I had been a better sex partner, lost weight, changed my hair color, he would have been pleased with me."

Following magical thinking is bargaining, the third stage of grief. God is often the object of the bargaining process. "Oh, God, I will serve You faithfully. I have not walked with You as closely as I should. I promise to read, pray, witness, be humble. I will do anything You say to save my marriage." Bargaining with God is in reality a form of manipulation. We try to manipulate God into restoring our losses.

Then follows the fourth phase of grief—sadness. This is an emotion we usually do not want to feel. It rolls over us like a dense, gray fog. Sadness is normal. It is a healthy emotion that visits us. In time, true sadness will reduce from a high intensity to a manageable low level.

It can take from six months to two years after a major loss before the fifth and final stage inevitably arrives: acceptance. Forgiveness can bisect the grieving process at any of the five stages. But it usually follows denial and precedes acceptance.

One can experience acceptance in at least one of two ways. Susan can accept Jerry's betrayal in bitterness. She can go on with her life, controlled at every point by the anger festering in her heart. That would be Plan A. There is a Plan B: forgiveness.

Part of our counseling involves prayer. These are deeply emotional, even unique prayers. Since Susan chose forgiveness, she prayed to transfer Jerry over to the Jesus Jail. She pictured our Lord nailing Jerry's selfish sins to the cross. She released him. That was hard. But something else was harder. Listen to her prayer: "Dear Father, I'm going to do the hardest thing I have ever had to do . . .

as an act of my will because I don't feel like it. I now fully accept upon myself all of the consequences of Jerry's sin against me. I even, as an act of my will, thank You for them." She sobbed. She did it. She said it. It was finished! She was free.

Why did she choose to pray that prayer? Susan knew something that's obvious, yet often overlooked or forgotten. She was going to live with the consequences from her divorce whether she accepted them or not.

My dear mother had to pay my father's credit cards off whether she liked it or not. Bankruptcy was not an acceptable option for Mom. She was raised on a small farm in Indiana with ten other children. Survival meant cooperation. Cooperation meant fulfilling responsibilities. The family's survival depended on the character quality of responsibility, not irresponsibility.

I wish I could report that my mother followed Susan's response of forgiveness, acceptance, and freedom. She didn't. In fact, I had to learn to forgive my mom and accept the consequences of her bitter response to my dad's irresponsibility. She often redirected her anger at him to us boys.

Susan, Mom, and I had little or no control over what happened to us. But we have all the control in the world in how we respond to what happened to us. Our response is potentially more damaging to us than what others did to us. I can choose to live by forgiveness in a place of blessing or in a prison of bitterness.

Forgiveness never depends on any response from the offending one. Our Lord Jesus didn't wait to be asked for His forgiveness when He cried out from the cross, "Father, forgive them; for they do not know what they are doing" (Luke 23:34). He didn't attach any conditions to the forgiveness, like, "Father, forgive them if they acknowledge all they did wrong and repent."

None of the evangelist Stephen's executioners repented before he died under the crushing hail of rocks. Dr. Luke records it this way: "Falling on his knees, he cried out with a loud voice, 'Lord, do not hold this sin against them!' And having said this, he fell asleep" (Acts 7:60). Stephen did what was right regardless of the response of those killing him.

Most of us unintentionally give the keys to our freedom to those who have hurt us the deepest. We are earnestly waiting for them to change, repent, feel sorry, or say, "I was wrong and understand your pain." For most of us that is not going to happen. They hurt us in their selfishness and immaturity. Don't expect them to humbly acknowledge their wrong in their current state of mind. Be deeply grateful to God if confession and repentance do happen. But either way, accept the loss and walk on in freedom.

Forgiveness and freedom don't necessarily restore trust in the offender, however.

FORGIVENESS AND TRUST

Susan's former husband wanted life to return to some semblance of normalcy after the divorce. For Jerry it was a new wife, a new life, and frequent visitation privileges with his kids. Since Susan was a Christian, he reasoned, she would forgive and forget and trust him now. Wrong!

Trust and forgiveness are not the same. Forgiveness is what we *grant*, regardless of the behavior of the irresponsible one. Trust is what the offender must *earn*. Susan did struggle through to forgiveness. That was in her circle of responsibility. But Jerry's frequent lies sowed a field of mistrust. His lifestyle and selfish patterns continued. He did nothing to rebuild the shattered trust.

Out of obedience to the Lord, Deidra did forgive Keenan for his misplaced priorities and for selfishly focusing on his own need for approval at the expense of her and the five children. Then she had to slowly begin to open up emotionally to him again. Keenan, on the other hand, had the responsibility to rebuild her trust that he would focus on his role as husband and father.

God recognizes that rebuilding trust is not easy. "A brother [or wife] offended is harder to be won than a strong city" (Prov. 18:19). Slip-ups will occur now and then. But humble acknowledgment of them continues the trust-rebuilding process.

Deidra sensed the genuine change in Keenan's heart and saw the extra effort in his actions. By the same token, she had to remove, brick by brick, the protective wall around her emotions. She had to learn to trust and to feel all over again. And to her credit, she did.

Steve and Amanda both had to start at square one to forgive and rebuild their trust in each other. Since each had been unfaithful, each had to ask and receive forgiveness. They both had to rebuild trust. To their credit, they did. It is out of their corrected failures that they lead marriage workshops in their church.

It is important to remember that forgiveness must be granted as soon as possible (Eph. 4:26). Trust, on the other hand, is earned and will take an extended period of time to develop. This explains why forgiveness alone does not mean the automatic restoration of relationships.

Forgiveness and Restoration

Shelia's dad was drunk nearly every night. As with most addicted people, he had a dual addiction. With alcoholics, it is usually sex. They do not particularly care whom they have it with, even if it is with their own children. This was just one of the big scars Shelia carried. Her parents eventually divorced, and her mother married a physically abusive man. The dread of drunken fights was replaced by fear of his abuse.

Shelia's stepdad had a paranoia that Shelia's mother would have an affair. He beat her unmercifully if she was just minutes late coming home from work. She had to account for every moment of her time. In turn, Shelia's mother took out her abuse on the children. Each night the children planned what they would do if Dad came after Mother or Mother came after them.

When Shelia became an adult, both the stepdad and birth mother grew more sophisticated in their abusive behavior. It became more verbal than physical. The stepdad never took responsibility for his behavior: "She made me do it." Her mother did the same: "If it were not for you kids, I would not need to do this." Blame shifting was the rule of the day. Neither adult took responsibility for his or her behavior.

Shelia knew Christ as her personal Savior. She, over the course of time, was able to face honestly the sin of her parents and forgive them. She still does not have a fully restored relationship with them. She dearly wants one, but there are actions prohibiting it.

First, the stepdad and mother still verbally attack and attempt to abuse her emotionally. To use her words, "They are both dangerous people to me"—not physically, but emotionally.

"But if Shelia has forgiven them," you may ask, "why don't they have a relationship?" Forgiveness lays a foundation for building a relationship, but it is not the whole structure. Just as salvation is the foundation of our Christian experience, it is not the whole of our Christian life. The apostle Paul clarified the difference between his role as an evangelist and the role of those who instruct and disciple new believers: "According to the grace of God which was given to me, as a wise master builder I laid a foundation, and another is building upon it" (1 Cor. 3:10).

Shelia began the bridge-building process with her parents, but the emotional assaults continued. Ongoing offensive behavior does not build trust or a relationship with anyone. Not only did Shelia's parents continue to hurt her, they did not take any positive steps to restore trust. The fallacy in their thinking was that forgiveness and trust are the same. They are not. Shelia's parents would not take any responsibility for their behavior. The apostle John described such denial: "If we say that we have no sin, we are deceiving ourselves, and the truth is not in us" (1 John 1:8). Continued self-deception restricts the personal power needed to rebuild any meaningful relationship.

Some would reason that if Shelia really forgave her folks, she would just forget the past and overlook the abuse in the present. That is as ludicrous as assuming that if my neighbor physically violated my daughter, I would prove the sincerity of my forgiveness by exposing her again to that potential abuser. Would I have to forgive him? Yes. Forgiveness, I grant. Trust, he earns.

Forgiveness does not relieve the offender from the consequences of his failure. In some rare cases, after restoration is effected, God bonds the relationship to be better than it ever was. This is not usually the case.

Husbands frequently say to me, "Why can't she just forgive me and move on?" They have difficulty comprehending that forgiveness can be granted right away, but trust takes time. She grants him forgiveness; he earns trust. Most men do not understand that forgiven offenses are easily reexperienced by their wives. Men tend to want as few consequences for their behavior as possible. I do too. But that is not life. It takes time to heal emotionally.

Husbands may process their failures at seventy miles per hour while their wives work through wounds at five miles per hour. When the apostle Peter compared a wife to a "weaker vessel" (1 Pet. 3:7), he referred to the physical quality of a valuable, delicate vase that is handled with great care. It in no way implied that a wife is inferior to her husband. Husbands are to "grant [wives] honor as a fellow [equal] heir of the grace of life." The apostle warned men that if they do not treat their wives with loving consideration and respect, they cannot expect to have their prayers answered.

In contrast, women tend to be more forgiving than men because of their greater desire to have a relationship with them (Gen. 3:16). Mutual restoration of relationships is in direct proportion to the changes we make in our attitude *and* behavior. In some instances, a man will restore his relationship with God and make major changes in his marriage, but his wife will remain entrenched in her bitterness, or do something equally worse.

Buck had been a hard-driving rancher, part-time car dealer, and owner and manager of large real estate holdings. Work and money were his gods. Through months of difficult counseling, Buck made major behavioral and attitudinal changes. But his wife, Ginger, refused to acknowledge any of his changes to him— although she would do so to me during our counseling sessions. She had a strategy. It was simple: "If I acknowledge or even praise him for his growth, he will quit trying." She purposed to manipulate him through her bitterness. This is the opposite of the ways of God.

The writer of Hebrews described Ginger's responsibility this way: "Encourage one another day after day, as long as it is still called 'Today,' lest any one of you be hardened by the deceitfulness of sin" (Heb. 3:13). Buck had worked hard to restore Ginger's trust. She was just as determined not to return that trust. He fulfilled his responsibility, but she would not fulfill hers.

God has designed a cause-and-effect world. What we sow we reap, in every endeavor including relationships. Yet God is rich in mercy and compassion toward us. We get more grace from Him than we deserve. We frequently fail to offer this same dose of forgiveness to each other. While God always gives us the desire and power to forgive, we can choose to resist this resource. He did not make us mindless robots. It is our loss if we do not respond to His provisions to heal relationships and work them out.

PURPOSE TO FORGIVE

In the spring of 1968 I finally located my dad. He had been living in San Diego and had given up alcohol some years before. I called him. The conversation was very pleasant. We did some surface chatting. I told him my wife and I were expecting our first child. We arranged a visit. It went well, and visits continued sporadically.

Before one of these visits, I was shocked by what I heard from God. He prompted me that I needed to ask my dad's forgiveness for stealing three of his silver dollars when I was ten years old. I'll never forget that struggle. I was a youth pastor in a large church. It had been the practice of my life for years to ask forgiveness for my sins, offenses, and failures. But when God urged me to ask forgiveness of my dad for that minor childhood theft, I was in disbelief. It was not in rebellious resistance; I just reasoned to myself, "My dad stole my childhood, failed on every front as a parent, and I am supposed to humble myself and ask him to forgive me for stealing three lousy silver dollars?" The prompting got stronger the closer the day came for Dad's visit. I had never before felt such intense conviction of sin and the strong urging of the Holy Spirit to confess it.

Dad's visit went well. He was his old, jovial self. Sober, my dad had the greatest personality one could hope for. But the visit was ending. It was getting late, and he had a long drive home. He said good-bye to my wife and our toddler. I walked him to his car at the curb. It was dusk and the streetlights had just come on. Now was the time. I had to do it. A pause came in the conversation.

"Dad," I began, "God has prompted me to ask you something. Do you remember the coin collection you used to keep in the top drawer of your dresser?"

I could tell he was searching his memory.

"Well, I stole three silver dollars from it to go to the carnival at my elementary school, and I wonder if you would forgive me for stealing them."

The years had been hard on Dad. Perhaps it would be more accurate to say Dad had been hard on himself through the years. He was old, tired, spent, and seemed even shorter in stature than I remembered.

He dropped his head and began shaking it side to side as he

raised both hands to grip my shoulders. He began to sob. Muffled between tears and gasps for air, he cried out to me, "Son, would you forgive me for all that I have done to you?"

"Yes," I said, choking on my own tears. "I did that years ago. I forgave you." Father and son slipped into a big bear hug. Dad's thirteen halting words washed away many years of feeling unloved, neglected, abandoned, and rejected.

With his face drenched in tears as from a fresh spring rain, Dad gripped my shoulders tightly again, nodded twice, and turned to get into his car. I stood on the curb, watching his taillights shrink into the last rays of the fading California sunset. I glanced up at the evening sky and closed my eyes and said, "Thanks." Now I understood God's prompting about the three silver dollars.

That hallmark memory has guided me these past thirty years. It reinforced a discipline of my life—to purpose to obey God, especially when I do not understand why. I literally cringe inside each time I imagine what I would have lost by not obeying God's prompting to confess my juvenile offense. Little did I know that harnessing the power of obedience in my own life would open the door for obedience in my father's life. I learned years later that Dad had been born again as a youth but remained stunted as a spiritual baby for most of his life.

From that experience I gleaned a principle that shines as brightly as the North Star to give me direction when I'm confused. It is, *Fulfill your circle of responsibility, regardless of others' irresponsibility.*

I do not think even a calculator could keep a running tally of the number of times since that event that I have asked myself, *What is my responsibility?* Then I tell myself, <u>*Now do it.*</u> My motto has become, "Be faithful in the face of others' failures." Obedience to the principle of fulfilling my circle of responsibilities gave me my father back. I am living proof of the power of personal responsibility in restoring fractured relationships.

If you have pain caused by others' failures, I encourage you to write out in detail all that you have gone through. Be honest. Tell it like it is. God gives grace only for the truth.

Then talk to a trusted friend, your pastor, or even a Christian counselor; ask him to pray with you. Using your list, tell God what happened and how it hurts. Tell Him you now transfer the irresponsible ones over to the Lord Jesus. Release them to Him. You deserve to be free. Finally, thank Him for what He is going to do in your life and also in the lives of others because of this trial.

You do not deserve to carry this weight another day. Transfer all of those who wounded you by their failure to be responsible to the Jesus Jail one at a time. Then walk away a free person.

For some, picking up the shattered pieces of Humpty Dumpty may mean attempting to restore a broken relationship; for others, it means picking up the pieces of their own lives and moving on. But it all begins with forgiving those who failed you by their irresponsibility.

<hr />

I have encouraged you up to this point not to assume others' responsibilities. But sometimes that is not realistic. What can you do if you *must* shoulder someone else's defaulted responsibilities? Mom showed me the way. It will work for you.

TEN

WHY PICK UP THE
BALL OTHERS DROPPED?

The banquet facility was packed. The president of the All American Home Center walked to the rostrum. It was time to honor a long-time employee for faithful, diligent service.

"Would Myrtle please come to the rostrum?" the president asked. Still spry for her sixty-five years, she approached the master of ceremonies. The reflection off the brass plaque danced on the ceiling. "In honor of your twenty-five years of loyal service to the All American Home Center," the president said, "we would like to present this plaque to you as a small token of our appreciation. May I also say that Myrtle has only missed three working days in her twenty-five years."

As if on cue, her fellow employees sprung to their feet in a thunderous, standing ovation. That honor had not been bestowed on any employee before, nor has it since. She was faithful to the end. Now she is retired.

The All American Home Center could count on Myrtle. My brothers and I could count on Mom.

It is now more than forty-five years since we held that family council in my brother's bedroom. The decision was to do whatever it took to keep the family together in light of Dad's total abandonment of the family. Dad abdicated all his responsibility to us. Now we had to assume it all. We were no longer the ideal family.

God designed the framework of the family. He assigned each person a role and responsibility, all balanced like a delicate mobile. Tremendous power is harnessed when family members carry out to the fullest their respective responsibilities. We have discussed many of these roles and responsibilities already. They are the ideal. But sometimes the ideal is broken. Sin has entered the world and death and destruction by sin (Rom. 5:12). Alienation, separation, loss, and pain have resulted. Like the broken eggshell of Humpty Dumpty, the pieces of fractured relationships, broken marriages, and shattered dreams lie scattered at our feet. Everything that is meaningful is smashed.

My dad shattered to pieces the ideal roles God had established for the Lynch family. The apostle Paul defined God's ideal this way: "Christ is the head of every man, and the man is the head of a woman, and God is the head of Christ" (1 Cor. 11:3). As the head of our family, Dad was decapitated by alcohol.

What do you do when one of the important persons in the family equation is no longer there? What happens when a lead player walks off the stage, never to return? What do you do when couples stop calling you for social get-togethers following your divorce? What do you do when the walls begin to talk to you in the emptiness of your home?

If the children are still at home, whom do you turn to for advice and to meet the discipline, instruction, and recreation demands? When something in the home breaks down, who will help? If your car won't start, whom do you know well enough to call for help? How do you make ends meet financially? How do you reenter the workplace? Who will take care of the kids? Where in the world do you begin when your ideal is smashed?

RESPONSE TO THE BROKEN IDEAL

Some Christians choose to minister to and learn from only those believers who fit within God's ideal. They don't allow those devastated by divorce to teach or share in any spiritual ministry. Some church programs fit only the original family model comprised of Dad, Mom, and children.

We all wish that no family would split apart. But it happens. How do we minister to those who have to assume crushing responsibilities when their family ideal is broken, especially when it is not their choice? The reality is that, in many cases, church, family, and friends see those struggling in broken relationships but close their eyes in denial or view the consequences of separation or divorce as due punishment from God.

It is true that God disciplines us when we disobey Him: "For those whom the Lord loves He disciplines" (Heb. 12:6). Yet many suffer innocently because of the sins of others. When Achan took a beautiful cloak, two hundred shekels of silver, and a bar of gold from the forbidden spoils of the conquest of Jericho, disaster ensued. And he wasn't the only one who suffered. Thirty-six innocent men needlessly died at the battle of Ai (Josh. 7:5). Thirty-six wives and their children were devastated by the loss of their husbands and fathers because of one man's selfish greed.

This ministry default is changing slowly across the landscape of the church, but its movement is at a snail's pace. Susan can attest to that. Where does she fit in the church with three daughters and no husband? What Sunday school class should she go to? What social events will she feel comfortable attending? When will she stop being condemned for a divorce that was not about her? When can she quit explaining why she is single?

With 50 percent of the "ideal" marriages disintegrating in our religious circles today, we can't afford to ignore the painful reality of broken families. We can share their burden by helping them see what is now in their circle of responsibilities, and what is in ours.

Accept It

An empty checkbook and a nearly bare cupboard helped us accept the reality of the broken ideal in the Lynch family. This acceptance is a vital first step. When one accepts the reality of a difficult situation, what happens is absolutely incredible. It can become a powerful launching pad to deeper trust, faith, and resources that one may not have been aware of before.

Carolyn's husband had been a pastor. He walked out on her and their two daughters. We helped her to accept and work through the devastating losses. She could not see how she was going to raise the girls, provide a house, car, clothes, food, and medical insurance. Meager child support did not begin to cover their basic needs. She felt powerless.

Carolyn did the next right thing—she cried out to God. He is creative. A thought hit Carolyn: *I am a good housekeeper. People need their homes cleaned.* She made a few calls. In less than a week she had two homes to clean. Referrals poured in. She researched methods of cleaning domestically and commercially. She incorporated timesaving devices. She had to start adding other women to her cleaning team because of the growing requests for her quality service.

I saw her at a social gathering months later. She told me about her business. She gave me a stack of her business cards with this instruction: "If you meet other women who have to go to work fast because of what they have been through, please have them call me. I will put them to work."

Where did this begin? It started with Carolyn coming to grips with the reality of the broken ideal. She tapped into the power of personal responsibility when she cried out to God and did the next right thing. She had to assume responsibilities that were not intended for her in the beginning. (This certainly does not mean she would have been wrong to have worked outside the home while married. It would be hard to emulate the Proverbs 31 woman without some fiscal involvement.) When Carolyn accepted the reality that she was going to have to be the responsible one in the family, she could then turn her energies into how to do it. My friend Max did the same.

You have already met Max. His wife left him with five children. The youngest was still a toddler. I can still see him today, thirty-five years later. He did the next right thing. All but the toddler were in school. He was a general carpenter and dry-wall man. Each morning as he loaded his tools in his truck, he included a playpen. Though he had to make other arrangements when the child became a preschooler, Max was able to take that child to work with him for almost a year. He was a devoted father.

God is creative and empowering when we finally accept the reality of the loss, turn to Him, cry out to Him, and do the next right thing.

My God Shall Supply

My parents had agreed early in their marriage that they would put my oldest brother through college, and then Carl would in turn put me through college. I would do the same for my younger brother, John. We brothers were four years apart.

After Dad abandoned the family, Carl took the money that was to have gone for my college education and put it into our house payments. I understood the necessity of it and agreed.

Upon graduating from high school and after a year at a community college, I entered Biola College. The cost difference between public and Christian college was drastic. I discovered that our church had scholarships for "needy" students. I applied.

To my pleasant surprise, I became a recipient of one of them. It covered about half of my tuition.

My home church sent me out to a rural mission church in Carbon Canyon an hour away from the college to help work with the young people. A man in my home church also found me a part-time afternoon job in a foundry. The little church helped with travel expenses. Then they asked me to quit my foundry job and pastor them. I was nineteen.

My home church licensed me for the ministry a year later. The men's brotherhood group bought me used cars because of the extensive amount of driving I had to do. A family in the little mission church set up a scholarship assistance fund to help struggling Bible college students. They sent checks to the college to help with my tuition.

I graduated from Biola College four years later, totally debt-free. This continued all through my three years of seminary. I returned for a second graduate degree and God provided again.

Years later I wanted to get my doctorate. I did not have the money. I asked the Father what He wanted me to do. I applied to a school and was accepted, and then came the bill for the first class. I had been asked to speak at a singles conference in Nebraska and received an honorarium gift for speaking. As I drove from the conference to Chicago for the first class, I opened the envelope. It was the exact amount I needed for that class.

Later my mother-in-law called and asked how school was going. She inquired how long it would take to finish the degree program. At the rate I was able to cover it financially, it was going to take a number of years. I was just happy to do it. She and Linda's dad overwhelmed me with their generous offer to help cover the expense. For a preacher to be without words is a sight to behold. Yes, we graciously accepted their offer.

Today I sit in my lovely office in Blue Springs and look at the wall across from my oak desk, where my diplomas hang. Every single one was made possible by many individuals and groups. My dad defaulted on providing for any of those degrees, but when I had to assume the responsibility for them, God generously provided. I can honestly say, "My God [did] supply all [my] needs according to His riches in glory in Christ Jesus" (Phil. 4:19).

Financial default is one thing, but spiritual default is another. Jean knew this firsthand.

SPIRITUAL DEFAULT AT HOME

Jean acknowledged that the ideal was broken in her home. Though she had become a Christian early in her marriage, her husband, Earl, was not a believer. Different men from our church reached out to him at home. He was cordial, respectful, and personable, but definitely not interested in spiritual things. He and Jean eventually had three children, but Earl defaulted in his spiritual responsibilities to the family. These kids were all in my youth group as teenagers when I was a youth pastor in Southern California, and they were exceptional in every way. But how could these sharp, spiritually alert kids come from a spiritually divided home?

My path crossed Jean's often through the five years I served as youth pastor. My wife, Linda, looked up to her as a godly woman and spent quality time with her. We saw that Jean's family got along better than most families where both parents were Christians. I personally learned a great deal from the inner workings of their home in spite of the husband's lack of involvement in the church.

The most important ingredient in their success was that Jean assumed the defaulted spiritual responsibility for the family. The positive results in her life, and now her adult children's lives, reveal the long-range benefit of her godly actions.

Jean started by assuming personal responsibility for her own words, actions, and attitudes before the Lord. Earl did not control her response to life. She acknowledged her full range of emotions and the reality of his actions. She never gave him the power to control her response to him. That remained singularly hers.

Next, she trained her children to be responsible before the Lord for their responses in life. She never allowed them to use their unsaved father as an excuse to default in their personal lives or in their church responsibilities.

Furthermore, Jean assumed full responsibility for her own spiritual growth at home. She attended most all church functions and taught in the children's Sunday school.

When it came to the personal disciplines of the Christian walk, she remained diligent and faithful. One personal discipline that was her hallmark was prayer. Any occasional restriction that Earl placed on her only drove her deeper into prayer. Her face radiated the reality that she had been with the Lord in a deep personal communion.

She was an ardent Bible student. She devoured the Word of God. She did not have the privilege or luxury of asking her husband biblical questions at home as urged by the apostle Paul (1 Cor. 14:35).

Honor and respect also clearly marked Jean's life (Eph. 5:33). She respected her husband. He was not an alcoholic or abusive person. He was not openly antagonistic to the family's involvement in the church, but he also was not the spiritual leader. But Jean's absolute trust in her heavenly Father gave her a stellar strength that allowed her to respect her husband.

Did Jean always agree with Earl? Hardly. But disagreement never created an opportunity or excuse for disrespect. I saw Jean and her children exhibit this same respect at church.

Jean led the way for her children in church involvement. She assumed the responsibility to have her children's church involvement reflect a healthy balance. Never did I see her make the church her husband's replacement. She did not fill the spiritual vacuum at home with feverish religious involvement at church. She consistently allowed her relationship with her heavenly Father to fill that void through His Spirit. Her church remained an avenue of service from the overflow of a personal relationship with God (John 15:5).

With Earl's approval, Jean led in prayer at mealtime. As the children became older they prayed. She prayed with them each night. She loved Earl and prayed for his salvation for more than forty-two years.

Jean taught the children God's Word at home. She never expressed anger at Earl for his failure to do it. Her kids had an incredible grasp of Scripture. They were leaders and examples in the youth group. Their godly mother instilled in them admirable qualities by means of assuming her husband's defaulted spiritual responsibilities. I was thrilled to hear recently that Earl finally did trust Christ as his personal Savior and has become very active in their church.

Jean is the most notable example I have seen of what Paul observed in Timothy's life—a strong spiritual influence: "For I am mindful of the sincere faith within you, which first dwelt in your grandmother Lois, and your mother Eunice, and I am sure that it is in you as well" (2 Tim. 1:5). His godly mother and grandmother taught him the holy Scripture from childhood (2 Tim. 3:14–15). All we know of Timothy's father was that he was a Gentile, most probably an unbeliever.

Timothy came to Christ under the direct influence of his mother and grandmother. Paul's reference to Timothy as "my beloved son" (2 Tim. 1:2) indicated his mentoring relationship with him. Paul filled the role of a spiritual father to Timothy in his later adult life.

Timothy had a difficult job in Ephesus—to instruct older men not to teach foreign doctrines (1 Tim. 1:3). He had no birth father to show him how to relate man-to-man. Timothy came from a home where his father undoubtedly defaulted in spiritual matters. Eunice and Lois assumed this responsibility and raised an outstanding young man. Later Timothy became Paul's companion when the apostle was lonely and discouraged. Yes, Eunice, Lois, and Jean had much in common.

Although Earl made it possible for Jean to express herself fully in her home and in her church, Susan's husband did the opposite. Jerry was not passive but active in undermining, impeding, and countermanding all of her spiritual influence. Susan faced a totally different picture at home with Jerry, her unsaved husband. It was a struggle for her all the way.

By the time Susan came to me, her husband, Jerry, had moved out of the home and a legal separation was in place. Immediately I was impressed with what Susan had done spiritually for herself and her daughters in the face of Jerry's open opposition.

Jerry not only did not pray but wore a disgusted look when Susan or the girls prayed at mealtimes. He emphasized that going to church was a waste of time, an activity for "weak old ladies." He planned fun family activities for Sunday morning and then asked the girls, "Wouldn't you rather go swimming, camping, or to an amusement park instead of going to church?"

Susan's response reminded me of Job. In all these negative attacks on her faith, she did not respond by cursing Jerry or God (Job 1:22). She took the initiative in spiritual and family matters in the face of Jerry's abdication of nearly all responsibilities. It was an uphill battle all the way, but she did the next right thing biblically. She did what she could.

Do What You Can

When the ideal is broken, the things that should be are not. What, then, is one to do? There are at least four questions to ask in determining what to do when you face assuming responsibilities that are not ideally yours.

THE TIME QUESTION

First ask, "Do I have time to do it?" Often I hear, "I will make time." Sorry! That is something only God can do. God created time and He is going to end it. Usually to "make time" means taking time away from something else. If it is free time, that's fine. But when you take on something else to the neglect of a legitimate responsibility, something could be terribly wrong. Keenan learned this the hard way.

We've already discussed Keenan's obsession with helping others. In those days, when the phone rang, Keenan was always the first to answer. At requests for his help, Keenan actually felt his adrenaline start pumping. Before he had made the agreement to check with his wife first, he would have bounded out the door, Mr. Fix-it to the rescue. Now, as a couple, they coordinate their ministry of helps. They take each request and together decide if they have time to accommodate it.

The apostle Paul connected time management with wisdom. "Be careful how you walk, not as unwise men, but as wise, making the most of your time, because the days are evil" (Eph. 5:15–16). It takes wisdom to distinguish between good, better, and best. We often rationalize about doing a good thing when we should do the better or the best thing. This is when we need to pray for wisdom from God, and if it is indeed from Him, it will meet all eight criteria of the wisdom from above (see chapter 6). *pg 107 begin*

THE QUESTION OF ABILITY

The second question to ask ourselves before assuming another's responsibility is, "Do I have the ability—mentally, physically, emotionally, spiritually—to do it?" Sometimes what's really needed is for the person abdicating responsibility to grow up. When parents step in and assume the responsibility to fix their grown children's or grandchildren's lives, they can get stuck in a rescue role, instead of a supportive role of encouragement and care. Grown children who do not shoulder their own responsibilities become a constant drain on their parents, mentally, emotionally, physically, and spiritually. Their issues would test the best pastor or mental-health professional.

My personal opinion is that parents who feel responsible to help should direct their adult children to those who can view the overall situation with more objectivity and hold them accountable for follow-through. An outside person may have a better ability to help or even be aware of something else—more resources.

THE RESOURCE QUESTION

The third question to ask before assuming an additional responsibility is, "Do I have the necessary material resources?" Material resources include finances and property; the key word is *material.*

What did I tell Mabel, a dear widow on a fixed income, who wanted to help her married children "just until they got on their feet"? The son, daughter-in-law, three kids, and two dogs were ready to move in with Mom in her one-bedroom, one-bath apartment. They said they could play like they were "camping out." Since her landlord did not care, Mabel faced the pressure to decide alone. With all the maternal desire of her heart she wanted to help. "I just can't turn them away!"

"Fine," I acknowledged, "but where will they sleep?"

"Oh, I guess I could give my kids my room. I could sleep on the couch and let the grandchildren sleep on the floor."

"How long could you do that?"

"Not very long. I don't sleep well as it is. I don't know how I could do it and keep up with my other obligations."

"Would you have to neglect some other important responsibilities to do this?"

"I guess so."

"Are you the best resource to help meet your son and his family's immediate and long-term needs?"

Some who are assuming others' responsibilities will use Scripture to support what they really are not able to undertake. One passage they'll quote is 1 John 3:17: "Whoever has the world's goods, and beholds his brother in need and closes his heart against him, how does the love of God abide in him?" Note it says, "Whoever has the world's goods." At this point I ask, "If God expected you to assume this responsibility for them, wouldn't God give you the resources to do so?"

"Yes, I know He would, but I just feel I should do something."

In Mabel's case, doing something would mean helping her son's family find someone else who has the resources to help. In many cases, immature adult children take advantage of a loving parent whose resources are limited. But when the resource question is pushed to its logical and responsible conclusion, it becomes evident what can or cannot be done and who is or is not able to help.

There is one more thing to consider before assuming others' defaulted responsibilities—the issue of authority.

THE AUTHORITY QUESTION

Bernard loved his granddaughter. There was nothing he wouldn't do for her. He had the time, ability, and more than enough resources to care for her. Her mother was a single mom. She changed jobs and boyfriends regularly. She lived from one crisis to another. Finally Bernard could not take it anymore. He wanted his grandchild to live with him until her mother got her act together.

"Are you planning to go to court and prove her an unfit mother?" I asked.

"Well, no. But she is!"

"How were you planning on getting custody?"

"Her mom is ruining her life. We can give the kid more stability."

"Are you planning on kidnapping her?"

"You just don't get it!"

"Bernard, do you have the authority to take this child without taking legal precautions?"

When one assumes responsibilities in this manner, he faces a violation of established authority to do it. He must be prepared to suffer the consequences.

There is another side to the authority issue. When authorities prevent or prohibit the obedience of God's clear commands, we must be prepared to disobey and be willing to joyfully suffer the consequences. When the apostles Peter and John were commanded by the Jewish council or Sanhedrin "not to speak or teach at all in the name of Jesus," they answered, "Whether it is right in the sight of God to give heed to you rather than to God, you be the judge; for we cannot stop speaking what we have seen and heard" (Acts 4:18–20). It is in our circle of responsibility to obey God first and last.

Then the high priests and their associates attempted to directly silence Peter and the apostles again by putting them in jail. This time Peter firmly stated, "We must obey God rather than men" (Acts 5:29). But it should be clearly understood, Peter was not violating authority to assume others' defaulted responsibilities. He was diligently endeavoring to fulfill his legitimately assigned responsibilities as commanded by God (Acts 1:8).

THE NEXT WRONG DECISION

Kitty had been married for seven years to the manager of a large chain discount store. Many of his employees were women. In time, he involved himself in affairs and a divorce ensued. Kitty was willing to rebuild the marriage; her husband was not. Years later Kitty returned to my office because of the conflicts she was having with her successive boyfriends.

Kitty knew Jesus Christ as her Lord and Savior. Active church involvement had always been her pattern of life. That did not change. Something else did. As I inquired into the various conflicts she was experiencing, they seemed to center on one complaint. She would date a particular man, and then he would start wanting his "space" and fade out of her life.

When I am talking to a man or woman who has failed in multiple relationships, I ask a revealing question. "Kitty, I don't need to know details, but are you sexually involved with this friend?"

The way this is answered can be more unnerving than the answer itself. "Yeah, so?" It is as if there is something wrong with me that I would even ask such an "obvious" question. "Yeah, so, what possible connection do my sexual habits have with what we are talking about?"

"Kitty, what needs are you endeavoring to meet in this relationship?" Few women who are involved in an immoral relationship say it is because they have sexual desires that need to be satisfied. Instead they say, as Kitty did, "I want to feel valued, honored, and loved. I want companionship and a deep, heart-to-heart relationship, a permanent one." There's nothing wrong with that.

Before you cast the first stone at Kitty, look at what needs you have that are or are not fulfilled. If you have these basic needs met, you may find it hard to identify with her. If you don't have these things, you can feel the same emptiness, pain, and loss she felt.

I have not been very effective in just informing people that their sin is wrong. They already know it and have justified it. Instead, I ask some questions: "Do you think God knows your needs?" Often God has been factored out of getting their normal needs met.

"Do you think God can meet your needs?" Here I usually get a look that says, "If He could, why hasn't He?"

"What do you think God feels about the way you are attempting to get your needs met?" Rarely do they say, "God thinks it is okay" or "I think He understands."

At this point I ask, "Is your way of getting your needs met working for you?"

Kitty's sudden glance down at the carpet answered that question.

An all-too-common response is, "Yeah, but God hasn't met my needs." In other words, "God has failed to give me a mate, and I don't think He will. I just have to do something now myself. God has defaulted on His responsibilities to meet my needs. Now I have to assume them and meet them the best I know how." Inevitably, this kind of thinking leads them to do the next *wrong* thing because they perceive God to be in default.

Is God in Default?

My mind often returns to the many chapel messages I heard at Biola College five days a week. I do not know if chapel speakers consulted with each other, but they frequently focused on the same handful of scriptural texts. One of the all-time favorites, which still rings in my ears almost forty years later, is an obscure story from 2 Chronicles. It has a direct bearing on Kitty's real needs and God's perspective on her needs. The passage says, "For the eyes of the LORD move to and fro throughout the earth that He may strongly support those whose heart is completely His" (16:9).

To this day I do not remember hearing one speaker who put that verse in its historical context. They merely challenged thousands of us students to be the one whose heart was completely His. Years later I studied the historical setting of this passage and gained a new appreciation for what God was saying to Kitty and me.

King Asa occupied the throne of David, ruling well the southern kingdom of Judah. He destroyed almost all the pagan objects of worship and urged the people to keep their covenant with God. Ten years of peace were shattered by the invasion of Zerah, the

Ethiopian, with a million-man army and three hundred chariots. As Asa drew up for battle, fear must have shot through his heart, but he did the next right thing. He prayed, "LORD, there is no one besides Thee to help in the battle between the powerful and those who have no strength; so help us, O LORD our God, for we trust in Thee, and in Thy name have come against this multitude. O LORD, Thou art our God; let not man prevail against Thee" (2 Chron. 14:11). The result? "So the LORD routed the Ethiopians before Asa and before Judah, and the Ethiopians fled" (v. 12). Great!

After many reforms, God gave Asa peace until his thirty-fifth year. Then it happened. Baasha, king of Israel, began to fortify the Israel-Judah border. Asa felt threatened by this defensive maneuver. The pain of potential attack and defeat shot again through his heart. But something different happened this time. Asa, out of fear, reasoned as Kitty did: "I am on my own. I have to do what I have to do to meet my needs. I can't count on God to be there for me." Asa felt God could not be trusted with his literal survival at this point. Asa may have felt God had defaulted on His responsibilities by allowing this trial to occur. The fact that there was an enemy threat on his border (a need) was proof God did not care and would not protect. The presence of an obvious need, in his mind, meant God was in default.

So Asa emptied the treasuries from his own house and the house of the Lord that did not belong to him. He sent the amassed wealth to Ben-hadad, king of Aram (Syria), to bribe him to break his treaty with Baasha. He did just that. Baasha ceased fortifying the border and the threat was over. Safety and security returned to King Asa in the southern kingdom. "A man's got to do what a man's got to do," became Asa's driving motto. Then came a knock at his door. It was the prophet Hanani, sent by God. One can almost see his head shaking from side to side as he rebukes King Asa for resorting to the king of Syria, and not the Lord God, to rescue him.

The prophet asked a convicting question: "Were not the Ethiopians and the Lubim an immense army with very many chariots and horsemen? Yet because you relied on the LORD, He delivered them into your hand" (2 Chron. 16:8). "You had a serious need," Hanani said. "What has been God's track record? What happened to your trust this time?"

Does the presence of an unmet need mean that God is in default? No! The need is an opportunity for God to meet it for your benefit and His glory. Or it can be an occasion to learn you can experience need and still be content (Phil. 4:11–13).

What is God searching for? He has put out an all-points bulletin in search of those whose hearts are completely His even in the midst of overwhelming situations. How does He find these loyal people? He either allows or brings deep needs into our lives to see if *we* are going to default in our ultimate trust in Him. Jesus tested His disciple Philip the same way in preparation for feeding the five thousand (John 6:5–6).

Kitty was so angry at her unfaithful ex-husband that she turned to herself to meet her needs. Her anger shut God out and left her trapped by the evil one. How so? Her behavior flunked the "wisdom from above" test. Her behavior was not pure, peaceful, full of good fruits, unwavering, and without hypocrisy (James 3:17). It was full of bitterness, jealousy, selfishness, and pride, was earthly, natural, and yes, demonic (James 3:14–15).

The presence of need is not evidence that God has failed. Instead, it is an opportunity for God. Denial of a need or inappropriately meeting a need grieves the heart of God. Experiencing need is not abnormal for a believer. The godly apostle Paul acknowledged to the church at Philippi, "I know how to get along with humble means, and I also know how to live in prosperity; in any and every circumstance I have learned the secret of being filled and going hungry, both of having abundance and suffering need" (Phil. 4:12). This brings us to the next right thing to do when faced with having to assume another's defaulted responsibilities to meet our needs.

ENTRUST YOURSELF INTO GOD'S RESPONSIBILITY

If asked to name one of the hardest disciplines of the Christian life, I would say, "Trust." You see, trust has to do with pain—emotional pain. The higher one's emotional pain threshold, the greater the ability to trust. The lower the emotional pain threshold, the lower is one's ability to trust.

We trust in direct proportion to our willingness to experience emotional and, in some instances, physical pain. The attempt to avoid all emotional and physical pain leads to a life of fear and the need to control. These qualities will not create a life of happiness.

Trust is like a thermostat. The higher you turn up your trust in the heavenly Father, the greater your inner peace. The lower you reduce your trust in Him, the less peace and greater fear you experience. The greater the trust, the more comfortable the climate. The lower the trust, the greater the cold and misery.

When one has experienced a great deal of painful loss, his ability to trust is often reduced. Loss can benefit us if it focuses our trust back on the Lord and not on temporal things or relationships. The downside of loss is if it decreases our trust in everything, including God.

Everywhere Jesus turned, He experienced loss. None of His half brothers or sisters believed in Him as Messiah and the Son of God before His resurrection. Although His disciples observed His ministry and miracles firsthand, they abandoned Him at the cross (Matt. 26:56). Jesus did every right thing and ended up alone. (Not lonely, but alone.)

There were two things Jesus did not do when painful things happened to Him. The apostle Peter said of Jesus, "While being reviled [verbally abused], He did not revile in return." Jesus was perfect in every response and every word He spoke. Second, "while suffering [physical abuse], He uttered no threats" (1 Pet. 2:23). But we still need to know what He did do.

219

While His disciples denied Him, abandoned Him, or hid, Jesus practiced a personal discipline that allowed Him to keep going. He did not do it just once; He did it often. This one discipline made it possible for Him to handle the extreme injustice, physical and emotional abuse, and abandonment by friends and family.

Jesus knew He could not ultimately trust His disciples or family. He was arrested, abused, and betrayed by the religious and civil authorities. He knew He could not trust them either. If people can trust in one of three levels of authority, Jesus always trusted in the top level. His family and disciples were the lowest level of authority. They failed Him. The religious and civil authorities, who declared Him innocent seven times, then killed Him, comprised the second level of authority.

The third and highest level of authority was His heavenly Father. The apostle Peter reveals Jesus' secret to a spiritually healthy response regardless of the depth of pain experienced: He "kept entrusting Himself to Him who judges righteously"(1 Pet. 2:23). Jesus moved His case to the highest court. How did He do this?

First, He entrusted or committed Himself to God. *Entrusted* means "to hand over," the way a prisoner is handed over to a judge. Normally a guard does this, against the will of the prisoner. In this case, Jesus willingly handed Himself over to His Father. He cried out on the cross, "Father, into Thy hands I commit My spirit" (Luke 23:46).

Second, in His humanity, Jesus had to *keep on* committing Himself to God. He did not do it once and for all. All during this brutal ordeal, our Savior had to repeatedly commit and recommit Himself to His heavenly Father. We see this repeatedly in His private prayer times. The deeper the pain, the more intense the commitment to God who judges righteously.

Each person God allows me to share this concept with is struggling through seemingly unbearable pain. Picking up the pieces of a shattered life, marriage, or relationship, especially because of others' sins and failures, is very hard for any of us to do. We find ourselves giving it to the Lord and taking it right back. Then we return to our spiritual senses and recommit to Him. Guilt engulfs us because of this vacillation. But take heart—Jesus had to keep on entrusting Himself to His Father too.

Every time Carolyn, who had been abused and abandoned by her preacher-husband, had a setback in her housecleaning business, she had to recommit herself to the Father. She had to reaffirm to herself that He knew what He was doing. Each time my rancher-friend, Buck, made a special effort to be sensitive to his wife and she refused to acknowledge or respond to him, he had to recommit himself to the Father. When Kitty finally made her commitment to follow the Lord in holiness with or without male attention, she experienced severe testing at every point. She had to cry out to the Lord regularly. Shelia had to gather strength just to be cordial and caring to her abusive parents. Approaching them was like staring into the barrel of a loaded shotgun with a hair trigger. She never knew when they were going to launch into an abusive tirade. She told me many times all she could do was go back to the Father for comfort because a fresh wound was so painful. But Shelia loved her parents and wanted to do her part to see them healed of their anger and bitterness.

Finally, notice the one to whom Jesus turned Himself over: "to Him who judges righteously." God stands in stark contrast to an unfair, unjust world. He knows every effort you have made to work out a difficult situation only to have those efforts rebuffed or misunderstood. How reassuring it is that the God of all comfort knows the truth and understands. This is crucial, because life as we know it is definitely unfair.

LIFE IS UNFAIR

My wife, Linda, and I invited Susan and her three young daughters over to our home for dinner. Our youngest daughter, Michelle, entertained Susan's children royally. I ached for them and for all the domestic conflicts they had experienced at their young age. They craved male attention. They enthusiastically received any small gesture on my part. I thought about how unfair life had been to them. These children did nothing to deserve what they had been through.

From time to time I have had to remind myself that life is not fair, and for very good reason. Satan is the prince of the power of the air, and he is not fair. His three-pronged strategy has always remained the same: to steal, to kill, and to destroy (John 10:10). He does his destructive work and then plants thoughts in our minds to blame God for what he did. We saw this in Job's marriage. After he and his wife had virtually lost everything, she bitterly urged Job to "curse God and die!" (Job 2:9).

Satan is not fair. God is. And in the end, God will make all the crooked ways straight. God judges righteously. He knows the truth. He keeps the score. He sees those who dropped the ball. With great accuracy He takes note of those who deny the faith and turn their backs on Him and on their responsibilities. They will give a full account to God for their defaulted responsibilities (Rom. 14:12). Let God demonstrate what His power can do to help you fulfill your responsibilities, especially when others default on theirs.

***

There is one final issue that is absolutely essential in understanding the power of personal responsibility. It can be the most freeing. It was for Marylee.

ELEVEN

How Will God Judge Me?

Marylee had one of the most gentle, quiet spirits I have ever seen. Rex, her husband, was totally devoted to control, outward appearance, and people's approval. Every decision was a political one—how he would look to others.

Marylee was a compliant pleaser, not so much to gain approval as to keep Rex's combustible anger from igniting. Any conflict tore her up emotionally. Marylee could not stand having someone upset with her, and this included God.

As we've seen in previous chapters, Rex refused to change his behavior, attitudes, and words. He rewrote his arguments with Marylee so that she was always wrong and he was always right. He reasoned that were it not for her behavior, life would work for him. He had also made this clear to his two former wives. He found fault with each of them.

Marylee carried through with each assignment and agreement made in my office. Rex, on the other hand, identified and indicated he would assume his circle of responsibilities but failed consistently to follow through. And that, too, was always someone else's fault.

Rex's irresponsibility was not what was bothering Marylee now. She was willing to take the emotional and infrequent physical abuse, not because she thought it was right, but because she struggled with fear—fear of God, not Rex. She asked, "Will God judge me if the marriage fails? I know this sounds silly, but I can't help feeling God is going to be upset with me and is going to judge me severely for all that has happened." Marylee reasoned that if she did everything God asked her to do and the marriage failed, she would still get the blame for it. If God did not judge her, He would at least strip her of any future reward she ever hoped to have. God would punish failure.

Revenge Is Inborn

Marylee is not unique in her reasoning. Revenge and punishment are universal human concepts. One of the consistent characteristics of all known cultures is the practice of exacting revenge or punishment. Even aboriginal tribes in remote parts of the world have revenge laws. If one tribal member steals another's pig, the natural thing to do is to steal his pig or, worse yet, to kill him for it. Mankind practices this eye-for-an-eye or pig-for-a-pig revenge principle instinctively, apart from any outside religious influence. The concept of revenge must be part of the sinful genetic code passed on from parent to child.

I personally believe that the human need for justice is part of God's general revelation in the heart of all men (Rom. 1:18–20). Many people reflect this sense of revenge or punishment in their relationship with God. They often view natural disasters or physical handicaps as punishment from God. Why? Because of an innate belief that sin causes all human suffering and, therefore, suffering is punishment. One hears this occasionally about parents whose child was born with a handicap or whose life prematurely ended through an accident or disease. Our Lord's disciples even reflected this common thinking.

One day as Jesus and His disciples passed a man with congenital blindness. His disciples asked, "Rabbi, who sinned, this man or his parents, that he should be born blind?" (John 9:2). They, too, believed that the presence of sin caused all suffering. In this particular situation, however, the man's blindness was not a matter of sin and punishment but instead an occasion for God to display His glory in a difficult situation (John 9:3). The disciples revealed man's historical fear of God's wrath. This fear wrongly concludes that God is going to punish us, whether or not we are responsible for the conflict. This perception is a no-win situation. But there is good news.

OUR CIRCLE ALONE

God will hold you accountable only for *your own circle of responsibility.* This truth set Marylee free. I can still see the relief on her face when she understood the liberating truth of personal accountability. I think it tends to be more freeing to women than men because women are more prone to struggle with guilt. Usually a man looks at a conflict in terms of "What's wrong with you?" while a woman thinks, "What's wrong with me?" This self-blame can come from her natural sensitivity to feelings of guilt or it can come from the false belief that if it is her fault, then she can fix it.

These false guilt feelings tend to make us vulnerable to taking on others' responsibilities. The result? We start to feel we are totally responsible. This false logic concludes that if we are responsible, then God is going to hold us accountable for everything. He will judge us accordingly.

It is absolutely crucial to realize that we will have to give an account to God only for what is in our own circle of responsibilities. This unnerves the chronic blame shifter, like Rex. Try as I did, I could not get Rex to focus on and fulfill his own circle of responsibilities. He literally obsessed on Marylee's behavior. It was a mind game. But there was one problem with this game: God was not playing.

Rex feigned spirituality to such a degree that he appeared to be well-nigh perfect. That was his public side. The private side was deceptive, cunning, and manipulative.

One might ask, "Doesn't he know he will have to give an account to God for his behavior?" That is no problem to him, for in his mind he has rewritten his wrong behavior so now it doesn't exist. Any wrong thing we pointed out in his life, he simply believes he had no choice but to do. In his self-deception, he was powerless. Marylee made him do it. Narcissistic people like Rex factor a personal God out of their day-to-day thinking and replace Him with a focus on human relationships.

Regardless of Rex's mental gymnastics, he *will* stand before God either as an unsaved man at the great White Throne Judgment or as a saved man at the Judgment Seat of Christ. It is not within the purview of this book to delve into these alternatives. It will be helpful, however, to distinguish between these two separate events for those who feel responsible to God for others' behavior and what they perceive God is going to do to them because of it.

THE WHITE THRONE JUDGMENT

The White Throne Judgment is in reality the "final judgment" designed for the unsaved (Rev. 20:11–13). Contrary to popular opinion, this judgment does not decide whether a person is going to heaven or hell. There will be no celestial scales to weigh good and bad deeds so God can determine one's eternal destiny. God will judge only the evil works of the unsaved. Then the sentence of the second death is passed upon them. Some may ask, "If they are all going to hell, why does God have to go through this process?" Simple. First, to pronounce the final sentence on an already condemned person. Second, to determine the degree of punishment (Luke 12:47–48). The believer is not part of this judgment of condemnation and punishment (Rom. 8:1–2). He will stand before God on different grounds and for different reasons.

THE JUDGMENT SEAT OF CHRIST

Second Corinthians 5:10 says: "For we must all appear before the judgment seat of Christ, that each one may be recompensed for his deeds in the body, according to what he has done, whether good or bad." To many believers, this sounds scary. But a study of the words Paul used will enlighten us about his meaning.

First, the word for "judgment seat" in Greek is *bema,* which denotes the place of an awards ceremony. In the Grecian games in Athens, the oval arena contained a raised platform on which an umpire or notable politician sat. After a competitive contest, the winning athlete stood before this person and received a garland. The other contestants received their rewards from the one seated on the *bema* or "reward seat." It is important to remember that this was never used as a judicial bench.

Next, since the judge is the Lord Jesus, who bore in His body all of our sin, the question of salvation is not the issue, nor is sin, whether committed before salvation or after. Not even the unconfessed sins of the believer are the issue. God went on record in the Book of Hebrews, saying that "their sins and their lawless deeds I will remember no more" (Heb. 10:17). A believer's unconfessed sin hinders fellowship with God now, but it does not change his eternal destiny (1 John 1:5–10).

Furthermore, the word *appear* could be better rendered "to be made manifest." What is going to be revealed? The true character and motives of the believer. God will reveal whether we served in our own energy for our glory or through God's Spirit to His glory.

If we served in the flesh for our glory, we will experience a loss of reward. But if we accomplished our works through God's Spirit for His glory, we will receive a reward. The issue is not reward or punishment; it is reward or no reward.

Many years ago a college friend copied an old poem in the fly-leaf of my Bible. It has been an important reminder to me as it depicts the day I will stand before my Savior.

His Plan for Me

When I stand at the Judgment seat of Christ
and He shows me His plan for me,
The plan of my life as it may have been
had He had His way and I see
How I blocked Him here and checked Him there,
and I would not yield my will,
Will there be grief in my Savior's eyes?
Grief though He loves me still?
He would have me rich but I stand there poor
stripped of all, but His grace
While memories run like a haunted thing,
Down the paths I cannot retrace.
Then my desolate heart will well nigh break
with the tears that I cannot shed,
I shall cover my face with my empty hands,
I shall bow my uncrowned head.
Lord, of all the years that are left to me
I give them to Thy hand
Take me and break me and mold me,
To the pattern that Thou has planned.

(Author Unknown)

The greater our efforts to bring glory to God, the greater our reward. As an act of grace, God will fill each person to his or her capacity to "proclaim the excellencies of Him who has called you out of darkness into His marvelous light" (1 Pet. 2:9).

When we fulfill our circle of responsibilities through the power that God gives us, He will reward us with crowns (Greek: *stephonos*, "victory wreaths") that we will enthusiastically place at His feet. We will have an enlarged capacity to praise Him for eternity because of our faithfulness to our responsibilities here on earth. Now our choice is clear.

JUDGMENT AND RESPONSIBILITY

One may rightfully question, "What does judgment have to do with resolving conflict?" There is a passage of Scripture I have purposely not mentioned yet. It is one of two passages that pointedly inform believers they will stand before God to be judged. The first of the two was 2 Corinthians 5:10. The next is found in Romans 14. There the apostle Paul used the circles of responsibilities concept to resolve a difficult conflict between two antagonistic groups of Christians. They collided over the issue of what was spiritually permissible to eat. Paul, in effect, told the mature group to stay in their circle of responsibilities and accept those weak in faith without quarreling over their immature opinions. He told the weak in faith not to judge other believers for what they allowed. Paul commanded each group to stop "looking down" on or judging each other because God had accepted them both (Rom. 14:1–3).

Paul reproved both groups for getting into God's circle of responsibility. "Who are you to judge the servant of another? To his own master he stands or falls; and stand he will, for the Lord is able to make him stand." He made it clear: "We are the Lord's" (Rom. 14:4, 8).

Then Paul rebuked the Romans for judging and rejecting each other with contempt. In this second major passage regarding the believer's judgment, Paul alerted believers to the fact that "we shall all stand before the judgment seat of God." We are soberly reminded that every knee shall bow to Him, "so then each one of us shall give an account of himself to God" (Rom. 14:10, 12). Paul firmly warned each faction to work out its conflicts by fulfilling its own responsibilities. Why? They would stand before the Lord and give an account for what they did to work out the problems, not what others failed to do. If they stayed focused on their own responsibilities, God would empower them to restore harmony in their relationships. As far as they were concerned, divine accountability was the key motivation to restore a broken relationship.

ACCOUNTABILITY: THE HEART OF RESPONSIBILITY

At the very heart of circles of responsibilities is accountability. Why? Because we have to ask ourselves two questions: *What am I responsible for, and to whom am I responsible?* We will fail to fully discharge our responsibility if we do not clearly understand that responsibility is not given to us in a vacuum. Responsibility has purpose and order because it issues forth from the very nature of God, the originator of purpose and order. It is to this God we must give an account. A spiritually mature person takes seriously his future accountability to God and is motivated to obedience by it.

Those who default in their responsibilities do so from selfish reasons and disregard their future accountability. When Susan's husband, Jerry, developed an interest in pornography, how far ahead was he thinking as to its effect on his marriage with Susan, let alone his standing before a holy God? When my dad wrote bad checks, maxed out the credit cards, and abandoned the family, how far ahead was he projecting into the future, and whom was he thinking about?

The awareness of ultimate accountability can be a relief or a grief. It can bring a sense of relief to know that on one hand, you will *not* be responsible for others' circles of responsibilities, just your own. On the other hand, it can bring grief to realize that you diminish your capacity to praise and glorify the Lord Jesus in heaven because of your failure to be a responsible person here on earth.

We live on one of three levels of motivation at any given

moment. First, we can be motivated for our own gain or fear of our own loss. Second, we can have a desire for others' gain and a fear of others' loss. Or finally, we can have a mature perspective, a desire for God's gain or concern for His loss. Immature people live primarily on the first level of gain or loss for self, factoring out any future accountability. Over the years I have seen that those who grow to understand the long-range view of life and eternity develop a track record of fulfilling their responsibilities. The immature stand around and ask, "What accountability?" They just never seem to get out of the toddler stage in their growth toward spiritual maturity. For the mature, no responsibility is too small.

No Responsibility Too Small

From time to time, a person with less offensive and hurtful behavior waits to fulfill her responsibilities until the major offender changes. Her sense of accountability is very weak. That describes the wife of my farmer-friend, Doug.

As I attempted to help that couple identify and assign responsibilities, and accept and fulfill them, I ran into a roadblock with Doug's wife. His behavior had so devastated her that she felt too weak to do anything. She felt he had so much to acknowledge and correct, compared to her, that she could continue her wrong behavior until he changed. I shared that she would still be accountable before the Lord for her circle of responsibilities, even though she felt she was less at fault.

No responsibility is too small to fulfill from God's perspective. It is not a matter of amount. It is a matter of principle. Jesus focused on the two crucial principles of faithfulness and obedience in a parable highlighting accountability.

A master had three servants. Before leaving on a business trip, he gave them silver to invest and gain a profit for him. Two of the three servants, through trading in the business community, doubled their master's investment. They identified their responsibility, assumed it, and fulfilled it.

Jesus emphasized the fact that the master did not just say, "Well done," but he rewarded their faithfulness with additional wealth, responsibilities, and the privilege of sharing in their master's joy.

Then there was the third servant. His responsibility was clearly identified. He took the silver and assumed the responsibility to invest or trade it. Then came the day of accountability. He had failed miserably. Was it for lack of information? Matthew wrote, "And the one also who had received the one talent [of silver] came up and said, 'Master, I knew you to be a hard man, reaping where you did not sow, and gathering where you scattered no seed.'" He knew his master's character. Then the servant defended himself, "And I was afraid, and went away and hid your talent in the ground; see, you have what is yours" (Matt. 25:24–25).

Fear of potential failure may have locked him up. In effect, deciding to do nothing was in itself a decision. His master would have been happy had he just put the talent in the bank and received interest. The judgment was severe. The servant lost the original talent of silver. He was called "worthless" and cast into "outer darkness" to experience deep pain characterized by "weeping and gnashing of teeth" (Matt. 25:30). Jesus punctuated the fact that the smallest responsibility is important to God.

God never holds us accountable, however, for what we cannot do or for what we do not have. He does expect us to do everything we are able to do with strength He gives us, and then, having done all, to "stand firm" (Eph. 6:13).

It was hard for Doug's wife to accept her own responsibility. She took the same attitude as Doug. He was not about to change until she met certain preconditions. She was not going to be responsible for her overspending until he was willing to develop a relationship with her. But when each of us stands before the Lord, we won't be asked to give an account for anyone else. God will ask only what we did with our own circle of responsibilities, even the small ones. The key issue is our focus.

CHANGE THE FOCUS

Doug's wife could not even respond to him emotionally. She could hardly think about, let alone do, the next right thing. I knew I had to encourage her to change her focus. Thoughts of Doug depressed her. I asked her to do something very hard: "Would you just put Doug out of your mind for a moment? Would you replace him with thoughts of the Lord Jesus?"

The expression on her face plainly said, "What does He have to do with Doug?"

"Just tell me what you know and think about the Lord."

It took a few minutes for her to clear her mind. Then her thirty-eight years of Sunday school, church, summer camp, and vacation Bible school flooded her memory. A pleasantness seemed to come across her countenance. For a few minutes we just talked and shared about our Lord. Then I asked her to read Colossians 3:23–24, substituting the word *Doug* for "men." Slowly she read, "Whatever you do, do your work heartily, as for the Lord rather than for—" she paused— "Doug." She continued, "Knowing that from the Lord you will receive the reward of the inheritance. It is the Lord Christ whom you serve."

My office got quiet. Thoughts of Doug had consumed her. Every waking thought was about him and how he hurt her and the girls. She made every decision from a "Doug focus." Whether the subject was avoidance, manipulation, or revenge, Doug was the picture in her mind. I gently asked her if she would be willing to replace Doug with Jesus.

"How?" she exclaimed. "Jesus does not harass me on the phone, shame me, criticize me, or act like a Dr. Jekyll or Mr. Hyde."

"How do you think Jesus took the excruciating pain of His brutal death here on earth?"

She slightly shrugged her shoulders. Then I asked her to read Hebrews 12:1–2: "Let us run with endurance the race that is set before us, fixing our eyes on Jesus, the author and perfecter of faith, who for the joy set before Him endured the cross, despising the shame, and has sat down at the right hand of the throne of God."

There are important insights in these two verses. The "race" is our life, complete with all its parts, especially the trials, temptations, and responsibilities. We are to run the race with "endurance." In the Greek this word is made up of two words; one means "under" and the other "remain or abide." It literally means "to remain under indefinitely with no hope of change or relief."

Many defaulted responsibilities that we must pick up and carry all but crush us. The word *endurance* refers to the ability to remain in a difficult situation with no prospect of relief. There is no light at the end of the tunnel. Light gives hope of relief soon. Endurance is the ability to remain in a difficult situation with no light or relief in sight.

The writer of Hebrews says to run under pressure with our eyes fixed on Jesus, not on a light of anticipated relief. There will be relief in heaven, but this is earth. This is what Doug's wife needed to do: replace her focus on Doug with a focus on Christ.

Next I pointed out *how* Jesus fulfilled His responsibility of dying on the cross—"who for the joy set before Him endured the cross." Jesus focused on the joy of returning to His Father and His glory. This is the same type of joy the Father has waiting for us.

Finally, after the ordeal of the cross, Jesus sat down at the right hand of the throne of God. It was finished. He had assumed the final triumphant position.

Our Lord had to first drink of the cup of suffering that He did not want to drink (Matt. 26:39). He asked His Father if it could be passed from Him. He submitted to His Father's will. He fulfilled the responsibility that He assumed in eternity past, before the foundation of the world. How did He do it? Jesus knew He was accountable to the Father and He was going to be greatly rewarded (Phil. 2:9–11).

The whole purpose of giving God an account of our fulfilled circle of responsibilities is so that we might be richly rewarded by Him. Then, with a powerful surge of gratefulness, we will cast our crowns at His feet and glorify Him forever. God has prepared us a place (John 14:2), a position (1 John 3:1), and a purpose (Eph. 1:12) in heaven. But that is eternity. Can I lose it all now?

They Can't Take It from You

Most of the apostle Paul's letters to churches or individuals addressed specific problems or issues. The letter to the church at Corinth was no exception. The issue of divorce, as it relates to Christians married to non-Christians, was raised.

Although the original question is not stated in the letter, we do have the answer. The question could have been, "Am I obligated to keep this marriage together at all costs, even if the non-Christian wants out?" Implied is, "Will God hold me accountable for the failure of the marriage if the nonbeliever wants to end it?" Perhaps a broader question could be asked, "Could the disobedience of another affect my reward or standing as a believer?"

There are conscientious Christian wives who anxiously fight for their marriages in the fear that God will harshly judge them if, for any reason, their unsaved husbands leave. They say, "God hates divorce. If my husband divorces me, will God hate me?" The apostle clearly sets the record straight. If the unbeliever is content to live with the Christian, the believer is not to send the unbelieving spouse away (1 Cor. 7:12–13).

But the confusing issue is, what if the non-Christian wants to leave? The Christian has God's full permission to let the non-Christian leave. The Christian is not obligated by God to force the unbeliever to stay in the marriage out of fear of what He will do to the Christian if this happens.

The broader application is clear. You should do all that is within your personal power to make the marriage work. But if the non-believer insists on leaving, let him go. The unsaved or disobedient Christian spouse can't take your reward away by divorcing you. You can still be a faithful person even if someone is unfaithful to you. Absolutely no one controls your accountability and reward but you. They can't take it from you.

Many people had turned away from the faith after the apostle Paul led them to Christ and discipled them. He felt the loss. He even felt that he may have worked in vain (Gal. 2:2). But after all the abandonment he experienced, and the apostasy and falling away he witnessed, Paul could confidently say from the dimly lit Roman jail cell where he was about to die, "I am already being poured out as a drink offering, and the time of my departure has come. I have fought the good fight, I have finished the course, I have kept the faith" (2 Tim. 4:6–7). Paul pictured his pending death like a drink offering poured out on the daily sacrifices (Num. 28:4–7). Praise to God.

Looking back over his life, Paul felt a sense of completion in the course laid out for him by the Lord (Acts 20:24). Though others failed him, he did not fail to fulfill his circle of responsibilities in spite of the setbacks, conflicts, disappointments, and persecution. Through it all he kept his faith and trust in the Father intact.

What kept him going through it all? He tells us: "In the future there is laid up for me the crown of righteousness, which the Lord, the righteous Judge, will reward me on that day; and not only to me, but also to all who have loved His appearing" (2 Tim. 4:8). Paul knew he was ultimately accountable for his circle of responsibilities to a Judge who was just and ready to reward him, not punish him.

I have seen this truth release fearful, confused people who felt partially or totally accountable for others' responsibilities. No longer do they feel that those who defaulted could rob them of their reward and relationship with God.

There is something else they can't take from you. Tonya knew this firsthand.

They Can't Take Your Peace

Tonya asked my wife, Linda, to go to court with her. The judge was going to declare the divorce final. Rodney, her Christian husband, had emotionally and physically abused her and the kids for years. She had held on in hopes he would change. He verbally beat her up with words like, "Submit, you witch." In time, she broke.

Tonya filed for temporary separation, hoping they would get counseling and the marriage would be saved. Rodney's ranting phone calls and threats continued. Tonya did everything she could. Now she stood before the judge who decreed the divorce final. Closing her eyes, she lifted her head to heaven to the righteous Judge and slowly nodded her head. She felt reassured. God understood. She had committed herself from the beginning to Him who judges in righteousness. This was not the way she wanted it to end. The ideal was broken. She had fought hard to keep her marriage together. She had fulfilled her responsibilities but received only physical and emotional pain. Amazingly, she kept her faith intact.

It was hard for Tonya to accept the reality that peace on earth might not come even if she worked hard to fulfill all of her responsibilities. Ever since the Fall of man in the Garden of Eden, the ideal and reality have been in conflict. What should not happen does. What God designed for our best gets broken.

Rodney caused Tonya immeasurable pain. He had the power to destroy their marriage and break up their home, but he could not snatch away her future reward for faithfulness (2 Tim. 1:12) or rob her of her peace (Phil. 4:7).

It is one thing to know we will someday face a righteous Judge who will richly reward us for our faithful efforts to restore broken relationships. But it is quite another to live day by day, purposing to do the one thing that will make it all possible. Joshua gave us a clue how to do it.

TWELVE

WHY SHOULD I BE THE RESPONSIBLE ONE?

A hot wind whipped across his suntanned face. Standing before Joshua was an expectant multitude that waited to hear his farewell speech. What would a man, born a slave in Egypt, say to a nation of thousands now free and at peace? What had his 110 years of walking with God taught him that would be important to them?

Joshua was at least eighty years old when he assumed the leadership of the nation from Moses. His mission was to lead the Israelites to conquer the land of Canaan that God had promised to them. His mighty conquest subdued six nations and thirty-one kings.

Would Joshua address the need of the nation to build strong families? That would certainly be appropriate. Would he reinforce the importance of a strong army and political stability? That would be fitting as he prepared to step down as their honored military leader. He chose instead to address the number one need of the nation: to be faithful to their covenant with God.

Because the covenant established through Moses at Mount Sinai was not everlasting, it had to be renewed with every generation. Joshua began by recapping Israel's history. He reminded the people of their primary circle of responsibility: "Now, therefore, fear the LORD and serve Him in sincerity and truth." To do that, they would have to "put away the gods which your fathers served beyond the River [Euphrates] and in Egypt"(Josh. 24:14).

Joshua knew he was not speaking to a completely convinced audience. So he challenged them, "If it is disagreeable in your sight to serve the LORD, choose for yourselves today whom you will serve: whether the gods which your fathers served which were beyond the River, or the gods of the Amorites in whose land you are living." Then in a clear, resounding voice, reflecting many years of hard-won conviction, he declared the hallmark principle of his life: "But as for me and my house, we will serve the LORD" (Josh. 24:15).

Had this declaration come from the lips of a young, idealistic warrior, hardly proven in battle or experienced in life, it would have been discounted as brash arrogance. Joshua and Caleb were the last living links to the nation's roots of slavery in Egypt. By now the Israelites were free and at peace in Canaan. Joshua's determination to serve God was galvanized through all the trials and battles Israel experienced to achieve this peace. Joshua had seen God tested in every way possible and proved faithful.

His declaration, "As for me and my house," starts with three important words—"As for me." Joshua had been a determined young man of faith when he was alone with no family. He was a responsible man in his youth in Egypt. This laid a foundation of dedication and determination that lasted his whole life.

We do not have a historical record of Joshua's early commitment that made him the epitome of singleness of purpose and dedication to God. How did he learn to accept responsibility and purpose to follow through? He is one of the few men of faith recorded in all of Scripture who, at the end of his life, was still a man of character and integrity.

Joshua developed self-discipline through acknowledging his responsibilities and fulfilling them wholeheartedly. Faithfulness and obedience were a way of life for Joshua because he purposed to remain responsible. It was not just a decision to be made and soon forgotten. Purposing to remain responsible before God became a way of life all his life.

A WAY OF LIFE

When I was a young boy, I invited Christ to come into my life and forgive my sin and be my Lord (Rom. 10:9). No one told me that there was more to the Christian life than simply making a "decision for Christ." I did not understand my responsibility now to cooperate with God and allow Him to change my thoughts and actions (Rom. 12:2). I mistakenly believed I could continue to live life my way with gusto, but with just an added religious twist. Wrong!

God does not call us just to make a decision to follow Him, but to adopt a new way of life patterned after Jesus, who is "the way" (John 14:6). The early Christians were identified as "belonging to the Way," even by their enemies (Acts 9:2). There was something noticeably different about their new lifestyle. It was based on the ways of God. One of God's ways involves identifying and fulfilling personal responsibilities, which have the power to restore relationships. It does work and it will work for you. You *can* work it out!

Dysfunctional ways of life, however, do not ultimately work. God cannot allow them to work for a Christian. Why? They are not patterned after His character or His design for us. There are patterns of life that seem right only because we were raised believing them to be right. Often the way that looks so right leads to death or separation (Prov. 14:12). This dysfunctional way can lead to emotional or physical separation and even divorce. Separation may come in the form of rebellious teenagers who turn their backs on God and the family. Separation may result from a workaholic spouse who runs from a difficult relationship at home and to admiration and recognition at work. A controlling, dominating man may cause his deeply hurt wife and kids to withdraw from him emotionally or even to leave him. Those who profess faith but continue to live an unchanged lifestyle may introspectively ask the same question my dad eventually did.

Many years after my dad and I had reunited, we were on a drive together. He was enjoying the scenery when he suddenly mused, "Son, today would have been your mother's and my fiftieth wedding anniversary." Then in a reflective tone he added, "I wonder what went so wrong."

I could tell his question was rhetorical, but I could not help but wonder as we traveled, *Doesn't he have a clue?* My dad did not appear to connect his selfish lifestyle to the resulting destruction of our family. No one told him of the power of personal responsibility in restoring relationships. As an adult child I knew personally the pain of a dad's failure to remain responsible in the family. But standing in stark contrast to my dad is Joshua, a man who did remain responsible and faithful.

BENEFITS OF RESPONSIBILITY

A question I'm often asked is, "Why should I be the responsible one? How is it going to benefit me to remain responsible when others are not?" There are at least eleven benefits in remaining responsible for our own circle of responsibilities. Each one is powerful and contributes towards the restoration of broken relationships.

1. TOTAL FOCUS

An athlete who breaks his concentration can expect defeat. By maintaining a steady focus, a believer, like an athlete, can be assured of a winning life with no regrets. The apostle Paul shared his secret of finishing life well, in spite of countless painful experiences. He revealed this to his friends at Philippi: "I press on toward the goal for the prize of the upward call of God in Christ Jesus" (Phil. 3:14).

What if Paul had to do that for only five or ten years? Anyone can hang in there that long! The fact is, Paul had been a believer for at least thirty years. It was not easy for him, either. Those were thirty years of total focus. He ran like a determined long-distance runner, listening to the cheers of the Old Testament saints who had gone on before him (Heb. 12:1). The lessons he learned from the popular Greek games he translated into spiritual realities for his race of life. Like athletes of old who look forward to standing before the earthly *bema* seat at the end of the arena, he, too, anticipated being called to the heavenly *bema* seat where his Judge sat ready to bestow a winner's reward upon him. Desiring to receive that reward kept him focused.

The concept of circles of responsibility can greatly aid our focus in difficult relationships. It helped Buck, that hard-driving rancher and part-time car dealer. He often asked what more he could do to improve his marriage with Ginger. She continued to attempt to control him with her anger and conditional acceptance. She stubbornly refused to acknowledge any of his changes for fear he would lose his motivation to change. Still, they continued to work together in their many business, ranching, and farming enterprises. I repeatedly said to Buck, "Stay in the pocket. Don't get outside or you'll get creamed." What?

Buck loved football. He knew what "staying in the pocket" meant. He knew I was referring to the quarterback staying inside his ring of defenders, who would make it possible for him to pass the ball downfield to a receiver. It is the quarterback's responsibility to look for eligible open receivers. It is the rest of the team's responsibility to protect the quarterback until he passes the ball to a receiver for a touchdown.

If a quarterback ever gets outside of his protective ring of defenders, he could get painfully sacked. I asked Buck, the quarterback in his marriage, to review for me the game plan that the Lord had given him. He painfully listed, "Listen attentively, acknowledge her emotions, avoid being defensive, speak in honoring tones, listen to her opinion, *ask* her instead of *tell* her, be gentle, be thoughtful." He recited this list like a memorized catechism.

Then I said, "Now what are you going to do?"

"I guess I'll stay focused and remain in the pocket." He got it!

Every decision Jesus made had one focus: His sacrificial death on a Roman executioner's cross. He willingly assumed the responsibility of the death penalty for our sin. Jesus moved through His brief three-year ministry totally focused on this decisive hour. When His mother wanted Him to remedy the problem of a depleted wine supply at a wedding feast, He responded, "My hour has not yet come" (John 2:4). The time for revealing who He was and why He came had not arrived. When His own brothers, who did not believe in Him, challenged Him to show Himself to the world prematurely, He responded, "My time is not yet at hand" (John 7:6). Because of Jesus' purpose even the religious leaders could not get their hands on Him to kill Him (John 7:30; 8:20). But in response to an inquiry by certain Greeks who wished to see Him, He declared, "The hour has come for the Son of Man to be glorified" (John 12:23). It was time.

Death for Jesus involved temporary humiliation, but soon He would enter into the glory that He had with His Father before coming to earth (John 17:5). Was this hour painful for Jesus? It had to be. He appealed to His Father that this hour might pass (Mark 14:36). Earlier Jesus admitted to His disciples that His soul was deeply troubled. He rhetorically asked, "What shall I say, 'Father, save Me from this hour'?" Jesus kept the focus of His life on His reason for coming. He reminded the disciples, "For this purpose I came to this hour" (John 12:27).

Although Jesus was always the one in total control, He delegated power to others to accomplish this final hour in His life. In the flickering torchlight, the crowd of religious leaders and military personnel came to the olive grove to arrest Jesus under cover of night. He met them with these words: "This hour and the power of darkness are yours" (Luke 22:53). They were now fully cooperating with Satan to murder the Messiah. Jesus stayed focused and self-controlled. No one was taking His life from Him; He voluntarily laid it down (John 10:18).

What did the hour mean to Jesus? It represented His circle of responsibility. There was to be only one mediator between God and man, Christ Jesus Himself (1 Tim. 2:5). There was to be one sacrifice, "the Lamb of God who takes away the sin of the world" (John 1:29). Our entire salvation depended on Jesus' staying focused on His responsibility. While the Savior agonized on the cross, Satan offered Him one more opportunity, through the taunt of a soldier, to prove He was the King of the Jews by coming down off the cross (Luke 23:37). Jesus had already performed all the miracles necessary to substantiate His Messiahship. Because He stayed focused, He stayed on the cross until He was able to cry out, "It is finished!" (John 19:30).

Jesus illustrated in His own life and death the incredible power to restore relationships through fulfilling personal responsibility— "God was in Christ reconciling the world to Himself" (2 Cor. 5:19). Your circle of responsibilities will benefit you by keeping you focused too. Not only will it help you stay focused, it will give a deep sense of a lifelong purpose.

2. PURPOSE

A disoriented airline pilot, after becoming hopelessly lost, announced on the intercom system: "Folks, I don't know where we are going, but wherever it is, we are making good time." That announcement capsulizes our culture: fast track, fast food, fast lane. One of people's most commonly admitted fears is aimlessness or purposelessness. Our culture is plagued with boredom, as we can see in the skyrocketing growth of the recreation industry. Boredom is characterized by high energy and no meaningful direction to release it: getting all dressed up and having no place to go.

I have never met anyone with a clear purpose in life who was bored. Being bored means you have nothing meaningful to do. Do? Fulfill your responsibilities. What responsibilities? Do the next right thing. The next responsible thing may be to rest, pray, call, write, study, exercise, encourage, teach, comfort, clean, cook, drive, worship, praise, witness, disciple.

One prevailing Christian responsibility, as it relates to unsaved people, is to witness (Acts 1:8) and then to disciple (Matt. 28:19–20). You never outgrow this responsibility. It is to be the purpose of your whole life. Grandma Harding underscored this to me.

I was speaking in a laypeople-helpers conference in Pennsylvania. The large fellowship hall was filled with people who wanted to sharpen their people-helping skills. All during the first session, I kept noticing an elderly lady hunched over a conference table taking copious notes. I felt flattered to see her listening so intently. My curiosity got the best of me. At the break I introduced myself and just had to ask, "How did the Lord lead you to be here today?"

"Well, young man," she said, as she pointed her index finger at me, "I'm ninety-two years old and I figure you're never too old to learn how to help someone. Besides, there is a young man I have been burdened for and I thought I could get something here today that just might help him."

I shook my head in amazement and said, "You are a real example to me. Your purpose has served you a lifetime." Grandma Harding died the next year. This saint knew she had a responsibility to fulfill the Great Commission until our Savior called her home. Our Lord's last words, "Make disciples," gave her a responsibility and purpose that lasted ninety-two years. Grandma Harding contrasted greatly with Maria.

Maria's gambler-father came to the United States without her or her mother. After he had a "lucky night," he sent for his wife and daughter. They were to book passage for New York on an ocean liner that departed from Cherbourg, France. Before the scheduled departure a physician discovered that Maria had an eye infection and refused to sign her immunization papers until the infection was cleared up. She and her mother missed that liner and took another ship. The liner they missed was the *Titanic.*

At ninety-four, Maria has outlived all her family. She recently threw away most all her family photographs. She summarized her life by saying, "Life's kinda funny. I mean, I missed the ride on the *Titanic,* and then I had TB [tuberculosis] and survived. And now I am all alone. My folks are gone. My boy is gone. And so I ask myself, 'Why am I here?' I ask that question all the time, and I don't have any answer. I really don't" (*Kansas City Star,* January 24, 1998).

"Why am I here?" The answer to that question should define our lives. Your answer will make the difference between meaningful satisfaction and miserable survival. When we fully accept God's call on our lives and fulfill it, we will not arrive at the portals of death asking Maria's haunting question, "Why was I here?"

When we abandon the God-designed responsibilities that define our purpose, we soon find ourselves on that aimless jet— "Wherever we're going, we're making good time." Circles of responsibilities are guaranteed to define your direction, sharpen your focus, and give you a definite sense of purpose.

Another personal benefit of purposing to remain responsible is the rewarding sense of accomplishment.

3. ACCOMPLISHMENT

The saying is true: "A mother's work is never done." I admire how my wife, Linda, has juggled her many roles as wife, mother, grandmother, home executive, and elementary schoolteacher. Add the roles of ministry office coordinator, conference copresenter, and manuscript proofreader and you have only begun to see the scope of her involvement in the lives of her family and others.

Linda is the first to admit her daily struggle to stay focused and not get sidetracked by many good things that are not her priorities.

One tool that helps is to identify what she is responsible for each day, then focus her energy to accomplish just those things. Jesus explained how.

Jesus revealed the secret of reducing stress and cultivating inner peace. "Do not be anxious for tomorrow; for tomorrow will care for itself. Each day has enough trouble of its own" (Matt. 6:34). To paraphrase: "Focus on today's issues. They will take all of your energies." When one deals with today's issues and fulfills them, he has accomplished much. He is ready to meet tomorrow's demands and responsibilities.

From time to time people in counseling ask, "Do you feel we are accomplishing anything?" Several questions help them gauge their own progress: "Do you have a clear picture of what you are responsible for?" Usually they answer affirmatively. Good. That is progress. That is an accomplishment. "Have you fully accepted your responsibilities before the Lord?" Usually an affirmative nod follows. That, too, is progress. "Are you fulfilling your circle of responsibilities on a daily basis?" If there is hesitation at this point I ask, "Are you fulfilling your responsibilities more now than you did before?" I applaud even the smallest accomplishment, for it shows change in the right direction.

Remember, the two things most hurting people want from those who help them is hope that they are going to get better and encouragement that they will be able to accomplish the tasks ahead. Fulfilling their circles of responsibilities gives them a sense of improvement and accomplishment that they may not have had before.

In meeting with Deidra and Keenan, who struggled with his misplaced priorities, I would inquire how the week went. Did Keenan check with Deidra before committing blocks of time to others? Each week she indicated that he was doing much better in that department. But her perfectionism sometimes kicked in and she would comment that Keenan still slipped up now and then.

With her all-or-nothing thinking, Keenan was either totally good or totally bad. Deidra had to learn from the Lord that changing words, attitudes, and behavior takes time. Circles of responsibilities give you a measuring rod, like highway mile-markers, to measure progress.

Fulfilling responsibilities accomplishes the goal that glorifies the Father. The Lord Jesus, in His high priestly prayer, made it clear: "I glorified Thee on the earth, having accomplished the work which Thou hast given Me to do" (John 17:4). Although the cross was still ahead, Jesus viewed it as already accomplished. Accomplishment meant glory to the Father.

Staying in your own circle of responsibilities keeps your life in focus and purposely directed. Then you, too, can confidently say at the end of your life, as Jesus did, "It is finished." It is accomplished!

Purposing to remain faithful in fulfilling your responsibilities will do something else for you. It will give you a sense of identity.

4. IDENTITY

Nick and Traci worked hard to reestablish a healthy relationship with Traci's mother. They both redefined their own circles of responsibilities. But something else had happened to Traci while she was growing up. Her identity was built on totally pleasing her divorced mother. Traci became so emotionally entwined with her mother that she had no clue as to who she was herself. As far as she could tell, she was whatever her mother wanted her to be. This mindset carried over to her friendships, dating, and her marriage with Nick.

Nick tended to be authoritarian in his home-management style. Control marked most decisions. Traci fit in perfectly with Nick, who took over where her mother left off. Mom, however, continued to tell Traci what to do, so Traci was torn between pleasing Mom and Nick. How Traci felt or what she wanted were rarely factors in the equation. She basically stuffed her wants, needs, opinions, likes, dislikes, and aspirations in an obscure, dark closet of her emotions, secured against any intrusion.

This is precisely why it was so hard for Traci to define biblical boundaries or limits with her mother. If I mentioned boundaries to Traci, she said two things. First, "What boundaries?" I then explained that they are healthy limits in our relationships. Next she asked, "Whose boundaries?"

"Yours, of course."

"I don't have boundaries."

"Don't you have any relational limits?"

"I don't know."

"Why?"

"I don't know what my limits are."

"Why?" I already knew.

"I don't know what I want in a relationship. No one has ever asked." Then the crisis hit: "I don't know who I am!"

People pleasers tend to lose their own identities in an insatiable desire to be accepted by others. Pleasers have a hard time taking care of just their own responsibilities because they do not know who they are and what they are legitimately responsible for.

Circles of responsibilities give people back their identities. How? To begin with, God gives each believer at least one spiritual gift (1 Cor. 12:7) to be used to benefit others. It is not to be buried and forgotten or laid aside for another's identity, expectations, or demands. God expects each one to use the gift(s) he has been given (1 Tim. 4:14). He does not give the same gift to every believer (1 Cor. 12:29–30); variety exists in the body of Christ. With the variety of gifts come varieties of responsibilities and expressions.

Next, God gives each of us natural talent and abilities—physical, emotional, and mental. He expects us to use those for His glory. Add together spiritual gifts, abilities, natural talent, and personality type and you wind up with an absolutely unique person in Christ. Your ultimate identity is to reflect Christ through who God made you to be. It is impossible to be a people pleaser and a God pleaser simultaneously (Matt. 6:24).

The apostle Paul did not lose his personal identity when he said, "I have been crucified with Christ; and it is no longer I who live, but Christ lives in me; and the life which I now live in the flesh I live by faith in the Son of God, who loved me, and delivered Himself up for me" (Gal. 2:20). When you read the Pauline letters, they still sound uniquely like Paul, not Peter. When you read the letters written by John, they have the earmarks of his style and personality.

The Scriptures did not originate with the human authors themselves. The writers spoke from God while they were carried along by means of the Holy Spirit (2 Pet. 1:21), the way a sailing ship is carried by the wind. God the Holy Spirit controlled the human authors of Scripture. These men were consciously involved at each step along the way; they were not in a trance or taking dictation. Yet God used their uniqueness at every point—who they were, their talents, gifts, and heritages. The authors identified what God wanted them to do, accepted it, and fulfilled it.

I personally know of few concepts that are more freeing than knowing clearly who I am and what I am called to do in Christ. This is absolutely the best avenue to express my spiritual gift because it is the way God intended it to be used.

David, the shepherd boy, could not fight the Philistine giant, Goliath, in King Saul's armor (1 Sam. 17:38–39) any more than we can express our uniqueness in Christ while trying to be like someone else. God gives grace only to do His will, not the will of others who would impose their agenda onto ours.

Another terrific benefit of remaining in our circle of responsibility is security.

5. SECURITY

We devise many strategies to make ourselves feel secure. Some choose money; others choose relationships. Still others find it in things. The aggressive ones attempt to find it in position. These things in themselves are not wrong. We all need some negotiable currency to live. Who does not need a relationship, whether it be a best friend, a mate, a brother, or a sister? As much as some of us strive not to accumulate things, most of us have more than we need. Possessions and money come and go. We all want to fit in, to belong, to be associated with or hold membership in something. But there is a more significant source of security: the knowledge and confidence that you are doing what you are supposed to do.

Our English word *secure* comes from two Latin words meaning "without" and "care." To be secure, one is relatively free from fear, anxiety, and doubt. One is confident and safe. A secure person is strong, stable, and firm.

I have watched many anxious faces relax into a quiet confidence when they understand their responsibilities and the next right thing to do. It is also a relief to know what they are not to do, what they are not responsible for.

Helen's adult son, Ron, as we know, was a drug addict. She came to understand she was not responsible for her son's recovery or to provide for him until he decided to get help for his addiction. She was to love him, pray for him, and provide a meal for him from time to time, but she was not responsible before the Lord to provide a launching pad for Ron. Of course she cared about him. She bore him. He was part of her. That would never change. But to continue to allow him to steal from her, to lie, to manipulate, and to exploit her financially was not being responsible but enabling his irresponsibility. Enabling is more motivated by self-protection than by self-sacrifice. Only when Helen was deeply convinced by God what her clear responsibilities were was she secure enough to treat Ron in a responsible way.

In a difficult relationship doing the next right thing may be hard. But a quiet, deep security develops from doing the clear will of God. Our Lord is the "anchor of the soul," both sure and secure

(Heb. 6:19). Security in belief births security in behavior. Identifying, assuming, and fulfilling responsibilities before God produces a deep sense of security second to none.

Remaining faithful to your circle of responsibilities, especially as it relates to relationships, delivers another major benefit. Anxiety is reduced to a minimum.

6. REDUCED ANXIETY

Rex, Marylee's husband, found counseling sessions a great source of anxiety. Anxiety is different from fear. Fear has an object. You can see the speeding car heading toward you and that a collision is inevitable. The car is a tangible source of fear.

Anxiety, on the other hand, is fear of the unknown. If you feel a car is going to dart out at you at any time even though you do not see it, that is anxiety. Anxiety is usually a concern in the basement of the mind, rattling around with disturbing yet indistinct noises that we cannot quite decipher. Rex was disturbed by anxiety.

The rattling noises of anxiety come from at least four sources. First, there is the fear that a truth may come up that we do not want to face. This heightened Rex's anxiety on a scale of one to ten to at least a nine. He knew there were truths about his character and behavior that he did not want to acknowledge, and he fought hard to keep them submerged.

Second, Rex was anxious about painful feelings. There were emotions that he had padlocked in the basement of his life for years. Any talk about hurts, losses, or conflicts only heightened his anxiety. He would rather have died than feel those emotions again.

Third, there were wrong motives that he did not want revealed. Rex was basically narcissistic to the core. He interpreted everything from his frame of reference. Like a child, he felt all of life, including relationships, was to revolve around him. The feelings of his wife, Marylee, rarely figured into his thinking. He met any discussion about his motives with attacks and the classic blame-shifting strategy.

But a fourth source of anxiety is more germane to us. Rex had a fear of anyone discovering the responsibilities he did not wish to acknowledge and fulfill towards his wife. When the conversation shifted to behaviors, words, or attitudes that he was responsible for in the relationship, his neck would begin to blotch. That is a telltale sign of anxiety. The body emits histamine into the bloodstream when it experiences anxiety. Red blotching of the skin is only one visual sign of anxiety.

In contrast, a great benefit of identifying, assuming, and fulfilling our circle of responsibilities is that unfulfilled responsibilities no longer rattle around in the basement of our thinking, causing anxiety that they will surface. When we begin to fulfill our responsibilities, we discover God's abundant grace ready and waiting.

I am encouraged many times to hear a sigh of relief when one finally acknowledges avoided responsibilities. When the person humbly assumes and obediently fulfills them, positive things happen. Defensive walls crumble. Hardened hearts melt. Stubborn wills obey. Broken relationships mend. Anxiety greatly reduces.

But this is only the beginning. Continuing to fulfill circles of responsibilities can lay the foundation for reduced tension in relationships.

7. Reduced Tension

We were taping the third of a seven-part *To Love and Cherish* television series for KCTV-50. Halfway through the program I asked Terry and Mary to come out of the audience to assist me in an illustration.

I gave one end of a four-foot-long rope to Terry and the other end to Mary, his wife. I asked them to put tension on the rope by pulling on their ends. Then I asked them to do something that I have asked scores of couples to do before: "I want you to reduce tension on that rope."

Mary dropped her end.

"No, you can't let go of either end."

She picked up her end of the rope again.

"Now reduce tension on the rope."

They both moved a few inches toward each other.

I turned to the audience and commented, "How easy it is to reduce tension on the rope and in a relationship if each one moves a little. It does not fix the problem completely, but it can reduce the tension."

Then I asked them to exert tension on the rope again. They were very cooperative.

Next I told Terry to release tension on the rope.

Both of them moved a few inches toward each other.

"No, Mary, I do not want you to move, just Terry."

They tried again. This time Mary did not move, but Terry did.

"Look, tension was reduced and only one person moved." This is exactly what happens when one or both persons in a relationship identifies, assumes, and fulfills his or her own circle of responsibilities. It may not fix longstanding, deep-seated marriage problems, but it will begin the process of building a less stressful atmosphere in which rebuilding can take place.

Not only will fulfilling circles of responsibility strengthen the relationship by reducing tension, it will reduce conflict.

8. REDUCED CONFLICT

Rex seemed to enjoy getting into an argument with Marylee. Arguments were one of his strategies to control her. Control was his tool for reducing his childhood fear of abandonment. He baited Marylee night after night. Out of self-defense she finally lashed back. The fight was on.

During one of Marylee's counseling sessions without Rex, we addressed this issue. She asked what she could do when Rex kept egging her on. Rex, as we've discussed, was a debater, a classic blame shifter, and a rewriter of history. Marylee was almost going crazy because of his ability to confuse her with twisted facts.

I suggested a simple way to reduce the conflicts. It would not fix the major problems Rex had in his personal life, but it could reduce the frequency and intensity of a conflict. "Marylee, pretend you are at a high-school dance and an obnoxious, unkempt boy asks you to dance. What would you do?"

"I would probably graciously decline."

"What obligation are you under to dance with this guy?"

"None, but I do need to be halfway civil to him."

"True. Now, when Rex starts pushing you to get into a fight, visualize him asking you to dance and graciously decline. He may get upset, pout, storm away, but simply tell him that you are not open to discuss this with him any further. Say that you will discuss it in the presence of the pastor or at our next counseling session."

There are clear biblical teachings that have a direct bearing on this response. We are told that if at all possible, and if it is within our power, we are to be at peace with all men (Rom. 12:18). Scripture also warns us not to have any dealings with an angry man (Prov. 22:24), and for good reason. When emotions are highly activated through anger, then logic and reasoning walk out the door. Rex used anger to win and control, not to bring peace. And finally, James underscored that "the anger of man does not achieve the righteousness of God" (James 1:20). Verbal fighting never produces the holiness that God desires we develop in a relationship. Conversely, it does destroy the work of God in people's lives.

Rex had real difficulty with Marylee's changes. Arguing was his unhealthy way of controlling her when he was afraid. Marylee's mature response only frightened him more, but it greatly reduced the destructive arguments.

9. Rebuilt Relationships
Circles of responsibilities can be the catalyst to rebuild a relationship. True, not every relationship is going to be rebuilt, but since we

are not omniscient, we do not know which ones will succeed. I often refer to the verse just mentioned, "So far as it depends on you, be at peace with all men" (Rom. 12:18).

I have watched impossible situations slowly reverse when just one person starts acting in a healthy, responsible way. I have seen an unyielding husband soften because of the positive changes in his wife. It has been encouraging to see a reluctant, distrustful wife join her husband in counseling because of the responsible change she sees in him. Frequently, the repentant attitude of the major offender translates to the mate as, "He or she must care." A positive change very often opens up the closed door of the heart of a hurting mate or family member.

Many times God reverses, suspends, or delays a pending judgment when an erring one repents, becomes responsible, and does the next right thing (see 2 Chron. 33:1–13). Yes, purposing to remain responsible can be an effective tool to rebuilding relationships. It can also be a powerful witness through your life.

10. POWERFUL WITNESS

Michelle, my youngest daughter, had just entered high school. We had started to attend a large church with an active youth group. The camps, retreats, and healthy social activities were a real encouragement to her. Many friendships developed. Eventually she was asked over to friends' homes.

Michelle had given some thought to what her convictions were. Entertainment was an area she had thought about. One evening a group of friends from church rented a particular movie. The popcorn, soft drinks, and dip were all part of the film party.

As the movie began, Michelle realized it was not a film she wanted to watch. Another friend also grew uncomfortable with the language and immorality. Michelle slipped out of the room, and her girlfriend followed. Her friend had a driver's license. Michelle asked if she would be open to going out and getting some ice cream. They did. She and her friend talked about the kinds of movies they would or would not watch. Michelle shared her standards. After the ice cream treat, her friend brought Michelle home early.

When Michelle came to the house, she looked a little discouraged. She reviewed the events of the evening. "I guess it means I won't have many friends unless I watch the sex and listen to the profanity." Convictions and friendship collided. Michelle wanted to remain faithful to her convictions, but she could see the cost was going to be great, even among church kids.

A few days later a letter came in the mail from a girlfriend who was not at the informal party. I am going to let you read it over Michelle's shoulder. It brought tears to my eyes:

Michelle,

Hey! I just wanted to drop a note to say thank you for allowing God to use you! You have impacted my life in many ways in the last two weeks of summer and I really don't know what to say besides keep up the good work.

Karen told me the other night how you . . . went home from John's because you won't watch movies over G or PG ratings (I don't remember which one). That stand really touched me. God needs leaders who are willing to stand alone for the kingdom and you showed me the other night that you are willing to stand alone. Whether you realize it or not you impacted many people over that movie and I admire you for it! It takes a lot to do something like that! I see your crowns in heaven stacking up! Not that you follow Him for that! I love you lots and I pray for you! Please let me know how I can pray for you.

Love,
Molly

I wish I could report that many girls now flock to Michelle because of her example. Sadly, that is not the case. She has had to face the serious reality of standing alone, even in Christian circles. When Jesus said, "The gate is small, and the way is narrow that leads to life, and few are those who find it" (Matt. 7:14), He was referring to belief in Himself, but the same principle applies to those who are Christians. Narrow is the way for followers of Christ's standards. These believers are not narrow-minded, but focused, purpose-minded.

Her peers and teachers honored Michelle for her character. When she identified her standards before the Lord, accepted them, and purposed to live them out in public high school, she was a witness to many. Biblical, responsible people will stand out. Jesus encouraged it this way: "Let your light shine before men in such a way that they may see your good works, and glorify your Father who is in heaven" (Matt. 5:16).

People who identify, assume, and purpose to remain responsible are indeed a rare breed and a great witness. But one other final benefit of remaining faithful to one's circle of responsibilities can be the greatest encouragement to you.

11. You Will Be Okay

Of all the questions I am asked, one continues to resurface whether spoken or implied: "Will I ever be okay?" Moses' farewell address to Israel answers just that question. He pointed to the two mountains before them. Mount Ebal loomed as a visual reminder to the nation that if they abandoned the Lord in disobedience they would suffer severe consequences. On the other hand, Mount Gerizim reminded them of God's promise of rich blessings if they were faithful to their covenants with God (Deut. 11:29).

"But," you may respond, "that was for the nation of Israel, not for us today." I wondered about that myself. Then I read a verse from the apostle Paul's letter to the Corinthian church: "Now these things happened to them [Israel] as an example, and they were written for our instruction, upon whom the ends of the ages have come" (1 Cor. 10:11). The word *instruction* comes from two Greek words meaning "to place or put" and "mind." Literally, it means "to place or put into the mind." To paraphrase this verse: "They were written from time to time for our instruction or to drive a particular point home."

What point is God trying to drive home through the two mountains that framed Joshua's farewell address? There is blessing and benefit for those who identify, assume, and continue to fulfill their God-given circle of responsibilities, *in spite of the lack of cooperation of anyone else.* You can be okay.

Mark and Kari worked with Pastor Tim for a while after our marathon session that one afternoon. They had been able to identify where they were *At* and where they could *Be* in their marriage. But in the end, both finally refused to accept and fulfill their respective responsibilities. I am grieved to report it will not be okay with them. At my last contact I learned that the family has virtually disintegrated. They failed to harness the power of obedience to work it out.

Marilyn and Bruce, after only one session, had learned where they were *At* and where they wanted to *Be.* They both accepted and fulfilled their individual circles of responsibilities and watched the power of personal responsibility restore their marriage. These folks became dear personal friends and have helped underwrite the ministry of Living Foundation Ministries for many years. They will do okay.

Doug, my farmer-friend, admitted he had been emotionally and sometimes physically abusive to his wife. This same pattern prevailed in his parents' home. Doug felt he was normal. In his thinking, his wife was the problem. She did learn to control her spending and became personally responsible. In response, God broke Doug. He finally acknowledged his emotional immaturity and the need to build a heart-to-heart relationship with his wife. His wife finally moved back home. Talking has replaced yelling, blame shifting, and name-calling. They now jointly handle their family finances. They did work it out.

Nick and Traci are doing great. This did not take a miracle but an act of decisive personal responsibility, which proved to be powerful in restoring a healthy relationship. Nick and Traci have both remained faithful in fulfilling their circles of responsibilities. Traci's mom even has a greater source of security now because Traci is acting in a more responsible, adult way. The enmeshment has all but ended, and they are relishing their new adult-to-adult relationship based on honor and a healthy love.

Susan originally never felt she could be okay after all she had been through with Jerry. But years later, she has done a great job with her three daughters. She is a physical therapist and loves to travel with her kids. She has learned firsthand the power of remaining faithfully responsible. She, too, will be okay. God's tools worked for her.

Helen is doing great too. Her crack-addicted son, Ron, is having to learn in adulthood what he did not learn in childhood: how to be responsible for his actions. When Helen stopped enabling him, an amazing thing happened. I am happy to report that Ron got the help he needed and day by day, he is doing much better.

Rex is a heartache. He sabotaged his third marriage. To this day I grieve for him. There were glimpses of hope that were dashed on the rocks of continued irresponsible behavior. Marylee went on to receive her master's degree and bought a small, comfortable home. For years she felt she could not live without Rex. She then replaced an unhealthy dependence on Rex with a balanced, healthy dependence on her heavenly Father. She has been fasting and praying for Rex. She knows that whatever happens with him, she is going to be okay.

Keenan and Deidra reported recently that they and their five children have never been happier. Keenan is no longer sprinting out the door to rescue or fix someone. He has identified, assumed, and fulfilled many of his family responsibilities. And an amazing thing resulted: the door of Deidra's closed heart has slowly cracked open. Trust did the work. Keenan's faithfulness accomplished for Deidra what hours of counseling could not do. I honor them both. They gave me permission to tell their story and use their real names. They still hit speed bumps in their relationship, like the rest of us, but they know now they are going to be okay. They knew they could work it out.

Shelia brings friends of hers into my office from time to time for counseling. A wondrous thing has happened: her mother has made a 180-degree change in her attitudes and behavior. She is no longer condemning or full of harsh criticism. Shelia is in shock. I wonder if this would have happened if Shelia had not stayed in her circle and remained faithful. This indeed is a miracle. Now Shelia reaches out to her parents from a position of spiritual and emotional health, not from neediness. Her cup is full (John 4:14). Her heavenly Father filled it. Shelia is okay.

Kitty, sadly enough, is not going to be okay. She has decided to move from one immoral relationship to another. She keeps making the next wrong decision. She is a gifted middle-management woman. But Kitty is heading for a bitter end unless she makes a change.

How about my dad? He now has more than seventeen years of sobriety. He has become a loving, giving great-grandpa. I am now his guardian, and Linda and I check on him regularly.

Yes, I have told you one account after another of men and women who had to face the reality of their responsibilities, assume them, and fulfill them. But I can say to you today from personal experience that without using this powerful tool, circles of responsibility, which is firmly rooted in the character of God, I would have lost my own father. God used my confession of sin—which was in my circle of responsibility—to powerfully restore one of the most significant relationships in my life. I can't help but wonder what's waiting out there for *you* when you identify, assume, and consistently fulfill your own circle of responsibilities.

Convinced? Not sure of your own personal power that God gives you to work out a difficult situation? John and Alice want to personally answer in their own words, "Does it really work?"

THIRTEEN

DOES IT REALLY WORK?

I wish I could report to you that everyone I have shared these principles with became a success story. Unfortunately, that is not the case.

Only one word distinguishes those who succeed from those who fail: obedience. The key is obedience to the ways of God as revealed in His Word.

John and Alice Bourdon are among those who did obey, and these principles changed their marriage and their ministry. Their story is amazing. Here it is, in their own words.

GREAT BEGINNINGS

JOHN

We would like to share with you how God has used the principles in *You Can Work It Out!* to impact our marriage and ministry. I applaud you for taking time to work on your relationships—I didn't think that was very important until three years ago. What we want to share with you is how God has worked in our lives to heal our shattered marriage.

I was born in 1952. My mother was an alcoholic; my father was strict and stern. At a very early age I learned to survive by being a perfectionist. It worked well in my life. I learned how to thrive by doing things perfectly.

I was saved while in college at Georgia Tech. Alice and I met there, and after I graduated with a degree in chemical engineering, we were married. We began our life together in Ohio. Then I developed a real desire to teach God's Word on the mission field, so we spent the next five years at Dallas Seminary. I continued to work full-time as an engineer while going to school. After graduating with a master's degree in theology, we went to the mission field.

While we were missionaries and teachers in Guatemala, my life looked pretty good. But then we had some problems with one of our kids, and as a result we returned to the United States and I took up engineering again. I became an elder at church, a leader in the evangelical community, and a well-respected engineer. My company flew me all over the world to teach seminars. Life looked pretty good to me, but it didn't to Alice.

ALICE

I couldn't have married anybody more different from me. John and I are exact opposites. I was raised in a Christian home and came to Christ as a six-year-old. I went to a Christian camp in the summertime and worked there in high school and college. I did things the way my parents, God, and others wanted me to. I wanted everybody to be happy with me, and I did just about anything to make that happen, short of being immoral.

John came from a fairly tense family where conflict was normal. If my family had a motto, it was "Keep peace at any cost." If you even dared to speak your mind about something, you were the black sheep of the family for causing disruption.

I grew up thinking that it was really godly to buy peace no matter what the cost. So I brought that mindset into marriage.

John, however, felt that being domineering and conflict oriented was the way to get things done. When you take somebody who wants no conflict and somebody who loves it—you can imagine what that produced. John spoke and I tried to please—and that was the dynamic of our marriage.

Early in our marriage that seemed to work pretty well. I was happy to make him happy, and he was happy to give the orders. Three children came along. Those years seemed to be pretty smooth. John was occupied with a lot of things, and I was occupied with the kids.

But once we left seminary, I had this feeling that things were not the way they ought to be. I was not very happy. I was anxious a lot of the time, wondering when John would next be unhappy and angry with me. It happened often. How much would it take for me to make him happy again?

One day John said, "You know, I think something's different about you. You have changed since seminary." I hadn't really changed—John had. He was just beginning to get uncomfortable and discontented with the life we led and the way I contributed to that life. He felt that if I would just perform better, our life would be a lot better.

While we were on the mission field, those conflicts became greater. There were lots of times when we could not communicate. I tried to explain to John that I wasn't happy, that I was troubled about the condition of our relationship, and he said, "Well, that's your problem. If you need help, go get some. But I don't have any problem with this relationship."

We left the mission field because of some concerns with one of our children. We went to Dallas, where John took a very high-pressure job. When I approached him then about my concerns, he said, "Oh, it's just because I am under so much pressure at work." So when it came time to leave that job in Dallas and move to Kansas City, I assumed it would cure all of our problems; in Kansas

City, John would have a less stressful job. But things didn't get any better. As a matter of fact, they got worse.

One day, looking at our two teenage sons, I realized they looked and sounded just like their dad. I started hearing the same words I heard from John: "Can't you do anything right?" "Don't you care about our family?" "Will you ever get this right?" There was a lot of anger, demeaning talk, and disrespect coming my way, not only from John now, but from my two sons. I finally came to the point where I felt like I couldn't take it another minute. John wasn't hearing what I was saying. He just kept telling me, "If you need help, go get help. I am perfectly happy in this relationship." I didn't know what to do or where to go. I had absolutely no answers as a Christian woman or a Christian leader about what to do to effect a change in my relationship with John.

In desperation one day I sat down and wrote a letter to John. I thought, *I am going to try just one more time to pour my heart out to this man.* Here is a portion of that letter.

My dear John:

I have been concerned about us for some time. I don't know exactly when the concern took a definite form, but I know that I have defended you against criticism from concerned friends for many years. There were concerns that you were too demanding, too critical, too driven, too controlling. Last year, though, I became aware that things were not getting better—but slowly and surely worse. It became clearly apparent that we were still on a downhill slide and that the kids were clearly paying the price.

I am concerned that you have no intimate relationships; not even our relationship is intimate. You do derive some emotional sustenance from our relationship, but the most intimate time in our relationship was during our courtship. It has steadily declined since then. You have pulled away and shut yourself off from me and refuse to allow anyone else to get close.

I am concerned as well that you don't deal with your emotions in a healthy way. You rarely express positive emotion. I do appreciate that you tell me that you love me, but love for the kids, support, encouragement, genuine interest, acceptance, pride, praise, contentment, joy, hope for the future, tenderness, and tolerance are rare. On the other hand, frustration, irritation, criticism, and anger are the hallmarks of your life. You are so rarely happy, satisfied, and content. And your expressions of anger are often thoughtless, tactless, mean, and at times, cruel. You seem to have no control over your emotions or the expression of them, nor are you concerned about their effect on others.

I have normally taken the brunt of your bad temper, and it was my choice to allow it to be this way, but when the hurt was directed at Josh and Michael and Molly, I couldn't make the choice that way any longer.

One other thing that concerns me is that you are so controlling. Being in control is not of itself wrong, nor is managing well your resources, but expecting to control other people and the details of their lives is not healthy.

I know that you have done none of these things intentionally. You are not by nature mean or unloving. That is what makes me think that you are deeply affected by circumstances beyond your control in your childhood that have shaped you into the man that you are today. I have tried to flex with our relationship for a long time. I have tried to see the positives in our relationship. But frankly, John, I am absolutely worn out. I don't know what the limit is of what I can bear and I don't want to find out. I do know that I can hardly make it through the day at times from lack of hope that it will ever get better.

I feel like I am living a lie to present ourselves as well-adjusted, happily married people with a few difficulties when I know we are in deep trouble. I battle with feelings of regret that we ever married, regret that somehow I have caused all this unhappiness, regret that if I'd stepped in sooner it would have been easier to rectify, regret that if I'd been a better wife and friend any problem that you faced as a child would have been erased. I battle bitterness against you because you don't seem to care. And when you do say that you care, you don't give these problems any priority. I battle feelings of fear of what the future holds, fear that you'll refuse to do anything about the problem.

I am relieved when you go on a trip because I don't have to deal with the problems directly for a while. Then I am very anxious before you come home. I have often thought of suicide, but I know that this would not honor the Lord and would only make life harder for the kids. I generally feel an overwhelming sadness that our situation is so grim and I seem so powerless to do anything about it.

In terms of what I look for and value in any relationship, I am receiving very little from our relationship. I treasure a friend who cares how I am doing spiritually, who wants to know how I feel, who cares about my dreams, who honors my values, who appreciates my opinions even if they are different, who supports and encourages my efforts, who picks me up when I fail. You do provide for me well financially, but I can't say that you are much of a friend to me. You are my companion, but not my friend. You don't seem concerned about my spiritual condition, you ridicule my feelings, criticize and demean my dreams, belittle my values, negate my opinions, discourage me, and beat me down when I fail.

John, I am absolutely committed to our relationship, but I am allowing our family to self-destruct by not intervening. It is like seeing someone having a heart attack and debating about dialing 911. If I continue to tolerate this situation, our children will think I am a fool or that I consider it . . . normal; . . . those are not acceptable alternatives. I do have a significant concern that you will not take this seriously or that you will refuse to make it a priority. . . . I must tell you, I will not wait.

JOHN

I would like to tell you that I was heartbroken over her letter. I wasn't. I threw it in the trash! Ninety-five percent of my life looked great, and the other 5 percent was miserable due to her hysteria. But for once she stood up and said, "We're going to get help," and for once I somehow knew she was serious. We went to our pastor and he listened to us for about five minutes and said, "Your problems are over my head" and sent us to Chuck Lynch.

Chuck met with us once, listened to me describe my life, looked at me, and said something that I will never forget: "You are a Pharisee!" It changed my life. As a Dallas graduate I have studied the Bible a lot, and it's not hard to see that a student of the Word and leader in the evangelical church and a Pharisee don't fit together. So through a process of meeting with Chuck over a period of time, God broke my heart. God used a process described in *You Can Work It Out!* to revolutionize not only our marriage but our family as well. It turned my heart around and started me on a journey toward maturity in Christ.

There are seven keys that Alice and I used to build harmony back into our relationship. You can use them too.

1. Identify the broken pieces. First, we had to honestly identify the negative words, actions, and attitudes that were creating disharmony. The place I had to start being honest was looking at Alice's letter and saying, "That really does reflect my life."

I will be honest with you: for a perfectionist, that was a hard process—to look inside expecting to see perfection but instead seeing imperfection and how wounded a creature I really am. We made a list of all the negative characteristics of our relationship.

If you were to sit down and describe your relationship, you might write down words like fighting, lying, pouting, critical, unfaithful, distrustful, vengeful, unloving, insensitive, perfectionistic, cussing, yelling, sarcastic, rejecting, blaming, undisciplined, harsh, unprotective, lonely, proud, controlling, dominating, overprotective, dishonoring, and disrespectful.

Remember, God gives grace or help only for the truth. We had to be honest. The truth exposes us, and it makes us vulnerable. But God wants us to be truthful.

2. Assign responsibility. It was here that we were introduced to the concept of circles of responsibilities. You know what I thought the size of my circle of responsibility was? The size of a pea. I made Alice's circle the size of a basketball. Why? Because I wanted to blame somebody else. If she was responsible for everything, then she was to blame for anything that went wrong.

We had to understand that God laid the basis for identifying and separating our circles of responsibilities. Romans 12:18 reads, "If possible, so far as it depends on you, be at peace with all men." In other words, as far as your circle of responsibility goes, be at peace with God, be at peace with yourself, and be at peace with your brothers and sisters. We had to identify who was really responsible for what. This was a tough, painful process.

We also added our biblical responsibilities to each circle. Each of us is commanded to love, forgive, encourage, pray, be Christlike, patient, and gentle. The fruit of the Spirit listed in Galatians 5:22–23 are other qualities we're commanded to have.

Finally, we were reminded that God has a circle of responsibilities too. Revenge is just one of these. We often try to take God's responsibilities on ourselves or shift all of our responsibilities onto God or each other. Instead each of us needs to identify our own circle of responsibilities both in a negative sense and in a positive sense.

3. Assume responsibility. Why was it important to identify and to assume our circles of responsibilities? Because we can separate these responsibilities in our heads, but assuming them happens in our hearts.

Identifying our responsibilities is not the same as assuming them. Chuck explained that blame shifting is one way we avoid assuming personal responsibility. Some of my favorite blame-shifting questions were: "When are you ever going to learn? When are you going to get your act together? When are you going to get this house clean? When are you ever going to fix a decent meal? When are you ever going to iron my shirts?"

Alice's favorite blame-shifting comments were: "Look who's talking! Well, that's the pot calling the kettle black. When's the last time you had *your* devotions? When's the last time you listened to the sermon? I'll do so-and-so when you do so-and-so. I'm not responsible for my behavior until you get your act together. So if you start being a leader in our home, then I'll submit. When you stop yelling at the kids, then I'll start paying attention to what you say."

These blame-shifting statements take the focus off the speaker and put it on the hearer, right where I would like to have it. I realized that blame shifting was the opposite of assuming responsibility. When those words come out of my mouth, I am not assuming responsibility for my circle. That's the Pharisee's ideal way of staying out of trouble. Anytime Alice came to me and said one of those blame-shifting things like, "Well, when was the last time you had a quiet time?" I knew she was attacking me, and I immediately began to justify myself and act defensive. And my self-justification helped me avoid personal responsibility.

ALICE

It also became important for us to learn to not assume the *other's* responsibilities. In assuming someone else's responsibility we often use guilt, shame, or blame to motivate one another.

Oftentimes in our relationship there were things that John wanted me to do because he didn't want to do them. For example, when the kids were misbehaving, he'd say, "You know, you are with the kids all day long, and they aren't behaving. What kind of mother are you?" John would use guilt to shift the blame and responsibility for the kids' behavior over to me because, of course, it was never a reflection that he wasn't a good father. He didn't want to take responsibility for that. So I would think, *Oh, goodness, maybe I'm not being a good mom. I need to really whip into shape here and get those kids to behave.*

4. Entrust yourself to God. Learning to entrust yourself to God when the other person has failed in his or her responsibility is not easy. It was very difficult for me to face the reality that I was responsible to change but John might continue the way he was. I really had no assurance that if I changed what I did John would change his way of doing things. He seemed to be unaware of some of his attitudes and behavior. But I learned that God would hold me responsible to do what He had called me to do; I wasn't to beat John on the head if he wasn't paying attention. I had to separate out of my circle of responsibilities what John was accountable to God for. I had to understand that I was responsible to provide a good example to our children of what it meant to be a godly person. Even if John never understood what he needed to do, I still could trust God to honor what I did.

5. Forgive the irresponsibility. If Jesus was nothing else, He was a God of forgiveness. John and I both spent much time in our counseling sessions asking and granting forgiveness. It was painful, but it was freeing.

JOHN

If you have trouble forgiving someone, you may be using one of the following excuses (I used several of them):

But I'm not angry.
But I can't forgive.
That's too big. I can't forgive that.
But someone has to pay.
But they won't even acknowledge what they did.
But I am living with the memories.

But I can't forgive myself.

But I can't forgive God.

But I'm not the forgiving kind.

But I can't let go.

But they'll only do it again.

Instead of hiding behind excuses, put yourself in Jesus' or the evangelist Stephen's place—both were able to forgive their executioners. That's what we are called to do through forgiveness.

6. *Remember, you are accountable to God alone.* We realized we each will have to give an account to God only for our *own* circle of responsibilities. God never commands us to be responsible for the actions of another. I will not answer for what Alice has done. I will only have to give an account to the Lord for what I have done, be it good or bad. And Alice will not have to answer for me.

7. *Purpose to stay responsible.* This is hard. For twenty-three years Alice and I had been doing it wrong. And now when we try to do it right, it sometimes seems unfair. We thought our dysfunctional system worked, but it really didn't. And it's painful to even acknowledge that I have a circle of responsibilities, let alone deal with it. But we wanted to save our marriage, so we committed ourselves to following through on our responsibilities.

A Process of Self-discovery

For me (John), this was a process of self-discovery. I honestly didn't know who I had become. When Alice wrote that eleven-page letter to me and I first went to see Chuck Lynch, I thought I was a really good guy. I was a successful businessperson and church leader, in control of my life. I had good quiet times and a good relationship with the Lord, I thought. I was almost perfect. Unfortunately, God didn't see me that way. That was the Pharisee talking—pure on the outside, rotten on the inside. Part of the process was to take a good, honest look at who I was and understand just how broken I had become.

I would like to share with you an excerpt from a letter that I wrote Alice a couple months into my recovery process:

> I feel like a blind man . . . who has been cured and is now able to see. And what I see is ugly. I have been devastated by the light which has come to shine within the darkness of my life. I have been amazed that I knew absolutely nothing of my sin or of the impact which it had on you and the kids. My powers of denial are tremendous. I feel a bit betrayed by our family and friends to whom this has been so obvious and who have remained silent. The realization of the magnitude of the pain which I have caused has come as a complete surprise to me. How could I have been so blind? The dependency of the frightened child within me and his fear of abandonment are so deep and so great that they permeate every aspect of my life. The events of these last few weeks have broken my heart and shattered my life, but they are nothing compared to the pain I have caused you over the last twenty-three years. You have every right to be angry, bitter, and to not trust me.

One of the things I learned in dealing with my own circle of responsibilities was that I didn't want any. My goal in life was to make Alice responsible for everything. Until I began looking inside and seeing myself for the sinner that I am, I didn't take responsibility for the things God called me to do. It doesn't do any good to try and push them off on Alice, because ultimately I am responsible for my own circle of responsibilities—as ugly and full of negatives as it may be, or by God's grace, as full of positives as it can become.

I learned that what made the difference between the negatives and positives in my circle was one word: choice! Romans 8 and Romans 12 explain that as believers we can choose to live a Christlike life in the power of the Holy Spirit or live in the deadening sin we know so well. What I had to realize is that being Christlike didn't feel comfortable. One of the hardest things for me to look at was that I really had become a Pharisee. I was perfectionistic. I was obsessive. I'd walk into a room and see everything that was out of order.

In the process I saw that placing things before God is called idolatry. I even placed Alice in my life where God should be, trying to get my emotional needs met by Alice, not God. My life was really messed up. My circle of responsibilities had collapsed so that I was totally dependent on other people. I had to recognize that I had the power to say no to sin. Christ gave me the power through the Holy Spirit to live as a different person. One of the hardest things for me was seeing that forgiveness is something granted, but trust is earned.

When God broke my heart, I turned to Alice and told her I was wrong, I really had been that blind man. I didn't know what I was doing. I wanted to be better. She forgave me, and I am earning her trust.

Furthermore, I realized I can't be perfect. The hardest thing for me was to accept forgiveness. It tore my heart right out of my chest and filled my eyes with tears. It was so hard to accept the forgiveness God has given me.

Recently my son, a freshman in college, was arrested. When we went to get him out of jail after twenty hours of mandatory confinement, he was scared to death to come out the door. In the past I would have killed him. Though he has seen a change in my life, he still came out with fear and trepidation. I greeted him with open arms. There was no judgment, only grace. He looked at Alice and me and said, "I was so afraid of how you would respond."

Alice looked at him and said, "Dad and I believe that we should give you as much grace as we've received."

Michael said, "But you've never needed as much grace as me!"

276

Experiencing grace allows it to overflow to those around us. That's what the process has done in my life. It has broken my heart. It has made me aware of who I really am. It has allowed me to accept forgiveness. And it all came from identifying and learning to stay in my own circle of responsibilities, not trying to shove that circle off on my wife, my children, or other people. The process was not easy.

SOMEONE HAD TO CHANGE

One person had to change before this process could begin to reverse itself in our lives. Chuck reminded us, the definition of insanity is doing the same thing over and over again, expecting a different result. I (Alice) was the one whose eyes opened first to the fact that our relationship and our family were not working. And a key principle to me for initiating the change in our family was circles of responsibility.

Another term for this is *boundaries*. Healthy boundaries begin and end at the edge of our circle of responsibilities. When I take responsibility for the things that are in my circle, including my walk with the Lord and being a good mother, wife, and friend, I establish and maintain healthy boundaries in my life.

This wasn't easy. I'd spent twenty years defending really rotten behavior on my husband's part. My friends used to ask, "Alice, why do you let him treat you that way?"

And I'd say, "Oh, you know, John can be such a nice guy." Denial! I wouldn't honestly look at what was not working in our marriage. I had to learn to speak the truth, and that was a really scary thing. I was living in a relationship where, if you told the truth, if you stood up for yourself, there was reprisal. It was hard to learn to say, "You know what? There is something in my circle that doesn't belong there. It belongs in your circle. And I'm not going to keep it anymore."

I had to be honest with myself about what I was contributing to the relationship. I had to stop living in denial and engaging in wishful thinking. Every time we went through one of John's rages, I'd get emotionally beat up. John would feel terrible about it and say, "I am so sorry," and bring me flowers. And I'd think, *Man, this is great. It's probably never going to happen again.* But it happened hundreds of times.

I had to separate my own circle from John's. And that was a difficult thing to do, because in his mind he had a very tiny circle. John earned a paycheck, came home, expected his dinner on the table. When his paycheck went into the bank, that meant that he was off the clock and he didn't have to do anything more. Everything else was in my circle of responsibilities. Now, that's much too big a circle for any person to assume. And so I had to separate out from my circle what didn't belong there.

John was not a very happy camper about having all that stuff dumped back in his circle. That started to make life a little bit uncomfortable for him. But we are creatures of habit and comfort, and we will not change when we don't have any motivation to change. We'd like to think we are really godly and spiritual and we'll make changes because it is the right thing to do. But that doesn't often happen. *We change only because it is too costly for us not to change.* To save our marriage, we both had to make room for new behavior and attitudes.

I had to realize that it was not my responsibility to make John happy. His happiness was his own responsibility. Can you imagine what a freeing thing that was? I no longer had to race around the house at ten minutes to five to make sure everything was in its place, the kids were clean, nobody was fighting, there were no dirty diapers, nothing was out of place, and dinner was almost ready so I could drop everything when he walked in the door and spend time with him. I was suddenly free from the huge load that I had carried for far too long. I finally realized that John's happiness, change, and godliness were all his responsibility and that God was never going to hold me accountable for those things.

Forgiveness was in my circle of responsibility, and some of those things that Chuck shares in his book *I Should Forgive, But . . .* absolutely stuck in my craw. I thought things like, *I could forgive John if he would just be genuinely repentant. I could forgive John if he would acknowledge how much pain I have suffered. I could forgive him when . . .* I realized that the longer I waited to forgive him, the more bitterness was going to build in my own heart. No matter how much I changed, no matter how much he changed, if that bitterness stayed there, it was going to eat me alive. So I had to learn to forgive even if John never said he was sorry, even if he never felt deeply enough how much pain he had caused me. I forgave him because God had forgiven me.

I needed to recognize that vengeance belonged to God. If John deserved to be punished for what he had done, it was God's job to punish him. It's true—sometimes I still feel the hurt. But forgiving is not the same thing as giving up the hurt. It means that you release that other person from the responsibility of what he did. You no longer hold it against him. You choose not to keep him in the jail of your heart because of what he did.

I'd like to tell you that we understood our circles of responsibilities one day and our marriage has been great ever since. But that's not true. I'm always tempted to go back to my old ways of responding because they are what feels comfortable to me. It was predictable. But as difficult as it's been, we know we cannot go back. It would mean death for our marriage and our family. So by the grace and strength that God gives us, we keep moving forward. We can see that God has better things in mind for us than what we've encountered in the first twenty years of our marriage.

LESSONS WE LEARNED

Unconditional love does not mean unconditional acceptance. I just assumed that if I kept loving John more and more, somehow our lives would get better. I never challenged anything he did. I let him speak to me any way he wanted. I let him do whatever he wanted. I jumped through hundreds of hoops trying to make him happy because I confused unconditional acceptance of wrong behavior with unconditional love.

Sometimes the most loving thing to do is not to accept what the other person does. You never stop loving him, but you don't always have to accept what he does. This was a tough one for me. But this is what setting healthy boundaries and defining your circle of responsibilities is all about.

Sometimes I have to stand in front of John and say, "Nope, we're not going there. If you want this conversation to go on, you are going to have to start speaking to me in a more respectful way because otherwise you'll find yourself talking to the wall." When I have to walk out of the room I start thinking, *Oh, man, that feels terrible,* because I spent forty years thinking that "peace at any cost" was a godly way to do things. I had to learn that loving confrontation is necessary and biblical.

I also learned that behavior we consider normal must be compared to the Word of God. I was raised in a Christian home where "peace at any cost" was accepted as a godly way to live, but it's not. John learned that anger and dominance were acceptable behavior patterns, but they aren't.

The struggle with old sin patterns is not over. It will continue. But our conflicts are less intense and less frequent. That is progress! We have developed better tools to deal with conflicts when they come up. I can't imagine what it would be like in our house if conflict no longer existed, because John and I both have such strong personalities. But now we have the biblical tools to help us work through them.

It is our sincere hope that sharing our story will mean that you won't have to start from scratch in figuring out for yourself how to harness the power of personal responsibility in restoring relationships. It has been a lifesaving tool in our lives. We hope it will be for you too.

John and Alice have "been there, done that." You may be there now, in a conflict with your parents, spouse, children, boss, or fellow parishioner. What have you done about it? I suggest you

- Identify what really happened in the conflict.
- Assign responsibility for each of the parts. Be sure you honestly assign to yourself what is legitimately yours.
- Assume your own assigned responsibility for the conflict.
- Fulfill all that is in your own circle of responsibilities.
- Remember that God has His own circle of responsibilities.
- Avoid assuming others' responsibilities.
- Forgive those who have defaulted on their responsibilities.
- Acknowledge God's grace when you have to fill in where others have failed.
- Remember, you will be held accountable to God for only your own circle of responsibilities.
- Purpose to be faithful in your own circle and enjoy the benefits of God's faithfulness.

Thank you for allowing me to have a part in your journey into Christlikeness. It will be my joy to learn from you how you did work it out and how you experienced firsthand the power of personal responsibility in restoring relationships.

CONFERENCE AND RETREAT TOPICS

DR. CHUCK LYNCH

- **Family Enrichment Seminars** (commonsense biblical help in dealing with conflict in the family, extended family, and blended family)

- **Freedom from Anger** (how to reduce anger in any relationship)

- **Freedom through Forgiveness** (practical help in removing the major hindrances to forgiveness)

- **How to Be a Biblical People Helper** (lays a foundation for helping people work through their problems in living)

- **Men on the Grow** (how to face your most difficult challenges and be successful and blameless)

- **To Love and Cherish** (how to develop a mutually fulfilling marriage)

For conference and retreat information:
Living Foundation Ministries
611 R. D. Mize Road
Blue Springs, Missouri 64014
(816) 229-5000
FAX (816) 229-5056